Francis Drake in Nehalem Bay in 1579

Setting the Historical Record Straight

Garry David Gitzen

2008

Francis Drake in Nehalem Bay 1579
Setting the Historical Record Straight

Copyright © 2008 by Garry D. Gitzen

For information: Garry Gitzen
P.O. Box 575, Wheeler, Oregon, USA 97147

Library of Congress Control Number: 2008909266

ISBN: 978-0-578-00625-3

Isnik Publishing, Wheeler, Oregon

Original Etching for Hard Cover Edition by: Lynn Thomas, Gilkey Award Recipient, Portland Art Museum
Cover Photo by Don Best showing the cities of Manzanita, Nehalem and Wheeler which border Nehalem Bay and Neahkahnie Mountain looming in the western sky.

All omissions or errors are the responsibility of the author.

In Memory of

M. Wayne Jensen, Jr.

1930 - 2005

ACKNOWLEDGEMENTS

I wish to acknowledge a deep, everlasting debt to the late M. Wayne Jensen, Jr., for this book could not have been written without access to the collection of over 600 books, 1000 photographs, original manuscripts, numerous drawings and maps reflecting 37 years of research into this book's subject. These documents cover years of tedious and physically tiring work, traversing the Neahkahnie Mountain countryside in order to establish that Francis Drake claimed this area (Nehalem Bay) as Nova Albion (New England) for Queen Elizabeth I. Mrs. Ruth Jensen has been of immense help as a sounding board and reference point for her husband's ideas and has provided a great deal of encouragement. Thanks to Phillip A. Costaggini for granting permission to reprint his thesis in Appendix I. Thanks to Samuel Bawlf and Bob Ward whose continued historical exposure of Oregon as a significant location of Drake's voyage has kept the quest for his true landing site alive. I thank Harvey Steele, former President of the Portland Archaeological Society, who encouraged me in the very early stages. Thanks to Tillamook County Commissioner, Charles Hurliman and Paul Levesque, Tillamook County Manager and Historian, for their belief in this book and for their ideas. Thanks to Ron Larson of HLB Engineering for the topographical maps, Peg Miller for her excellent editing skills, and her undying support and love. Thanks to David Dillon for his suggestions regarding structure and Bob La Du for fact-checking and Herb Beals for his expertise on early Spanish explorers. I so appreciate Dan Ayers, Charlie Fuerstenau, President Tom Mock of the Nehalem Valley Historical Society, Ken Painter and Mike Woodward for their enthusiasm; climbing cliffs and hillsides of prickly blackberries, trudging through mud and pushing through chest- high prickly salmonberry bushes. A big thanks to Beverly Anderson of the Tillamook County Library; I couldn't have completed this book without her assistance in locating hard-to-find books from large and small universities around the world. Thanks to Ray Shackelford for his support, Dixie Edwards of the Watershed Garden Works for her wapato and Henry Diem who, in 1986 introduced me to the Pacific Northwest aboriginal Indians.

PREFACE

The story is well known to school children and anyone who remembers a bit of English history. Francis Drake boldly sailed his ship, the *Golden Hinde*, into South and Central American ports to plunder silver and gold from amongst Spanish warships, serving notice that the fledgling British maritime empire was ready to challenge Spain for a share of the New World and the adjoining Pacific realm. Considered a pirate by Spain and a somewhat dubious adventurer and explorer by the English, Drake has been regarded by many Americans as a mere footnote to our early maritime history. Growing up in the San Francisco Bay Area of California, Drake's voyage was a more familiar subject to me. Nearby in Marin County lay Drake's Bay and several purported sites for his summer anchorage in 1579. When I was in school, in the 1950s, a brass plate that had been discovered on the Marin peninsula appeared to provide solid evidence for Drake's visit and claim of New Albion for his sovereign majesty, Queen Elizabeth. Despite contentions and continuing speculation about the specific location of Drake's northern California landing (Bolinas Bay, Tomales Bay, Drake's Estero, Drake's Bay, and San Quentin Bay are but a few of the proposed sites), the evidence seemed overwhelmingly in favor of the Marin County coast as the landing site.

First, there was the journal kept by his chaplain, Francis Fletcher. This was published in 1628 as *The World Encompassed* and it is still the primary source for descriptions of the landscape, fauna and flora, and Native Americans encountered. Despite some obvious gaps in the timelines provided, most historians believed that the bulk of Fletcher's account pointed to a central California location for the New Albion harbor. This was reinforced by maps published during the late sixteenth and early seventeenth century. One map provided an outline map of the harbor and indicated a latitudinal position of about 38° N, clearly indicating present day Marin County. Further studies of Native American folkways by Alfred Kroeber and others also seemed to support a Marin location, consistent with the Coastal Miwok culture. Thus, when the brass plate described by Fletcher, eagerly sought by California historians, was "discovered" in 1937 (originally found by a chauffer in 1933), the case seemed closed. Local enterprises were delighted and the Drake and *Golden Hinde* motif was thoroughly incorporated into restaurants, hotels, and Chamber of Commerce literature. To suggest that the jury might have delivered its historical verdict a bit prematurely was tantamount to blasphemy. Who was to doubt the experts, the manuscripts, the maps, and, of course, the infamous brass plate? Case closed.

Not quite. Other historians, many of them amateurs with a particular interest and expertise in marine navigation, viewed the record differently. The first map referring to Nova Albion, the Molyneux Globe, was produced in 1592 and marked the site at about 50° N. The famous harbor outline depicted on the margin of the Hondius Broadside map of 1595 (date is disputed) didn't quite fit the outline of contemporary Marin County coastlines. Not a problem, replied the traditionalists. Coastlines change, sandbars shift, erosion works its inevitable way, and this particular area lies along the Andreas Fault. Several large and well-documented earthquakes would alter coastal details considerably. Trying to align the Hondius outline with contemporary landforms was a good part of the mystery/history aficionados.

Other critics were uncomfortable about the application of Fletcher's descriptions to Miwok culture in 1579. No other Europeans had visited with, or documented, life styles of these peoples until the arrival of the Spanish over two hundred years later. Were the dwellings described by Fletcher comparable to dwellings encountered during the 1700s, not just in Marin County, but at numerous sites for other tribes along the Pacific coast? Gitzen examines this issue and raises new questions about the round dwellings of the Miwok and Nehalem natives. Most sources on Drake dismiss this as a dwelling type for any but the coastal Miwoks.

Then, in 1971, a serious challenge to the brass plate was issued. It wasn't the first challenge and some authorities had been skeptical from the beginning. The plate was deposited at the Bancroft Library at the University of California, Berkeley, as prestigious a home as any historical artifact could hope to have. Advances in metallurgy by the 1970s had made it possible to re-examine the manufacturing processes and reconsider the status of Drake's metallic declaration. It was determined that the plate was a hoax, made of rolled brass typical of an early twentieth century technique. Although the inscription cleverly imitated the text of Fletcher's journal, the perpetrators had been ignorant of another simple fact. The "brass" referred to in sixteenth century parlance, was in most cases lead, a much easier material to work with and inscribe. Subsequent investigations not only proved to all but the most stubborn that the plate was of recent manufacture, but the groups responsible for the intended practical joke were brought to light. As Gitzen states, the case was unraveling, but the evidence still favored Marin County.

My interest in the story involved a biological perspective. An acquaintance of mine, Mr. Fred Garland, had been following the historical debates and he had his own ideas about the anchorage site. Although his "safe harbor" was also in Marin County, we spent some time debating the various descriptions in *The World Encompassed.* I became especially fascinated with the identity of the so-called "conies", numerous medium-sized mammals described by Fletcher. The British referred to rabbits as conies, but Fletcher's description didn't match these or other obvious animals of the region. As a biologist, I became intrigued with trying to establish the biogeographical basis for the journal and for Drake's onshore activities. After considering a number of animals that might be the models for Fletcher's "conies", I must conclude, in agreement with Gitzen, that river otters may well be the mysterious beasts. Whether their numbers were ever as great as those described by Fletcher is unknown, but trapping and habitat destructions over the past two hundred years have undoubtedly impacted their population.

What if the Marin location was not correct? What other lines of evidence might point to other localities? First of all, England and Spain were on the doorsteps of war. The competition for trade with eastern Asia, especially Cathay (China) was about to plunge the two countries into open hostilities. Drake's disregard for the Spanish claim to the Pacific Ocean, backed by the Vatican, didn't ease tensions. Although the Queen officially looked the other way, her financial backing of Drake's expedition was all too apparent, especially to King Phillip's ever-present spies in her court. But an even more formidable reason lay beneath the surface of exploration and glory for Queen and Country. The quest for a northwest passage, the fabled Straits of Anian, had already been undertaken by another English navigator, Martin Frobisher. Discovery of such a shortcut from Europe to the Far East would bypass the Spanish maritime gauntlet in South America. Was Drake simply trying to circle the globe while financing his trip at the expense of Spanish treasures? Unlikely that such a venture would have been permitted, much less financed, by Elizabeth for the sole purpose of irritating so formidable a foe. On the other hand, discovery of such a passage would have guaranteed the Crown, and Drake, of continuing revenue far beyond the acquisition of a few ship cargoes. Thus, the discovery that the latitude markings on some of the early maps may have been altered on subsequent publications provides a meaningful context for cartographic deception.

Spain had only moved into Mexico by the 1570s. There was no presence in Alta California when Drake departed Guatulco with a considerable load of plundered silver and gold. He set out across the Pacific, supposedly heading home via the East Indies and Africa. The Pacific route was familiar to the Spanish since their trade galleons plied the southern crossing to Manila and the more northerly return to Acapulco. This brought them back to the California coast, usually between 35 and 42° N. Drake had left captured Spanish and a Portuguese navigator (Nuno da Silva) behind to inform the Spanish of his intentions. However, several early maps describing his route shows the *Golden Hinde* moving westward then turning sharply northward before falling back to the western coast of North America. How far north did he venture? Another controversy loomed, based both on other historical documents and on more recent findings and proposals.

Francis Drake's cabin boy and companion during the voyage was his cousin, John Drake (Sometimes referred to as his nephew but Zelia Nuttall's *New Light on Drake*, pg. 3, and pg. 21 states, "[John Drake] was established as a cousin of Captain Drake.")
As Garry Gitzen will inform you later in this book, John was taken prisoner during a subsequent voyage and subjected to the inquisition while held in Lima, Peru. In his recorded statements, John consistently informed the Spanish that a northern extent to at least 48°N was reached during the summer of 1579. This would place Drake somewhere near the Straits of Juan de Fuca. If so, did Drake believe that he had found the Straits of Anian? Would this not have been a precious discovery to keep from the Spanish? It wouldn't have been the first or last time that maps and other documents pertaining to discoveries have been changed to mislead one's enemies or competitors. Relating to this is the shroud of secrecy imposed on Drake and his crew when they returned to England. The ships logs, journals and maps were confiscated and placed in the Tower of London. It was only after the death of Drake in 1596 and Queen Elizabeth in 1603 that accounts, including that of Fletcher, began to surface. Unfortunately, Drake's original materials have never reappeared and may have been lost in one of the fires that subsequently destroyed parts of the Tower of London.

What was the fate of the bark (or frigate, as it is sometimes described) that Drake captured off the coast of Nicaragua (modern day Costa Rica)? Referred to as Tello's bark, the smaller boat accompanied the *Golden Hinde* to Mexico and sailed out into the Pacific with Drake, manned by several of his crewman, never to appear again! All further mention of the boat, as well as the fate of approximately 12 to 15 men, is missing from Fletcher's account. Lost at sea or unto another destination? By the time of the anchorage to career and repair the leaking *Golden Hinde*, the bark and its crew no longer exist. It is mentioned by John Drake, in his second deposition, as being present at the New Albion site. Is this boat buried somewhere along the northwest coast, in a bay or a river inlet?

And so we come to Gitzen's research on Nehalem Bay as a proposed anchorage site. What is it about these amateur historians, each brazenly challenging the Ph.D.s and learned experts who have made their scholarly pronouncements on what happened, when and where? Should we even bother to read their accounts, much less take them seriously? What do they know or what have they learned that the professionals have missed? Garry and others like him will be the first to admit that historical research is not their day job. It doesn't pay the bills. Their investigations and opinions are often met with disbelief, or quiet amusement bordering on contempt, from the academic establishment. I know, because I am part of that academic status quo. Peer pressure and respect for a hierarchical system of mentors and formal credentials can be overwhelming; outsiders should tread softly, if at all. Yet, one can turn to several other disciplines to observe the value of amateur endeavors in discovery. Astronomy, in which dedicated amateurs contribute to the discovery of new comets and other celestial features, is one. Amateur naturalists, especially in Britain and Europe, have contributed immeasurably to our knowledge of fauna and flora. In many cases, their findings and publications not only supplement the work of the professional, they may represent the only work on the subject.

I had ventured to Nehalem Bay following the stories and legends of buried treasure and markings that may or may not have had an association with Drake. The survey stones on display at the Tillamook County Museum are particularly fascinating; Gitzen relates their story in some detail. Are they and the local area around Neahkahnie Mountain related to Drake's northwest voyage? Honestly, I don't know. I met Garry during that trip in 2007 and I listened intently to his story. Although *direct* evidence for the multitude of New Albion claims is still to be found, one statement does appear to be defensible. The jury is still out! There is a growing body of evidence that at least part, if not all, of Drake's excursion may have found its way to Oregon, Washington, or beyond. What would it take to convince the historical establishment? The remains of the New Albion encampment or Tello's bark would seal the deal. So would an uncompromised discovery of the real "brass" plate. If some of the treasure, with its Spanish foundry markings, were discovered, the case for an Oregon landing would be substantial. How timely, if such evidence were to present itself as Oregon begins its 150 year anniversary celebration of statehood. The tragedy is, that except for Garry Gitzen, Bob Ward, and a few other mavericks, no one is looking or even willing to investigate the potential sites where this evidence may have been waiting for the past four hundred years plus.

Therefore, my hat is off to this small group of persistent historians, amateurs or not, who seek the truth and are willing to challenge the orthodox establishment. I commend them, and the volume you hold in your hand, for your studied consideration. If you like a mystery, an historical puzzle based on real life events, then join us for a fascinating trip into the past, an inquiry into what may have been. Better yet, acquire a few of the many books listed in the reference section, then come to the Oregon coast, visit the Tillamook Museum, and poke around the Nehalem Bay region. Do the ghosts of Drake's men whisper in the wind? Enjoy!

Lawrence W. Powers, Ph.D.
Department of Natural Sciences
Oregon Institute of Technology
Klamath Falls, Oregon
07 June 2008

TABLE OF CONTENTS

AMERICA
INDIA NOVA
TERRA AVS
TRALIS NONDVM
COGNITA
HAITI
EL MAR PACIFICO

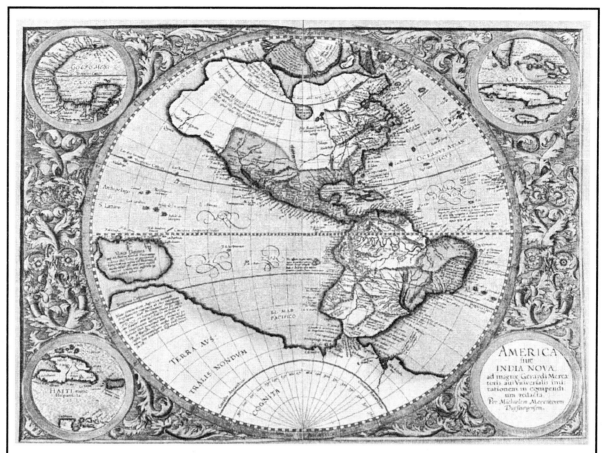

Gerard Mercator – Gemma Frisius America map circa 1570
The known world at the time of Francis Drake's voyage of circumnavigation

INTRODUCTION

On December 13th, 1577 Francis Drake, under license from Queen Elizabeth I, took his now-famous ship, the *Pelican* out of Plymouth, England and sailed through the Straits of Magellan and become the first Englishman to sail into the Pacific Ocean, at which time, he renamed his ship the *Golden Hinde**. He then sailed up the coast of South America, where, with license from the Queen, he took on supplies and goods by trading, exchange or confiscation from Spanish ships. He then sailed to the Pacific Northwest at 44° and then to 48° north latitude in the summer of 1579, until he entered into a fair and fit harbor for his five-week stay in Nehalem Bay to repair his leaking ship.

* Hinde has been Anglicized when spelled Hind. This text will hold to the original spelling of Hinde throughout unless quoting source materials.

Alongside Magellan's *Victory* and the *Titanic*, the *Golden Hinde* takes its place in history as one of the best known ships for its circumnavigation of the world between 1577 and 1580. For thirty years, the *Golden Hinde* was pictured on the English half-penny to commemorate this astounding achievement.

Who was Francis Drake?

In 1568 Drake was in command of his first ship with his cousin, Sir John Hawkins, who was the leader of the five-ship merchant trading expedition to the Caribbean. After a storm damaged their ships while in the Gulf of Mexico, they were granted safe port for repair on a small island south of Vera Cruz at San Juan de Ulúa. Due to unfortunate circumstances, a few days later, on September 23, 1568 they were deceived and attacked, resulting in only Drake and Hawkins's ships surviving. In addition to the loss of three of their five ships, they lost over 200 men including a brother, John Drake. Hawkins and Drake failed to receive reimbursement from King Phillip II of Spain for the deception and loss of goods. Consequently, it's been said that Drake was driven for the rest of his life in the pursuit of justice and restitution from the Spanish king and Viceroy Martin Enriquez.

On his circumnavigation voyage (1577-1580) Drake rounded the Magellan Strait and progressed up the coast to the city of Guatulco in Southern Mexico. Here, he put all men ashore who were not Englishmen; this was the beginning of his secret trip. According to one of Drake's best friends and Spanish captive, John Oxenham who under oath to the inquisition at Lima, Peru said Drake was to find *"settlements here* [of unclaimed lands] *in some good country"* (Zelia Nuttall, *New Light on Drake, A Collection of Documents Relating to His Voyage of Circumnavigation 1577-1588,* London MDCCCCXIV, pg 1-5) Unfortunately this is also where the reliable record of Drake's voyage ends.

Until now, where Francis Drake landed the on the Pacific coast to repair his treasure-laden *Golden Hinde* has been contested among professional and amateur historians. Robert F. Heizer, Berkeley California Professor of Anthropology, in his 1974 book *Elizabethan California* makes the case for the mystery, *"Mainly for the reason that no solid new evidence is available and the debate consists of special pleadings."* He refers to groups or individuals who have presented unfounded factual data or mainly conjectured ideas as to the true location of Drake's repair.

We will explore the surveying, navigation, geology, ethnology of the aboriginals, geography, and cartography and with patience, the reader will discover, in greater detail than previously presented in any other media; Francis Drake was the first European to interact culturally, spiritually and physically with the Pacific Northwest coast Indians. *The World Encompassed,* a primary reference in writing this book is the diary written by Reverend Francis Fletcher on the voyage, describes Portus Nova Albionis (Port of New England) as the site of Drake's landing which took place, as we shall see, in present day Nehalem Bay, Oregon.

The creation of a book consumes your life completely and becomes very personal. Great care and considerable research has been taken to insure accuracy of the information at the time of publication. I have drawn on periodicals, speeches, journals, diaries, letters, maps and surveys, memos, and histories in an effort to remain objective while maintaining the true context of quotes and references in this book. To those who teach writing I say: this book may not be the best written, but to the historian I say, this is the best book ever written on the subject by its references, documentation and footnotes. Let the following chapters and appendices begin correcting the history of Francis Drake's Pacific coast landing site.

To those who reject my conclusions and documentation, I would ask, what hard facts do you have to support your theories, without special interests? I challenge the detractors to put my evidence against yours, as to where Drake landed the queen's "treasure ship" in the summer of 1579 and to recognize the true history.

This document is neither a Native American artifact guide nor meant to promote archeological treasure hunting. In the words of Dr. James Delgado, the executive director of the Institute of Nautical Archaeology at Texas A. & M., had this to say in an essay comparing professional archeology to treasure hunters,

"The issue is one where the flash of gold and silver obscure or overwhelm the type of careful work that yields treasures of a different sort. We base our opposition to treasure hunting on the track record of those years of lost opportunities and lost history..."

June 17, 2008

Wheeler, Oregon

VERA TOTIVS EXPEDITIONIS NAVTICÆ
ADDITA
ASIA
TERRA AVSTRALIS

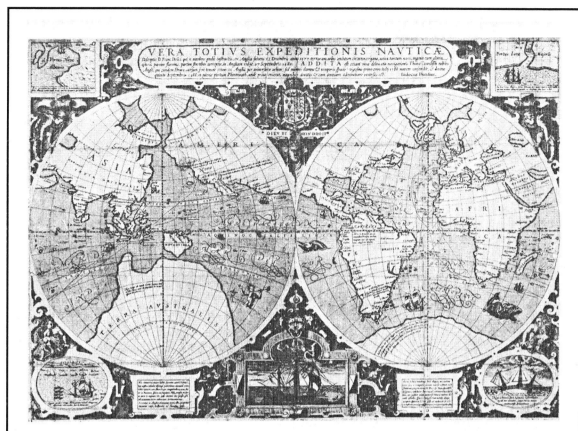

Fig. 1 Jodocus Hondius World Map commemorating Drake's path on his 1577-1580 circumnavigation voyage. The first copperplate map after Drake's return circa 1593-95. Approximate size 3 by 4 feet. Courtesy Maritime Museum, Rotterdam

Chapter 1 Discovering Drake's Nova Albion

In 1974, with the approaching 400th year anniversary of Francis Drake's landing on the North Pacific shores, scholars presented their cases for a national landmark of their proposed sites to the State of California Sir Francis Drake Commission, as to which bay; San Francisco Bay, Bolinas Lagoon or Drake's Bay being the true site where Drake repaired his ship for five weeks in 1579.[1] The commission concluded by stating that it would, "take a leap of faith rather than fact to register Drake's Bay or any other California bay as an historical landmark".

After four hundred years of mystery, including nearly two hundred years of controversy, we still have no solution to the Drake anchorage riddle.[2] The mystery for over 400 years of where Francis Drake careened and repaired his ship during five weeks in June and July of 1579 will now be exposed to those with open minds. Since formal boundaries were yet to be defined as Oregon, Washington and British Columbia, everything North of New Spain (Mexico) was designated, California. Francis Drake never set foot in what we know today as California, but instead he was in Nehalem Bay, Oregon.

AREAS OF DOCUMENTATION

In the process of setting the historical record straight, this book will cover areas in greater detail and historical documentation than what's been written concerning the time Francis Drake spent in the Nehalem Bay area from June 17th through July 24th 1579.

Four major 16th century sources, will be examined to show Drake's landing site. They are:
1. *The World Encompassed*, a journal by Reverend Francis Fletcher who was with Francis Drake on his circumnavigation.
2. The Jodocus Hondius Broadside Map circa 1593-1595
3. The Nicola van Sype Map
4. The John Drake Depositions to the Spanish Inquisition of 1584 and 1587.

Additionally, 20th century contemporary geological and anthropological documents, located throughout and in the Appendices, will be major sources affirming the location of Drake's landing.

In order to establish Drake's historical moment in time and place, it is necessary to examine a multitude of historical vignettes, by using various documents, maps, doctoral and master theses, and photographs to develop a complete and accurate mosaic to establish Francis Drake's Pacific Coast landing in Nehalem Bay.

We will compare Nehalem Bay with California theories of Drake's landing site and it will be for the reader to decide which bay is the true site after examining the following topics:
- Surveying
- 16th and 20th Century Maps
- Symbolic Sovereign Acts
- Topography

      o Indian Ethnology, Anthropology and Language

      o Flora and fauna

      o Geography

NEHALEM BAY, OREGON - NOVA ALBION

Nehalem Bay is along the North Oregon Coast less than forty miles south of the Columbia River. Nehalem Bay lies at 45° 41' north latitude, borders Neahkahnie Mountain to the north and Cape Meares headland which is sixteen miles to the South.

As we will see, confirming Nehalem Bay, will be through multifaceted corroboration. This will not be through allegorical contemporary documents, but new evidence presented for the first time and with historically documented facts throughout when comparing the above list with the diary of Drake's voyage titled, *"The World Encompassed"*. We'll see that Nehalem Bay is where the aboriginal natives treated Drake as a god and king and where he made his claim for Queen Elizabeth I of the unexplored North American Continent and called those lands Nova Albion. Topographical maps, geological features, ethnology, language and the first documented land survey made in the New World will show that Francis Drake landed his leaking ship for five weeks in Nehalem Bay.

Upon Drake's return to in England in 1580, the Queen took charge of all charts and logs with the intention of keeping the information out of the public realm and more specifically, out of the hands of the Spanish. To accomplish this veil of secrecy, she issued, as she had done at other times, an order "Under Pain of Death"[3] for anyone releasing information about the voyage. These priceless historical charts and logs have not been seen since that time, perhaps lost to fires or wars. It his hoped that additional documentation of the Drake voyage will come to light because of this book.

Looking for a place to careen his ship by laying it on its side to clean and re-tar the leaking seams, on the 17th of June 1579*, Francis Drake and his crew came to a bay along the Pacific Coast of Oregon. He anchored his ship, the *Golden Hinde,* at the mouth of Nehalem Bay while he scouted in his pinnace, an open rowing boat with single sail carrying up to 20 men, using a log & line to determine the depth and width of the channel.[4] He looked for a defensive position against potentially hostile Indians, which he experienced the previous year with the Patagonia Indians of Argentina who had wounded him in a surprise attack. Also, he wanted to be out of sight of the Spanish whom he believed may have followed him. At the rear of the bay, protected from the prevailing northwest winds of summer and out of sight of ships sailing past, yet close enough to the main channel, the *Golden Hinde* was off-loaded and his fort of stone was constructed (see in Chapter 3).

* Add 10 days to the present calendar because the English used the Julian calendar until 1595.

DRAKE – THE 16TH CENTURY NAVIGATOR

Having anchored to repair his ship in Nehalem Bay, Francis Drake was in command of the first landing of Europeans in the Pacific Northwest. The *Golden Hinde*, the most complex machine of its time, came to rest with its crew in a small bay bordered with lush evergreen forest, trees 20-30 feet in circumference and 250 feet tall, and surrounded by rolling hills and mountains. Drake and his crew lay 21,000 miles from England, the furthest one could travel in the unknown New World, a triumph of seamanship.

> On 14 April, 1579, Gaspar de Vargas. Chief Alcalde of Guatulco [Southern Mexico], who had been a captive of Drake, reported to the Viceroy Martin Enriquez, *"Francis Drake is so boastful of himself as a **mariner and a man of learning** that he told them* [Spanish prisoners] *that there was no one in the whole world who understood the art of navigation better than he."*[5]

To put this event into historical perspective, when King Henry VIII of England died in January, 1547, only thirty years before Drake sailed, not more than a few Englishmen were interested or trained in the practice of oceanic navigation.[6]

- A contemporary of Drake's, Captain Martin Frobisher, during his voyage in 1576 to discover the Northwest Passage by sailing over the top of North America to

China from the Atlantic had the same problem of all navigators of the time, "...*all arose from the inability of navigators to determine their longitude, and to the diverse and at the time unknown currents in these regions making their reckoning erroneous... (Frobisher's) chart is important for its arrows indicating the amount of variation observed and for the position of the observations, and is the earliest chart to have such notations. It is thus one of the earliest English scientific records relating to magnetism, and provided data that enabled Robert Norman to prove the inequality of magnetic variation in* <u>The New Attractive</u>*, five years later in 1581.*" [7]

- At the time of Drake's voyage, there were less than a handful of English-language books on basic math of geometric surveying and navigation and it was still an imprecise science. The best instruments had been devised many centuries prior and were not very exact in their measurements or calculations. In fact, the calculations for navigating by the stars were still considered somewhat magical and rarely did sailors lose sight of land to navigate.

- The earliest navigation books were a new science to the untrained common English seamen. Gemma Frisius's, *De Principiis Astronomiae & Cosmographiae* was the first description of navigation using the stars for triangulation and first published in 1530. Copernicus published his treatise on the solar system with the sun being at the center in 1543. These books, yet to be published in English, were the beginnings of open-ocean navigation by using the sun, moon and stars to determine latitude, longitude, time and day.

In 1547 Dr. John Dee a Gemma Frisius student and Queen Elizabeth's I appointed court astrologer, was at that time, the leading English mathematician in England. Dr. John Dee was adviser in mathematics and navigational applications to the Muscovy Company which had been formed to trade and explore the new world. Dee had trained Martin Frobisher, a Drake contemporary, before his voyages to the North American Atlantic seacoast in 1576. [8] Other English writers of navigation and surveying were father and son, Leonard and

Thomas Digges, who had published *Tectonicon* in 1556 and *A Geometrical Treatise Named Pantometria* in 1571.   John Dee, Leonard and Thomas Digges each had contact with the Queen's court and through contemporary 16th century contacts were, at some level, influential to Francis Drake's navigational education before he left on his circumnavigation voyage.

Nuno da Silva, a Portuguese pilot captured by Drake off the coast of Africa in 1577 and released in Guatulco, South America in 1579, described the three navigational books Drake carried,

> *"While in Guatulco Drake took out a map and pointed on it how he had to*
> *return by a strait* [this was the Strait of Anian, now proven fictional Northwest
> Passage] *which is in 66° and that he did not find it, then by way of China* [he
> would sail home]. *He carries 3 books on navigation, one in French L'Art de*
> *Naviguer, Lyons, 1554, one in English (either, Eden's translation of Cortes's*
> *work, The Arte of Navigation, London 1561 or Bourne's Regiment for the Sea,*
> *London 1574) and another, the account of Magellan's voyage, in a language (da*
> *Silva) did not know either Maximilian of Transylvania's De Moluccis Insulis,*
> *Rome and Cologne, 1523 or, Pagafetta's Le Voyage et Navigation faict par les*
> *Esponolz ec isles de Mollucques, Paris, 1525."*[9]

Of these, Cortes and Pagafetta are the current historian's choices of Drake's books.

General Drake, as he was addressed, being the leader of the expedition, with navigation of the open seas an emerging skill for seamen and with his only navigational instruments being a magnetic compass, sandglass, cross-staff, astrolabe and a log & line; became the first European captain to sail a ship around the world (Magellan's ship is credited as the first European ship), sailing more than 40,000 miles . He was the finest English commander of a fleet of sailing vessels, skilled in navigation and was devoted heart and soul to God, Queen Elizabeth I and England.

THE DRAKE LAND CLAIM

Demarcation line of the Drake land claim to North America
Demarcation line of the Drake land claim to North

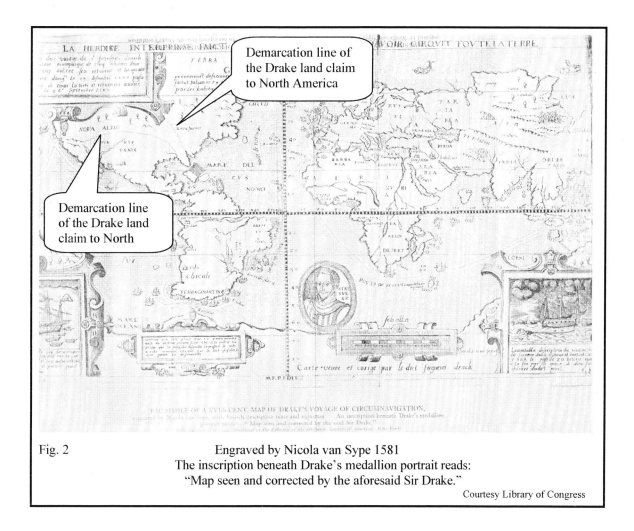

Fig. 2 Engraved by Nicola van Sype 1581
The inscription beneath Drake's medallion portrait reads:
"Map seen and corrected by the aforesaid Sir Drake."
Courtesy Library of Congress

The Library of Congress states, "One of the greatest cartographic treasures of the Elizabethan era is a map bearing the legend "*Carte veuee et corige par le dict sieur Drack*" ("A map seen and corrected by the aforesaid Sir Drake") see fig. 2. [10] Notice the North American continent depicted on the van Sype map with dotted lines extending from the west coast to the east coast.

Zelia Nuttall was a researcher of Mexican archaeology at the Mexican National Archives in 1908. She accidentally discovered the Spanish Inquisition Declaration of Nuno da Silva as to how and when he was taken prisoner by Francis Drake while sailing near Africa. Shortly afterwards Nuttall discovered many other unknown Spanish documents describing Francis Drake's voyage along the coast of South America in 1578-9. Nuttall brought to light an almost unknown map engraved by Nicola van Sype. Nuttall has this to say about the Nicola van Sype map,

> "On reading the inscription stating that the map was "seen and corrected by Drake" to be seen under his medallion portraite, the question naturally presents itself, what were the "corrections" made by Drake's hand?[11]

Nuttall continues,

> "It took some time before I grasped what I now believe to be the full significance of the two lines of demarcation which can be seen drawn on the North American Continent. One extends from the Gulf of California to the Mississippi river across the Continent, roughly marking the former border of the United States and Mexico. The other encloses "New France," the French possessions on the eastern coast of North America. These obviously indicate an intention to map out a "New England" embracing the entire North American Continent north and west of the limits assigned to New Spain and New France, including a tongue of territory stretching southward, separating these and terminating in Flordia.
>
> Whose hand but that of Drake, the explorer and discoverer, could have had the audacity to set limits to the Spanish and French possessions in America, and whose mind but his could have conceived, at that early period, the thought of so vast a country colonized by people of English extraction?
>
> It thus appears as though the present occupation of the North American Continent by the Anglo-Saxon race is after all, but a realization of what may be called Drake's Dream."

Drake's bold attitude of claiming so large an area might cause one to ask how he could have claimed the east coast when he wasn't there. Drake didn't need to be in all places to claim territory (though he had east coast knowledge from his previous trading explorations); only to know that the Spanish had not landed further North of 38° on the west coast. This he knew from captured Spanish maps showing Monterey Bay which is 36° 45' north.[12] He would have seen no need to place crosses or plaques on every hilltop to make a sovereign claim for England and his Queen. Francis Fletcher, Drake's minister on the voyage and author of *The World Encompassed,* states the Spanish had never been, in this place and their discoveries were "many degrees Southward of this place."[13] When the Spanish resumed exploration in 1774, they skipped the latitudes between 38° and 48° north, recognizing Drake's claim.   Also, why would Drake, with a leaking treasure-laden ship, ever want to sail any closer to Spanish territory than need be, when he believed the Spanish could be searching for him?

It makes perfect sense to say that Drake never landed any further south than 44° north latitude which is what John Drake, Francis's cousin, said; they came in at 44° north and went to 48° north. After John Drake returned in 1580, he sailed again in 1582 with the ill-fated, circumnavigation plan of William Fenton to establish trading partners. Because of storms and Fenton's errors in judgment, instead of sailing around Africa, they sailed west to the Brazilian coast. Here, John Drake wrecked his ship and was subsequently captured and gave two of his uncensored depositions (see John Drake depositions below). John Drake would not have known that Fletcher wrote 38° in his journal *The World Encompassed* [14] published in 1628.

The van Sype map shows a line across the entire North America from the west coast to the Atlantic Ocean, corrected and plainly claimed by Drake with his approval.

JOHN DRAKE

John Drake was Francis Drake's cousin, a 16-17-year-old cabin boy when he left Plymouth and Drake's closest confidant during the 1577-80 circumnavigation. Captured Portuguese pilot da Silva, in his deposition of May 1579 to the Spanish Inquisition, [15] indicated that John and Francis Drake would spend hours in the *Golden Hinde* cabin and da Silva saw John drawing in colored shorelines so that any navigator who followed would recognize the locations. (see Chapter 2 "Deos" for additional drawing of shore lines)

After John Drake returned to England in 1580 he gained command of his own ship and set sail with four other ships, planning to repeat the Drake voyage into the South Seas and claim Spanish treasures. Neither the expedition nor John Drake were to be so lucky; his ship was wrecked while trying to negotiate a river he had navigated previously with his cousin, Francis Drake and he was captured by the Spanish and spent the rest of his life in South American prisons.

During his confinement, John Drake gave two well-published depositions to the Spanish Inquisition describing his participation in the 1577-80 voyage.[16] Both in 1584 and again in 1587, he said they (Francis Drake and crew of which John Drake was a member) came in at 44° north latitude and sailed to 48° (see Appendix IV). When John Drake was asked about the 30 to 40-foot ship known as Rodrigo Tello's Bark, which Francis Drake had captured while off the coast of New Spain (present day Nicaragua), John Drake said they left the bark in California. In 1579, everything north of New Spain was considered California. When John Drake says they left the Tello's Bark in California, he was referring to Nehalem Bay, Oregon.

THE PLATE OF BRASS HOAX

According to Francis Fletcher, Francis Drake made a formal claim of the Nova Albion territory in 1579 for Queen Elizabeth I by inscribing a "Plate of Brass" and fixing it to a large post.[17] (Note: the *Anonymous Narrative* states that a plate of lead was used and not a plate of brass.)

The authentic plate of brass has yet to be found. However, a bogus plate was produced in Northern California in 1936 and was believed by many, for forty years, to be the authentic plate. The perpetrators of this astonishing charade were members of the California Historical Society [18] who duped their unknowing colleague, Herbert E. Bolton, distinguished professor of California history and director of the prestigious Bancroft Library at the University of California Berkeley. Samuel Eliot Morison said of Professor Bolton and the "plate of brass",

> *"(he) begged his students to keep their eyes open and if it were found, bring it to him, provided an irresistible temptation for some joker to have fun at the expense of the distinguished professor."*[19]

Professor Bolton believed the fake plate to be real and he solicited other professionals to verify its authenticity. Bolton had Professor Colin Fink and Professor E. P. Polushkin examine the plate and they confirmed the forged plate of brass to be genuine.[20] However, a July 1977 report which was signed by James D. Hart, Director of the Bancroft Library states,

> "*The most recent, although by no means the most precise, public challenge to it [Plate of Brass] was that made by Samuel Eliot Morison in the second volume of his book <u>The European Discovery of America</u>. His conclusion was firm: "'Drake's Plate of Brass' is as successful a hoax as the Piltown Man or the Kensington Rune Stone.*"[21]

Professor Robert Heizer, University of California at Berkeley, one of the leading professional ethnographic authorities, relied heavily on the authenticity of the "plate of brass" in his 1947 thesis to prove the California Miwok and Pomo Indians were the natives Drake came into contact with in 1579.[22] In 1974, then believing the plate was a hoax, Heizer states,

> "*we have to admit **we know very little about the particular form of Indian culture… and even the native language spoken there** [Northern California Miwok/Pomo] **up to about 1800 A.D. is in some doubt.**"* [23]

We will see in Chapter 4 that the Indians Drake met were the Nehalem.

An investigative report was conducted by the Bancroft Library in 1977 and they concluded with the opinion that the "***plate is a modern forgery*.**",[24] The plate is no longer on display at the Bancroft Library nor are there any plans to reinstate its former authentication. Some amateur and professional historians continue to accept the plate as real. Although a proven fake, over the past 75 years, many historians and readers of history have taken for granted that the plate is real because, once written, even if incorrect, history takes on a veneer of fact unless the record is put straight.

UNRAVELING THE DRAKE RIDDLE

This long-standing mystery began to reveal itself in 1968 when M. Wayne Jensen Jr., a 35 year-old archaeological student at Portland State University, along with a partner, Donald Viles, a Garibaldi printer, mapped numerous cairns and marked rocks on Neahkahnie Mountain in Tillamook County, Oregon. After extensive research, Jensen and Viles theorized that Francis Drake was the initiator of these marked rocks.

It was not until Jensen and Viles had ended their partnership that Jensen arranged in 1978 for a surveyor, Phillip A. Costaggini (See Appendix I), a master's candidate at Oregon State, to document the cairns and marked stones, shedding significant light on the mystery. Costaggini's thesis concluded that the area was a 16th century survey site and Francis Drake would have been the only logical choice to have performed such a survey, as we will see in Chapter 2.

Sir Francis Drake
Plymouth, England bronze 1883

Chapter 2   Neahkahnie Mountain Survey

EARLY EXPLORER LAND CLAIMS AND THEIR SOVEREIGN SYMBOLIC ACTS

Other than Francis Drake, explorers of the period never sailed any further than 42½° north latitude. Spaniards Juan Rodriguez Cabrillo and Bartolome Ferrelo (who took over command after the death of Cabrillo in 1542), sailed as far north as 42½°, the present border between California and Oregon. Although they claimed land to Miguel Island, Mexico,[1] no mention of other land claims or landings were known to have been made.

Early land claims are as follows:

A. Portuguese Captain Diogo Cao in 1483 carried stone pillars to Southern Africa [2] with partial inscriptions which were set up to mark possession. The pillars were called *Padroes.*

B.   Bartholomew Dias set up Padroes on the east coast of Africa in 1488 to mark another Portuguese land claim. [3]

C. Spaniard Balboa in September of 1513 assembled a heap of stones to take possession of the South Sea [Pacific Ocean] and the name of the King of Castile was inscribed in stone. [4]

D. Elizabethan explorer Captain Martin Frobisher stacked rocks into cairns as sovereign symbolic acts of claiming land for the queen on his voyage of discovery to Nova Scotia in 1575-6. [5]

E. At about the same time Drake was engaged upon his voyage of circumnavigation, Martin Frobisher was actively pursuing his 2nd voyage of discoveries on the northeastern coast of what is now Canada. On July 20, 1577, an anchorage was made in Jackman's Sound where Frobisher and his company went ashore in order to take formal possession of this region in the vicinity of Hudson Bay. A description of the ceremonies performed are described by Frobisher:

> *"After this order, we marched through the Countrey with Ensigne displaied, so farre as thought needfulle, and now and then **heeped up stones on high mountaines and other places in taken of possession**, as likewise to signifie unto such as hareafter may chance to arrive there, that possession is taken in behalfe of some Prince, by those who first found out the Countrey".* [6]

F. Sir Humphrey Gilbert, another Elizabethan explorer who made a notable voyage of discovery, set sail in the summer of 1583. His fleet came to anchor in St. John's Harbor, Newfoundland and on August 5th the rite of taking possession was performed by the following acts:

> *"And afterward were erected not farre from that place the Armes of England **ingraven in lead** [bold underline by author], and affixed upon a pillar of wood. Yet further and actually to establish this possession taken in the right of her Majestie, and to the behalf of Sir Humphrey Gilbert knight, his heires and assignes forever; the General granted in fee farme* [ownership forever] ***divers parcels*** [suggests surveying of the land] *lying by the waterside, both in this harbour and elsewhere".* [7]

This same manner describes the claiming of lands by Drake in the *World Encompassed* by means of a survey and engraving a lead plaque and affixing it to a tree, post or pillar of wood.

G. On a voyage of discovery to the Northeast in May of 1580 by English Captains Arthur Pet and Charles Jackman, their barks *George* and the *William* became separated in a storm. The log of the *George* states on the 22nd of June:

> *"The wind blewe very much with great fogge, we lacking Water and wood bare within an Island where wee founde great store of wood and water, there were three or foure goodly sounds. Under two points there was a cross set up, and a man buried at the foote of it. Upon the said crosse Master Pet did grave his name with the date of our Lorde, and likewise upon a stone at the foote of the cross, and so did I also, to the end that if the William did chance to come thither, they might have knowledge that we had been there..."*

This illustrates the placing of markers and the carving on stone were characteristic actions of English seamen to let others know of their presence. [8]

H. While at Port St. Julian, Argentina in 1578, Drake's crew,

> *"...engraved in the stones, ... As a memorial of our generals name* [Drake] *in Latin, that it might be better understood, of all that should come after us."* [9]

These are all examples of land claims where stones served as markers and symbolic acts to take possession of lands. Viewed in this context, the monument survey rocks and cairns on Neahkahnie Mountain left by Drake were consistent with the time period to claim land for the queen and confirm the discover's ownership percentage, as she had licensed Gilbert in 1578. It might be said here, no survey or marked rocks or cairns has ever been found in or around any Northern California bay.

GOALS OF THE GREAT VOYAGE

The opening paragraph of Reverend Francis Fletchers *The World Encompassed* lays out the purposes of Francis Drake's circumnavigation of the globe. Many historians will agree that one of his prime goals was to lay claim to large areas of the unknown world, keeping pace with Spain and Portugal for lands to trade and colonize.

The opening paragraph of *The World Encompassed* states:

"Others not contented with school points [book and classroom mathematics] *and such demonstrations have added thereunto their own history and experience. All of them in reason have deserved great commendation of their own ages and purchased a just renowned with all posterity. For if a **surveyor*** [bold by author] *of some few Lordships, whereof the bounds and limits were before known, worthy deserves his reward for his work, not only for his travel but for his skill also measuring the whole and every part thereof did a good job measuring a few bits of land which was already delineated by fences, trees, houses, churches and towns:"*

This passage is stating that a surveyor is entitled to his just rewards from his study of surveying and his physical energies. This is obviously referring to Drake being entitled to a percentage of ownership to the lands he discovered under the license given by the Queen, just as she had given to English explorers Gilbert and Sir Richard Grenville. Grenville was to take the voyage of circumnavigation but the Queen changed to Drake. [10]

Fletcher goes on with:

*" how much more, above comparison, are their famous travels by all means possible to be eternized, who have bestowed their studies and endeavor, to **survey and measure*** [bold by author] *this globe almost immeasurable?"*

This states for those who measured the world under great hardships and danger, deserve large rewards.

Fletcher continues with:

*"Neither is here that difference to be objected, which in private possessions is of value: **Whose Land Survey you?*** [bold added by author] *for as much as the Maine Ocean* [Pacific Ocean] *by right is the Lords alone, and by nature left free, for all men to deal withal, as very sufficient for all men's use, and large enough for all men's industry".*

Here Fletcher is stating it doesn't matter who owns the land, only that the survey is to be completed because God has provided this planet for all men's trading and colonization.

Because Drake's log and maps were taken by Queen Elizabeth I on his return in 1580, these documents of his voyage have never been seen in public. When Fletcher writes, *"Whose Land Survey you?"* verifies a "survey" of some kind of land measurement took place by using sightings of the sun, moon and stars which were measured numerous times a day for a navigator of oceans or surveyor of lands. The Neahkahnie Mountain countryside was an area of land Drake surveyed and claimed for England.

THE TRAIL TO DISCOVERY

The compelling and groundbreaking discovery of hard evidence that Francis Drake was in Nehalem Bay in 1579 is rewriting the Pacific Northwest's first contact history, exploration and colonization of the North American Continent.[11]

Remarkably, the late M. Wayne Jensen Jr., of Tillamook, Oregon, former Director of the Tillamook County Pioneer Museum, is at center stage of this discovery. This fascinating story of deciphering the true meaning of the Neahkahnie Survey Rocks located on the North Oregon coast at 45° 45' north latitude provides strong evidence of Drake having landed in Oregon. A professional 20th century survey of the Neahkahnie Mountain Survey Rocks and Cairns, directed by Jensen, is described in Samuel Bawlf's book *Sir Francis Drake's Secret Voyage to the Northwest Coast of America, AD 1579* as **"...the most important artifact of Elizabethan science yet found in North America"**.[12]

In 1971 during a speech presented at the Neahkahnie Community Club in Manzanita, Oregon by Jensen and co-discoverer of the puzzling marks, Don Viles (deceased 1989), they revealed the meanings behind the markings on the basalt rocks laid out upon the mountain's faces and pastures.

Jensen was the leading authority[13] of the inscribed stones and cairns which dotted Neahkahnie Mountain facing the ocean in a southwestern exposure. While in his teens, Jensen became interested in collecting materials about the area around Neahkahnie Mountain. Today the Jensen Collection contains books, manuscripts, research papers and original interpretative materials collected over a 40-year period covering early Elizabethan, Spanish, Dutch and French explorers, all of whom preceded Lewis and Clark's 1805 journey to the Pacific Northwest. A large group of these materials pertain to Sir Francis Drake and the discovery of the carved rocks and cairns leading to the theories of their origin.

Theories of the Rock Meanings

There have been varying theories as to how the carved rocks and cairns came to be laid out on Neahkahnie Mountain. When the early pioneers arrived in the late 1800's, pirate treasure was the leading theory to explain the marks and lettering on large rocks after hearing stories of gold from an early surveyor [14] (See Appendix I Costaggini Survey) Additionally, the Spanish Galleon *San Francisco Xavier* c. 1705, while returning from the Philippines, wrecked near the mouth of Nehalem Bay, adding to the theory of treasure, though the only things of real value ever recovered were well-traveled beeswax chunks, up to forty pounds each, which even Lewis and Clark mentioned in their journal.

WASHINGON
OREGON
COLUMBIA RIVER
ASTORIA
NEAHKAHNIE MT.
SURVEY SITE
NEHALEM
MANZAN
Nehalem Bay
WHEELER
PACIFIC OCEAN
NEHALEM RIVER

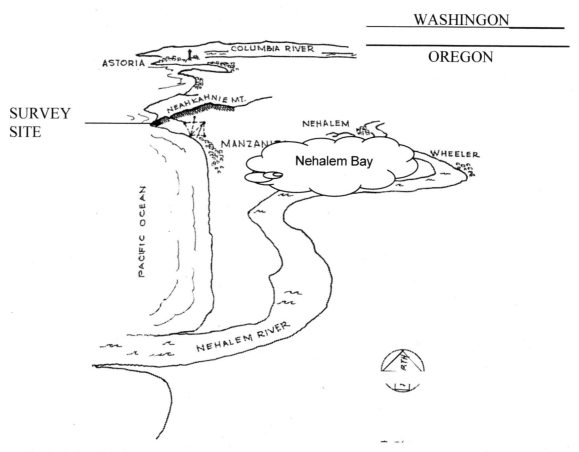

Fig. 3 Columbia River to the North of Neahkahnie Mountain and Nehalem Bay to the south.
Drawing by Doug Stahr

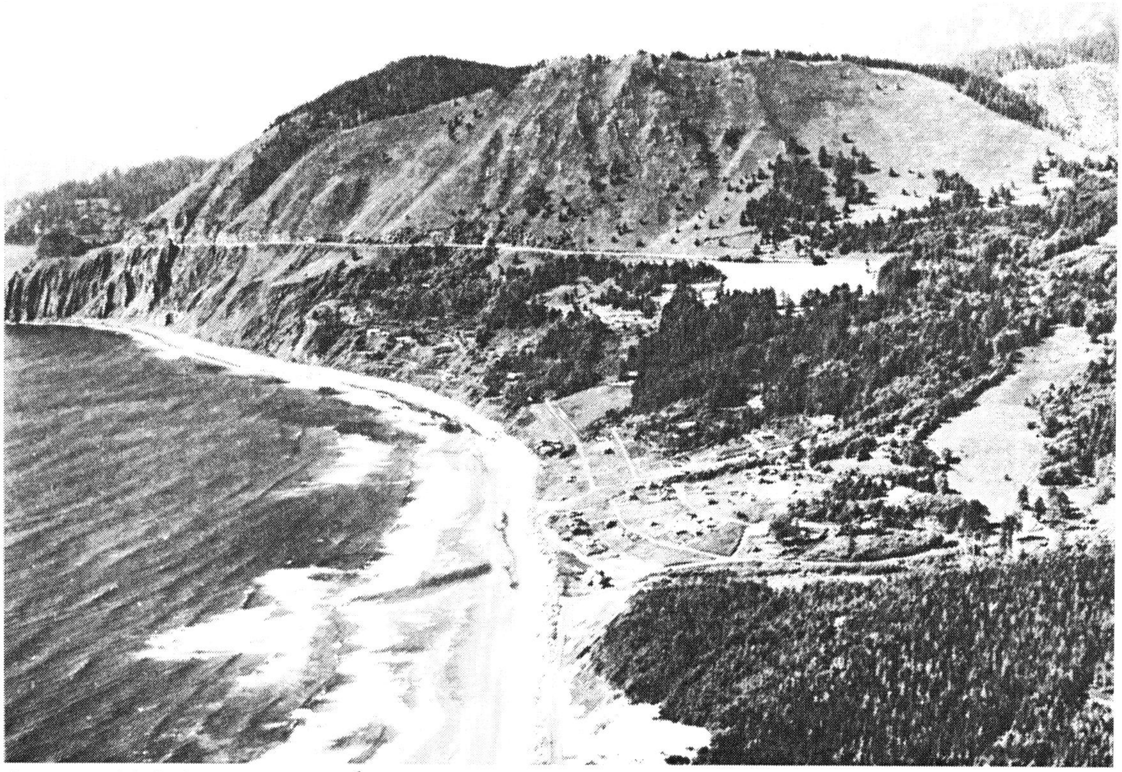

Fig. 4 Neahkahnie Mountain 45 degrees 44 minutes 38 seconds north latitude circa 1950
Courtesy Jensen Collection

THE DRAKE SURVEY

Jensen and Viles theorized, after researching other potential explorers in 1970 determined that Drake conducted a survey on Neahkahnie Mountain. Very few men in England in the 16th century could navigate in the open ocean without the coast in sight. Using the stars, sun, and moon to navigate and using crude instruments by today's standards, with no more than basic addition, subtraction and division skills - such were the limit of the seamen's tools. Standardization for recording surveys was non- existent and although Jensen and Viles'specific interpretations of all the marks on the stones may not always be correct, their conclusion of a Drake land claim was correct. Research of these markings has led to a direct link to the Copernicus system published in 1543 as well as other 16th century mathematical symbols which point to the Queen's augur, John Dee and the English translation of Euclide[15] for which Dee wrote the preface.

Drake was the best navigator of his time, sailing and surveying without a telescope which was not invented until 1600.[16] The sextant[17] wasn't invented until the 1700's, chronometers not until the mid-1700's,[18] chains and rods were to come into use after 1600. Traveling the ocean blue, observing the ocean swells, the movement of the heavenly bodies and using basic instruments of astrolabe,[19] magnetic compass,[20] sand glass, log & line[21] and cross-staff,[22] which used simple measurements of degrees and minutes, then converted into leagues, miles, furlongs, passes or yards and recorded on charts and plats, Drake navigated the globe. These were the instruments with which Drake navigated and these were the same instruments he used to perform the survey on Neahkahnie Mountain in the middle of summer, 1579.

Neahkahnie Mountain was a unique and special place to make a survey. At 1631 feet, it's the highest location directly on the Oregon coast between British Columbia and Northern California. It is bordered to the north by the Clatsop Plains whose topography runs flat for 150 miles up the central Washington coastline. Francis Fletcher described such topography while sailing south from 48° north after being in what we know now as British Columbia.[23] Neahkahnie Mountain was also bare of trees to the ridgeline because the Nehalem Indians burned the trees to encourage the growth of wild food sources for the natives and provide grazing for the large herds of elk to facilitate hunting.

Soon after the Jensen and Viles partnership ended, Jensen's correspondence reflected his continued search for the proof of Drake's landing on the Oregon Coast. There are letters from all over the world to the great institutions of learning and archival repositories. There are letters from individual researchers who were contemporaries of Jensen who were researching the archives pertaining to Drake and his crewmembers and supporters i.e. Hawkins, Elizabeth I, Essex, and others. There are diaries, journals or logs of Drake contemporaries - Hawkins, Cabot, Cavendish, Fenton and Frobisher, as well as first-hand experiences of the members of the crew during his circumnavigation - Francis Fletcher the preacher, John Drake, his cousin and cartographer.

Later explorers' journals such as Captain Cook and Captain George Vancouveralong with Perez, Martinez, Bruno de Hezeta, Bodega y Quadra and Malaspina, John Meares and Robert Gray were compared with each of their types of navigation and survey methods.[24] The technology available to 17th and 18th century explorers, their symbolic sovereign acts practiced in the claiming of new lands, all pointed to Drake making the survey on Neahkahnie Mountain, as he was the only 16th century navigator to travel so far north. The next explorer after Drake was in 1774 when the Spaniard Perez explored British Columbia and southern Alaska. Spanish explorers, Hezeta and Bodega made claims at Trinidad Harbor, California 41° 3'N latitude and Point Granville, Washington 47° 18'N. These were the only explorers after 1579 to essentially be dependent on dead reckoning surveying and navigation. Additionally, the Spanish style of land claim was to put up crosses and bury bottles containing documents. Therefore; they would not have made the type of survey found on Neahkahnie Mountain.

INCISED ROCKS

Since the discovery of the cryptic rocks by the first pioneers, there have been many theories as to the meaning of the mysterious Neahkahnie Mountain rocks and cairns. Most often when the stories are told there is mention of vast quantities of beeswax. There have been tales of wrecked ships, gold, treasure, and mysterious activities on the mountainside as well as Indianstories of white men coming to these shores at some time in the dim past.
[25]

As these tales have been handed down, it's been told that invaders made strange carvings on some rocks and buried a chest with a slave's body thrown upon it, that his spirit would protect the treasure. [26] The Indian legends were given credence because an early settler, while plowing a mountainside field one day, suddenly hooked his plow into two huge stones bearing strange markings. [27] This strangely marked rock is now known as the "W" Rock, seen in fig. 6 and 21, which will be explained further.

Fig. 5   Wendle's Rock
Courtesy Jensen Collection 1969 ©

Named for the man on whose property
the rock was found, 200 ft. from
the ocean on a small knoll.
Rock was chalked for better photograph.

Fig. 6   'W' Rock
Courtesy Jensen Collection 1969 ©

Known as the "W" Rock for the large
'W' carved on its face. Found near the
the beach while pioneer was plowing.

Fig. 7 BKS Rock   Known as the BKS rock for large carved initials.
Courtesy Jensen Collection 1969 ©

The BKS Rock was found along beach front, north of the W Rock. Some marks may be
graffiti as well as mathematical equations and symbols.

Not only had the Indian legends contributed to tales of pirate treasure, but there were the remains of shipwrecks near the mouth of the Nehalem River channel[28] within half a mile of Neahkahnie Mountain. With shipwrecks long before the white man and Indian legends, people felt that pirate gold could be the only answer for the strange inscribed rocks. For more than 100 years men have been satisfied to search for gold on Neahkahnie's slopes and shores by digging holes and sinking shafts using imagined maps and theories from all over the world trying to decipher the meanings of these rocks.

Fortunately, between 1969-1971 many additional carved rocks and cairns were to be found by Jensen and Viles, which until that time were unknown and were then recorded for the first time.

UNDERSTANDING THE MEANING OF THE ROCKS

Don Viles had spent many years looking for the treasure and in an effort to solve this mystery; he sought out Wayne Jensen in 1967. Wayne was a fourth-generation Tillamook County descendent and he'd been methodically collecting quantities of printed material about the Neahkahnie mystery and was independently working on his own theory to decipher the rock inscriptions.

The *North America's Hidden Legacy At Neahkahnie Mountain 1579,* by Don Viles in 1982 relates,

> "*We* [he and Jensen] *started our physical search from a seafaring angle. It dawned on us that the marks on the rocks represented 'shots' or compass bearings; that someone had taken a 'fix' on something, or in other words taken a compass bearing on a specific object or place.*"

Fig. 8   Angle Rocks A & B
Rocks are chalked for better photograph.
Courtesy Jensen Collection 1970 ©

Fig. 9   Angle Rock C.
Courtesy Jensen Collection 1970 ©

Viles goes on to say,

"Our first compass-bearing plot produced a stone with many strange marks. (see fig. 10) The marks later proved to be measurements and angles. Also on this stone was the word 'AUGUR'. It took us quite some time to decipher the marks on this rock. Some of them were Roman numerals; some were Latin italics, and some, although they looked like Roman capital letters, were actually angles and bearings."

Fig. 10   M. Wayne Jensen Jr. at AUGUR Rock
1969.   Courtesy Jensen Collection 1969 ©

Fig. 11   AUGUR Rock markings
Courtesy Jensen Collection 1969 ©

29

Their first line of thinking was that this had been a Spanish ship that was wrecked and that her crew had buried the cargo close to shore where it could be easily retrieved at a later date. The Spanish measurement unit *pie*, which is approximately 11 inches was used in their search of Neahkahnie Mountain.

> *"I don't think Wayne has ever forgiven me for that one,"* said Viles. *"He cut tons of brush so we could make a metal detector search. The only thing we found was that we had purchased a fine metal detector that would stand up in the worst of weather and that a Philippine bolo knife is the world's best brush cutter."* [29]

Since using the Spanish *pie* for a measurement unit produced no results, they changed the plotting to use the Spanish *vara*, a measurement of approximately 35-1/3 inches, which was used in Spain and Mexico in the 16th and 17th century.

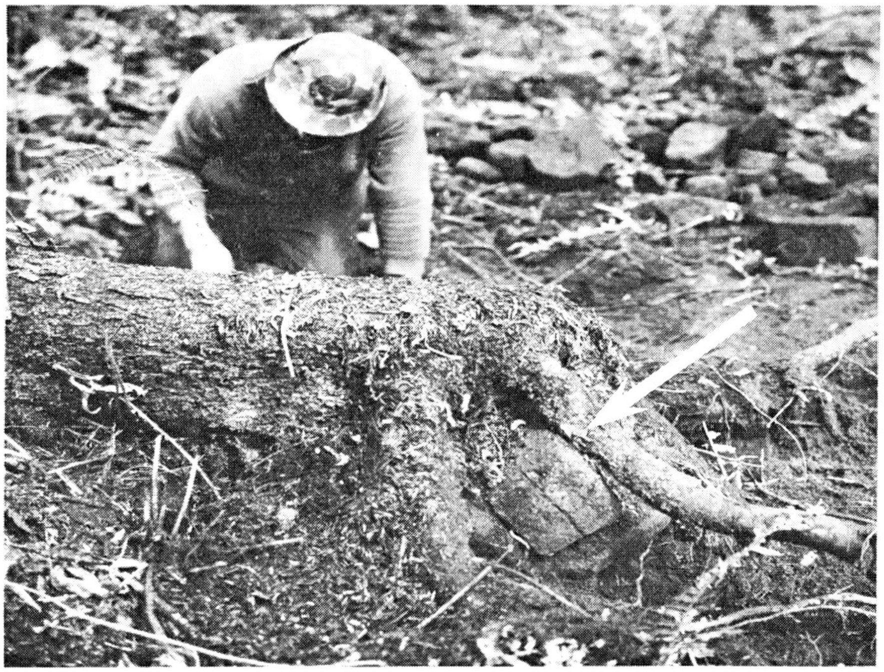

Fig 12 Viles digging out Measurement Rock Monument in 1969 from 100 year-old spruce root. Measurement Rock Monument is lying on its side with the top of the rock showing. Root sample document contained in the Jensen Collection (see below)
Courtesy Jensen Collection 1969 ©

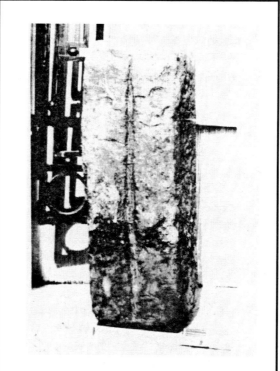

Fig. 13   Measurement Rock Monument
Known for the 36 inch incised marking
along three surfaces of the rock.
Courtesy Jensen Collection 1969 ©

Under the Measurement Rock Monument which was laid atop of a cairn of rocks two feet high and 10 foot around.(see fig. 15) At a depth of two feet a charcoal sample was taken and sent to the University of Georgia and on June 2, 1975 a report was issued[30] stating: *Sample UGa-1003 has been dated from the large pieces of charcoal from beneath the cairn known as the North Mound is 855 B.P or A.D. 1095.*

B.P. meaning before present (1975) the charcoal samples could be as old as 855 years. (See Appendix V)

The new unit of measure produced immediate results. Suddenly many more discoveries of additional markers and cairns were made, one of which produced the "Measurement Rock Monument" (see fig. 12 and 13). There were over 40 such markers and cairns which took much effort to build. These rock mounds were 2 feet high and 10 feet in diameter.

The Measurement Rock Monument is significant not only because it was shaped into a rectangle, the bottom flattened and has carved grooves up two sides and across the top measuring a total of 36 inches, **an English yard**, which was used in Drake's time. The Measurement Rock Monument is also the eastern point of the baseline measurement for the survey. The baseline on the eastern edge is the Measurement Rock Monument and the western point rock is known as the Ekahnie Rock (see Chapter 4 Indian Legends).

By using the English yard, Jensen and Viles could now plot positions or definite points to either find a marked rock or a hole where a "treasure hunter" had previously found a rock or cairn. They found numerous rocks and cairns on each face of Neahkahnie Mountain, some of which have yet to be surveyed.

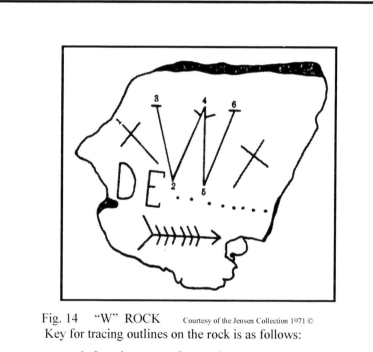

Fig. 14   "W" ROCK   Courtesy of the Jensen Collection 1971 ©
Key for tracing outlines on the rock is as follows:

    1. Location on top of mountain

    2. Survey Rock No. 1

    3. High point on mountain

    4. North end meridian baseline

    5. Wendle's Rock (so named for the original finder of the rock)

    6. Location lost to logging

Courtesy Jensen Collection

The sets of marks in fig. 14 were found on one of the stones discovered by late 19th century settlers of Neahkahnie Mountain. The stone was set close to the beach, on the southwestern side of the mountain.

The current research indicates the 'W' and the "crosses" [31] represent a combination of sun and star sighting points to determine the longitude, date and time of day. Gemma Frisius in *De principiis astronomiae…Deque usu globi*, 1530 was the first to realize that by using an astrolabe for the determination of azimuth of celestial bodies and by determining the bearings of terrestrial landmarks with repeated observations at several stations, a network could be drawn on paper which would give, by the intersections of corresponding points, a map of the countryside surveyed. [32]

One of the books Drake carried with him was the *Art of Navigation* by Spaniard Martin Cortes compiled in 1545 and first published in English in 1561, making it the first English translated navigation book written which uses the declination of the sun in determining the day of the year and latitude. [33] The "DE" research indicates declination along a meridian and the dots represents the path to take and following the arrows to the omega, the last letter in the Greek alphabet Ω., which is carved at the top of the right-hand cross shown on figure 6.

The north meridian end point is the cairn in which the incised rock of an English yard (36 inches) is located at point 4, see fig. 14.

The western baseline point is located from point 5 and then west to Ekahnie Rock, not pictured in fig. 21. (see Chapter 4 Indian Legends and Appendix I) This western baseline point contains John Dee's monas hieroglyphica of 1564. [34]

As court-appointed mathematician and astrologer, it would have been appropriate for John Dee's monas hieroglyphica to be the official stamp of an English survey. Dee wrote the preface to the first translation of Euclid[e] from Greek into English in 1570 and was a consultant who trained early navigators of the 1560-70 London Muscovy Company. D.W

Water, *The Art of Navigation in England in Elizabethan and Early Stuart Time*, refers to him in this way,

> *"The manner in which Dee, in his preface, handled his subject as a whole was masterly, while his detailed analyses of the arts of navigation and hydrographs, to name but two, have never been surpassed."*

The "arrow fins and points" on the 'W' Rock are believed to be measurement points or locations where measurements were taken on the way to the north mound where the Measurement Rock Monument was found. (See fig. 17 Wayne's Rock and fig. 18 Dual arrow points.)

Sixteenth century surveyors were proprietary about their work and with each plat they would use their own methods, symbols, letters and scale of measurement because there was no standardization at the time. The 'W' rock in photo 10, along with mathematical computations and the acts of cairn-building and the marking of rocks represents the land claim of a large proportion of the North American Continent between 38° and 48° north latitude by Drake. Determining longitude and latitude, day and time of year and by the creation of a survey map of the Nehalem Bay and Neahkahnie Mountain countryside, were the actions of this historic event. Drake's incising of these rocks and cairns became a symbolic signal to all who came after, that this land was claimed by the English.

Fig. 15   Early Measurement Rock Monument Cairn with moss removed

Courtesy Jensen Collection 1970

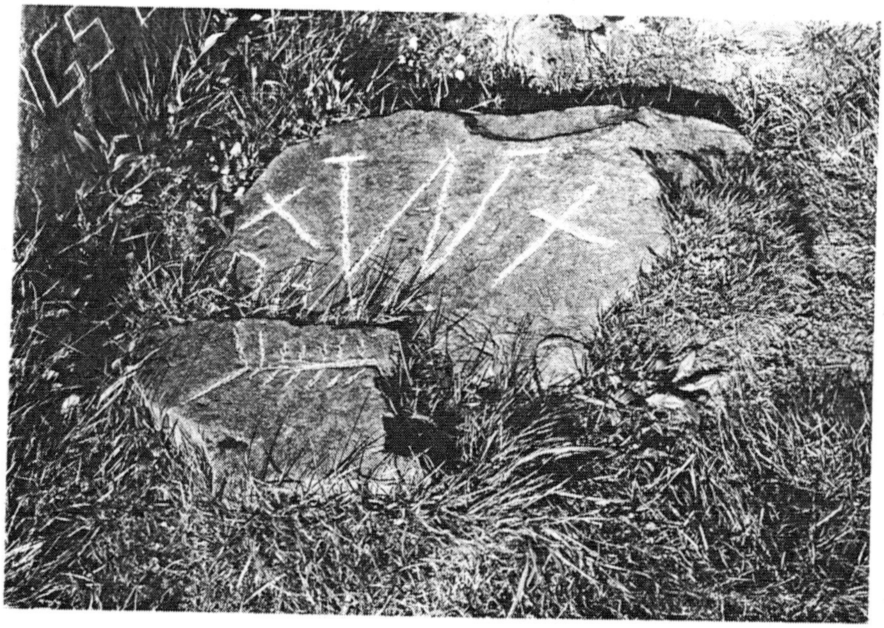

Fig. 16 'W' Rock and BKS Rock as found near beach

Courtesy Jensen Collection

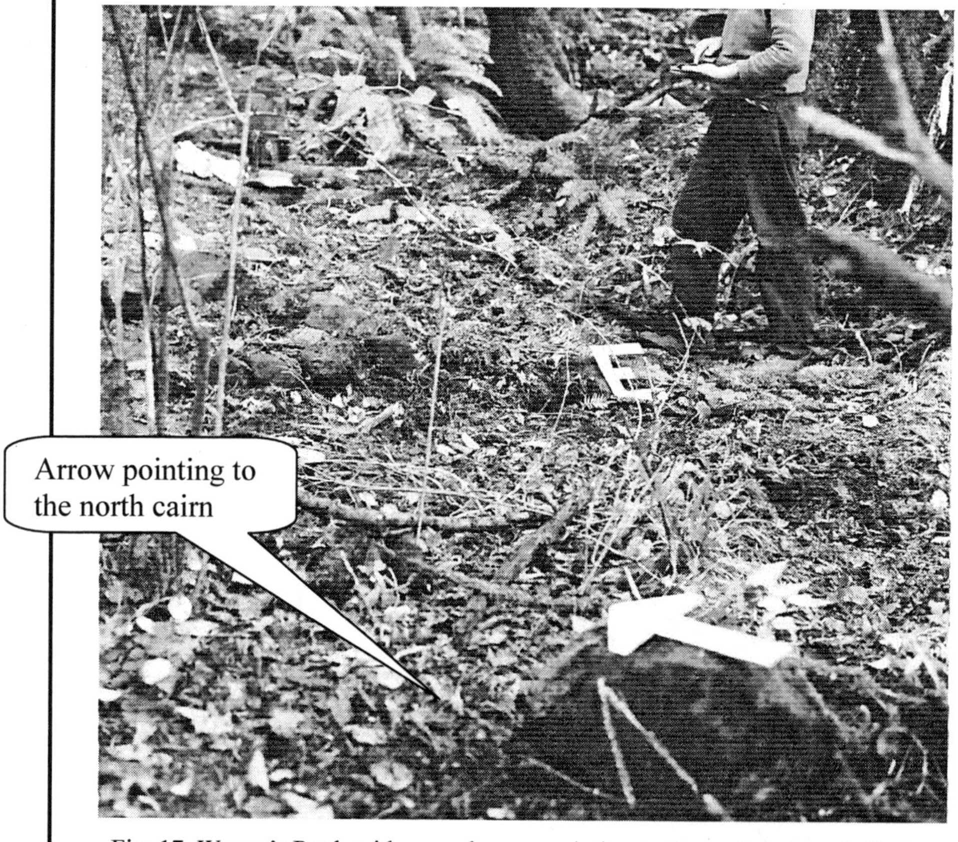
Arrow pointing to the north cairn

Fig. 17 Wayne's Rock with carved arrow pointing to the north cairn, chalked.

Courtesy Jensen Collection 1973 ©

Fig 18 Double Arrow Points   Courtesy Jensen Collection 1973 ©

ADDITIONAL CLUES TO THE SURVEY

It was now apparent that Jensen and Viles were not going to find a ship's cargo high on the mountain and that this was indeed an ancient survey. The question now became; "Who did it and when?"

Their first big break came when they noticed "*Dios*", meaning God in Spanish was misspelled as "Deos" on a Central American map of Panama drawn and written in the hand of Sir Francis Drake or one of his crew in 1595. (See Fig. 19 and 20)

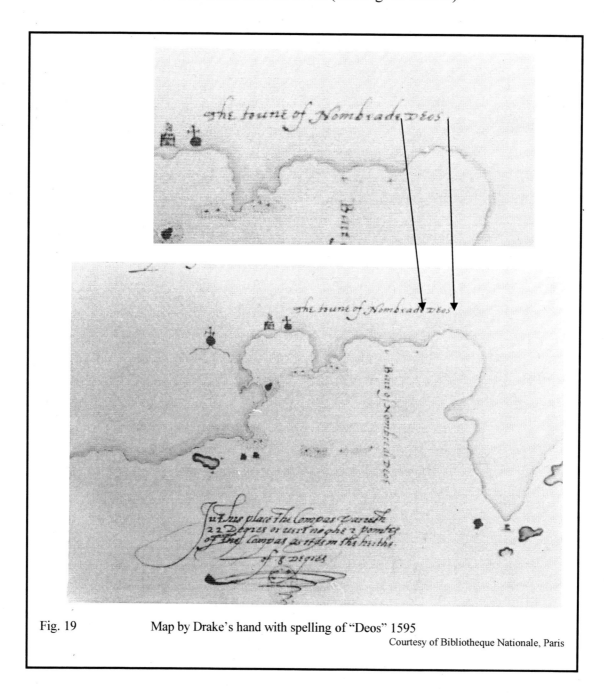

Fig. 19 Map by Drake's hand with spelling of "Deos" 1595

Courtesy of Bibliotheque Nationale, Paris

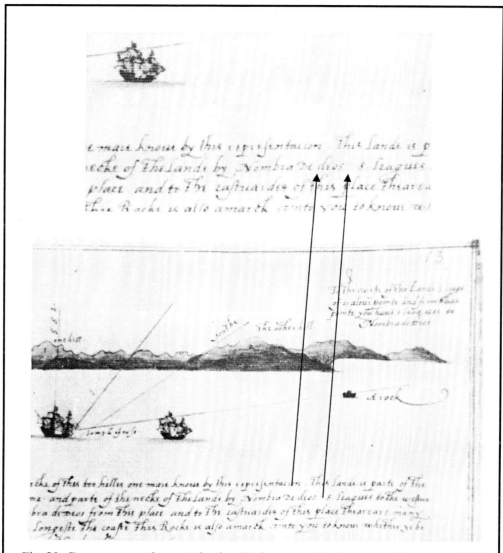

Fig. 20   Deos map was drawn at the time Drake was on the East coast of Panama in 1595. View of *Nombra de Deos,* where the Spanish treasure ships loaded their gold and silver on their return to Spain.   Courtesy of Bibliotheque Nationale, Paris

The watercolor above (fig. 19 and 20), made during Drake's last voyage to the Spanish Main (1595-1596), showing the care with which the sixteenth century seaman noted details of sea and shore. Today's sailor could easily orient himself by means of these graphic notes.

At the same time, Jensen remembered a drawing he had in his collection, showing the same spelling of *Deos* on the 'W' rock found in the late 1800's (see fig. 21 below). Up until that time it was considered the work of a prankster who didn't know how to spell *Dios* with an 'i' as in Spanish.

3.3"
DEOS
DE
8 inches thick
Sketch of rock at Nehalem, Oregon
B. F. H. Shepherd Oct 22" 1895
37 years ago

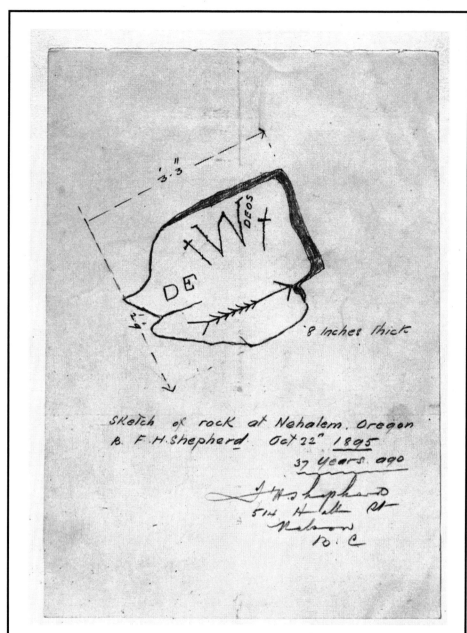

Fig. 21 Sketch of rock at Nehalem Oregon by F. H. Shepard 1895 found 1858.
Notice "DEOS" alongside the right vein of the 'W'.
Courtesy Jensen Collection

It was at this moment that they connected the rocks and cairns to an English yard and to Francis Drake instead of a Spanish survey.

With the research effort now directed at Drake and with the discoveries made from their ground search, Jensen and Viles had found evidence of the earliest white contact with the natives of the North American continent, along the Pacific Northwest on Neahkahnie Mountain. [35]

WHO ELSE COULD HAVE MADE THE NEAHKAHNIE SURVEY ?

16th and 17th Century Explorers

Only a very limited number of explorers could have made the survey; Cermeno, Vizcaino, Cabrillo and Ferrelo are the exclusive members of this group.

On his return from the Philippines to Acapulco in 1595, Spanish galleon captain, Sebastian Rodriguez de Cermeno was to explore the Northwest coast. Drake's voyage, without doubt, had some bearing on this Spanish venture. Cermeno wrecked his ship, the *San Augustine,* in Drake's Bay on Point Reyes, California. He and his crew made it to Acapulco, Mexico in a small open boat. A popular theory by historians was that Drake had landed at what is now Point Reyes, California, or one of the other small bays in Northern California area, because of the connection with Cermeno's artifacts left at Point Reyes. Cermeno and his crew never made any land claims and were lucky to escape with their lives.

Sebastian Vizcaino was sent out of Mexico, or New Spain as it was called, to make a northern voyage of discovery in 1602. He landed only as far north as Monterey Bay of which he recorded and mapped. Possibly he believed that the possession was taken by Cermeno of Drake's Bay in 1595 and had rendered it unnecessary to claim land further south. [36] Vizcaino was left with a decimated crew and came back with tales of fantastic places of snow-covered mountains, large forests and of terrible seas. Historians, for the most part, have never believed his story and have labeled him a poor sailor. He was credited with going only as far as Bodega Bay, California at 38° 19' north latitude.

Spaniards Juan Rodriguez Cabrillo and Bartolome Ferrelo sailed about the 42-1/2° north latitude in 1542-3, which is near the present day Oregon-California border although they did not land until Monterey Bay.

Explorations on the Pacific coast ceased for some time after Vizcaino returned in 1603. Cabrillo, Ferrelo, Cermeno and Vizcaino, could not have made the survey because none of these men traveled above the 43rd degree north latitude.

18ᵗʰ Century Explorers

Northern California remained deserted until 1769 when Upper California was taken by the Franciscans of the 18ᵗʰ century. Later, 18ᵗʰ century explorers sailed by Nehalem Bay on their way to Alaska for coast surveys. These were the English explorers - James Cook in 1778, George Vancouver in 1792, and the Spanish explorers - Perez in 1774, Bodega y Quadra in 1779, Esteban Martinez in 1788, Malaspina in 1791, and Juan Martinez in 1793. None of these explorers were carving stones or erecting rock cairns or doing surveys with 16ᵗʰ century surveying instruments. These 18ᵗʰ century surveyors were using more modern techniques of the "running surveys" and had chronometers to conduct large land surveys by timing how long it took from one point to another for triangulation.

James Cook would not have gone ashore to fix positions by regular triangulation; the framework of his surveys was the astronomically-based Lunar Distance method to determine positions of his ship and of coastal features. The scale of his charts had to be derived from the computed distances between fixes, to which the ship's dead reckoning from compass and log was adjusted. [37] Vancouver also used the running survey method because of the large amount of land mass he was to survey; and with the use of a chronometer to determine his position, he was able to complete the task without numerous landings.

All of the Spanish explorers sailed from Mexico to Alaska without stopping between 38 and 48 degrees north latitude.

16ᵀᴴ CENTURY SURVEYING METHODS AND INSTRUMENTS AND HOW THEY CORRESPOND WITH THE NEAHKAHNIE SURVEY

16ᵗʰ century surveying starts with the basic instruments; magnetic compass, cross-staff (sometimes called a profitable staff) and the astrolabe. The astrolabe was used chiefly for the purpose of navigation in the vertical position. It also could be used as a plane table instrument when turned horizontally and fixed in a firm position to make sure of its correct North-South orientation. This dual use was common in the early stages of European and especially in English surveying methods. By integrating a compass with the astrolabe it became a useful plane table Theodolite. The Theodolite or astrolabe was an instrument used by English navigators and surveyors to measure horizontal and vertical angles of sky and topography in graduated degrees around its perimeter. The existence and use of the Theodolite could not have occurred without Humphrey Cole, master instrument maker during the last half of the 16th century. Cole was the maker of Drake's astrolabe which was carried on the circumnavigation voyage of 1577-1580 (See fig. 22). [38]

Dr. R. T. Gunther's *The Astrolabe: its Uses and Derivatives* states that the astrolabe has merit of being portable, of being usable on the moving deck of a ship, and of being accurate in proportion to its diameter and to the skill with which it is constructed. The great two-foot astrolabe weighing over 30 pounds and constructed by Humphrey Cole located in the University of St. Andrews collection is considered the most important of these instruments. Gunther states Cole is certainly to be regarded as the leading scientific instrument maker of the Elizabethan age. [39] Gunther goes on to say, "The date 1575 upon the large instrument indicates that it was in making at the time when Humphrey Cole was engaged in the instrumental equipment for Martin Frobisher's first voyage of discovery in search of the Northwest Passage to China. An extant bill-of-lading shows that Cole provided 50 pounds worth of instruments for the voyage, and an "astrolabium" was included in the list.

At the same time, so large and weighty a disc as this astrolabe at St. Andrews could not have been used on a moving and insecure platform, such as a deck of a sailing-ship. It appears Frobisher provided himself with one and he would have intended it for use on shore.[40] In Thomas Blundevil(l)'s *New and Necessarie Treatise of Navigation 1613* he states, "broad astrolabes, though they be thereby the truer, yet for that they are subject to the force of the wind, and thereby very moving and unstable, are nothing meant to take the Altitude of anything, and especially upon the sea." [41] It's known that Frobisher built cairns and this large type of astrolabe shows the cairns were used to conduct land surveying as Drake did on Neahkahnie Mountain.

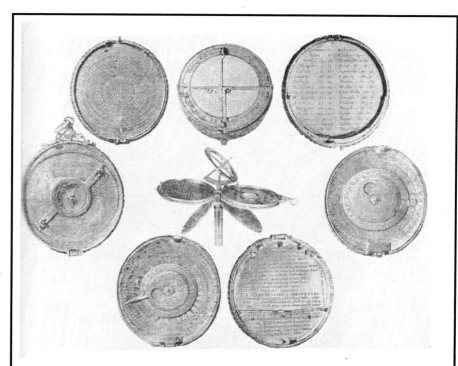

Fig. 22 Astrolabe, Theodolite and Dials by Humphrey Cole, dated 1569
This pocket astrolabe and dials are traditionally described as having belonged to Francis Drake
Courtesy of the Trustees of the National Maritime Museum, Greenwich

Other instruments, used to lesser extent, were the carpenter's square and quadrant, which were also integrated into the Theodolite (Horizontal Plane Sphere see fig. 23) which was used by William Bourne to perform his triangulation Survey of the Gravesend, English countryside in 1572 (See fig. 30 Bourne survey). [42]

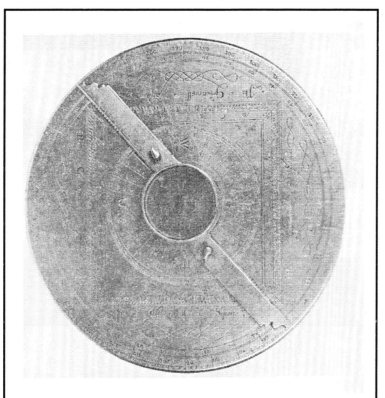

Fig. 23 Horizontal Plane Sphere (plane-table astrolabe)
by Humphrey Cole, dated 1574 Notice the compass in the
center of the instrument designed for horizontal use for surveyors.
Courtesy of National Maritime Museum, Greenwich

One of the instruments which Martin Frobisher used on his 1576 voyage, was a Horizontal Plane Sphere made by Humphrey Cole. In *The Seamans Secrets*, 1595 by John Davis, he considered it one of the navigator's necessary instruments,. It was used for fixing positions by bearing and distance, or if the navigator was a skilled surveyor, for triangulation survey work. The Horizontal Plane Sphere in fig. 23 is interesting for its outer gradation dividing the circle into 360°, its inner gradation dividing each quadrant into 90°, its innermost graduation of the rhumbs [compass points] winds, and those of the "The Geometrical Square' used in survey work.

The geometrical square was a primitive scale for finding distances. Even after triangulation was introduced in the middle of the 16th century, surveyors continued to be chiefly interested in <u>distances and heights</u> rather than angles. A quadrant, or quarter of a geometrical square, will usually be found upon quadrants (four quadrants equal 360° circle) intended for use in survey work, and a double quadrant on the lower half of the back of planispheric astrolabes [planispheric astrolabes were used to sight the sun and stars.

The planispheric astrolabe was used in a vertical position. The basic difference between positions is sighting holes for the sun being smaller than those for sighting stars which were larger]. The sides of the quadrants are usually divided into 12, 60, 100 or 120 divisions, the more numerous subdivisions being a refinement of the instruments of the 16th and 17th centuries. They correspond to imperfect tangent and co-tangent scales. This planisphere forms the base of Humphrey Cole's Theodolite of 1574 which was derived from Waldseemuller's Holimetrum of 1512 with the additional of a nautical compass, a development probably first made by Gemma Frisius about 1530 in which he used a stand-alone compass. In Cole's instrument the compass forms an integral part of the instrument about which the vertical semi-circle rotated. [43]

The research shows the "┼" on the 'W' Rock (fig. 6), was used to illustrate that a cross-staff was used to measure the height of Neahkahnie Mountain.

The triangle on Wendle's Rock (fig. 5) is incised with the number 1632, which indicates the height of Neahkahnie Mountain using the cross-staff. The U.S. Geological Survey states Neahkahnie Mountain is 1631 feet high.

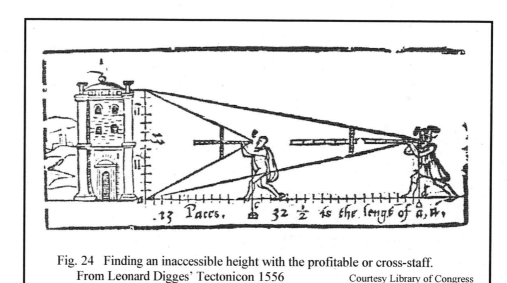

Fig. 24   Finding an inaccessible height with the profitable or cross-staff.
From Leonard Digges' Tectonicon 1556   Courtesy Library of Congress

The making of this profitable
Rodde or Staffe.

WE shall prepare two small, streight, stiffe, round, or rather square rods of mettall or of wood, well plained of like bignesse and length. Although it make no matter of what length, yet to auoide the errours, which little instruments, and short staues bring, and also to beare with the rude unwonted handling of such Artificers: let our Rods bee each fiue, or at the least thrée foote, and euery foote diuided in 12. euen parts or Inches, as yee see a. b. and c. d. These Rods must bee forged with a voyce in the end of them to ioyne readily tenne or sixe foote in length, (when time requireth) as the figure e. f. sheweth. Also yée must get (by the helpe of some Craftesman) foure other like Rods, the longer g. 2. Foote: the next h. 1. Foote: the other i. 6. Inches, then k. 3. Inches, the last and shortest l. 1. Inch, and ½. Each of these must haue in their middest a hole, that the long staffe of ten foote may bee put through them, and they moued on him at pleasure vp and downe, alwayes cutting the longer staffe e. f. Squirewise, and made to tarry on any diuision,

G as

3. Ynches.
6. Ynches.
1. Fote.
2. Fote in length.

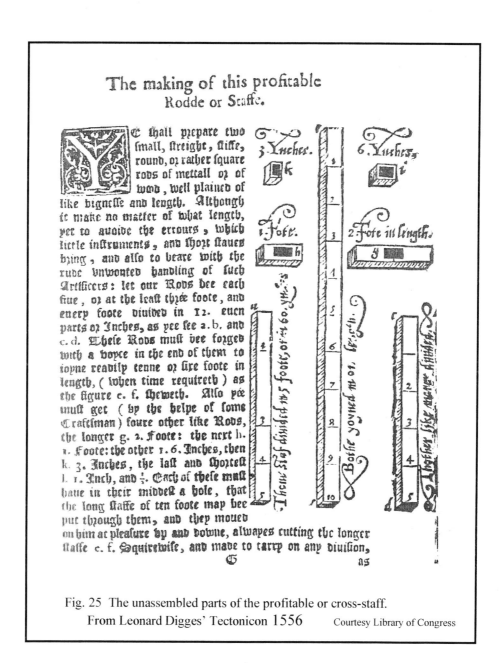

Fig. 25 The unassembled parts of the profitable or cross-staff.
From Leonard Digges' Tectonicon 1556 Courtesy Library of Congress

MATHEMATICIANS

Mathematician Thomas Digges (1546-1595) was a pupil and friend of John Dee, the Queen's mathematician and wrote some of the first English books on surveying. Digges was frequently named, along with Dee and Thomas Herriot, as one of the three leading mathematicians of their day in England. [44] Thomas Digges edited and published the book that his father, Leonard Digges, began, titled *A Geometrical Treatise Named Pantometria* which revealed the Theodolite for the first time in the 1571 publication. At that time, very few English books existed pertaining to mathematical measurements of land surveying.

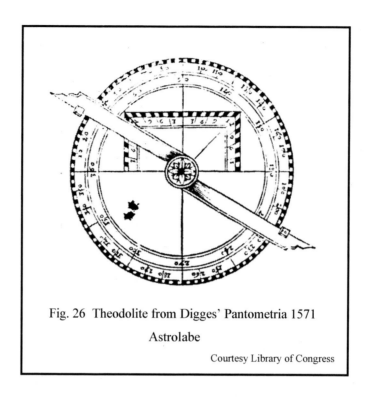

Fig. 26 Theodolite from Digges' Pantometria 1571

Astrolabe

Courtesy Library of Congress

In Digges' 1571 *Pantometria* his geometrical surveying goes through the general mathematical principles and surveying methods to arrive at distances and areas. Leonard Digges and his son Thomas wrote the first English books devoted to surveying. These were the earliest examples of teaching the mathematical methods which could successfully be used by an educated English surveyor.

Pantometria has 35 chapters which cover a range from elementary to countryside surveying examples. Of these, we will examine two:

1. Chapter 34 begins,

> *"To draw a plat of any coast or country containing the true proportions...without Arithmetic."*

Leonard Digges's example (fig.27 below) shows two compass rose points, A and B, measuring the top left quadrant of a land area being measured by using triangulation.

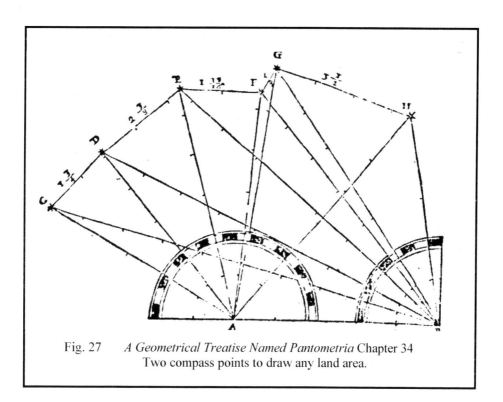

Fig. 27　*A Geometrical Treatise Named Pantometria* Chapter 34
Two compass points to draw any land area.

2. Chapter 27 begins with a description of how to use the instrument called a
Theodolite. While describing its use in the first paragraph of the instructions
Digges states,

> "*...noting diligently the angle or angles of position upon some flat
> stone* [bold added by the author] *or table prepared which angles
> here correspond with the compass and the mountain, trees, hills,
> rivers, buildings or villages or cities.*"

The Rays Rock (fig. 28 and 29) found on Neahkahnie is such a **flat stone.** Digges
recommends recording the mountain tops, rivers, trees, coast line and bay. The Rays
Rock was discovered on Neahkahnie Mountain by Jensen and his crew in 1972.

Fig. 28   Rays Rock North with moss removed. 12-72
Rays were chalked for photographic reasons
Courtesy Jensen Collection 1972©

Fig. 29   Rays Rock North
Courtesy Jensen Collection 1972©

The rays carved in stone (fig. 28 and 29) correspond to the compass rose points (fig. 27) and in fact, the Rays Rock is a compass rose point used to measure points on Neahkahnie Mountain and beyond. *Beyond*, because there are other points on the northeastern side of the mountain which Jensen found which have not been measured to date. The Neahkahnie survey covered a large area, just as William Bourne's Gravesend, England countryside survey covered a full 10 miles (see Bourne Survey below).

BOURNE SURVEY – FIRST 16ᵀᴴ CENTURY SURVEY

William Bourne made the first recorded survey of a complete township and surrounding area in his *Treasures for Travelers 1574*, and his survey is similar to the layout of the Neahkahnie Survey. Bourne, a one-time innkeeper, wrote in the popular science style which led to significant developments in many phases of navigation and surveying. [45]

Important features to notice on the Bourne Gravesend Survey (see fig. 30) are the distance measured, the two compass rose points, the scale or legend and the crossing points or intersection of the lines radiating from the compass rose points. The common features of the Neahkahnie and Bourne surveys are:

1. The distance covered by the survey is some 10 miles of countryside.
2. The two compass points of the Rays Rock are used to measure angles and land areas.
3. Each has its own scale; Bourne's is shown, the Neahkahnie survey needs additional research to identify its scale.
4. Basic triangle geometry was used for surveying distances between points.

Figure 6: Bourne Survey
Scale: 1: 52,800
A triangulation problem of William Bourne. From the Sloane ms. no. 3651 in the British Museum.
(Courtesy of the Director.)

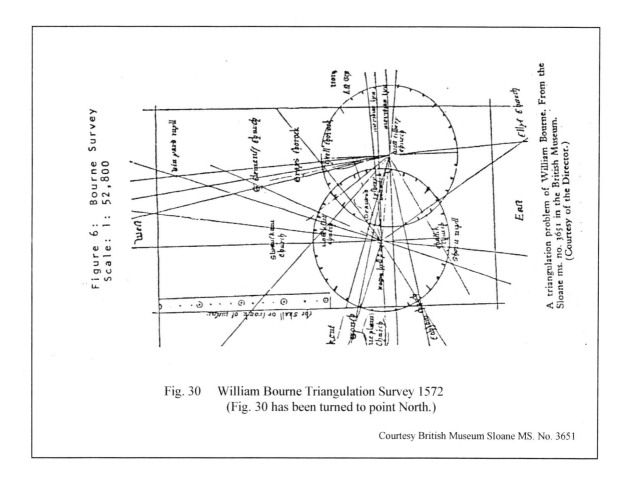

Fig. 30 William Bourne Triangulation Survey 1572
(Fig. 30 has been turned to point North.)

Courtesy British Museum Sloane MS. No. 3651

When measuring the points, Bourne used inconsistent scales for his measurements as did many of his contemporaries. Sometimes he would use paces, furlong, mile and yards all within the same survey. Additionally, his scales would not be in equal increments; as in the Gravesend Survey the circle dots were for 4 miles and the dots themselves were for 1 mile. Today, we would use 5, 10, 100 or more equal increments. Each surveyor in the 16th century had his own method of scaling the survey. This is one of the reasons the exact measurements and legends used on the Neahkahnie Mountain Survey have been indecipherable to date.

It should be mentioned again that no other country at this time was performing surveys using these methods. This English survey on Neahkahnie Mountain in all probability was performed by the hand of Drake and carved by a member of his crew.

20TH CENTURY PROFESSIONAL SURVEY

In 1977, Wayne Jensen, then Director of the Tillamook County Pioneer Museum, contacted Professor of Civil Engineering, Robert J. Schultz, P.E., P.L.S., A.S.C.E., Oregon State University to arrange a survey of the cairn mounds and rocks on Neahkahnie Mountain. A masters candidate at the time, Phil Costaggini, volunteered to perform the survey over the following three winters, when the foliage was at its minimum, to record the rocks and cairn locations, their interrelation, the type of survey, and to determine who might have made such a survey.

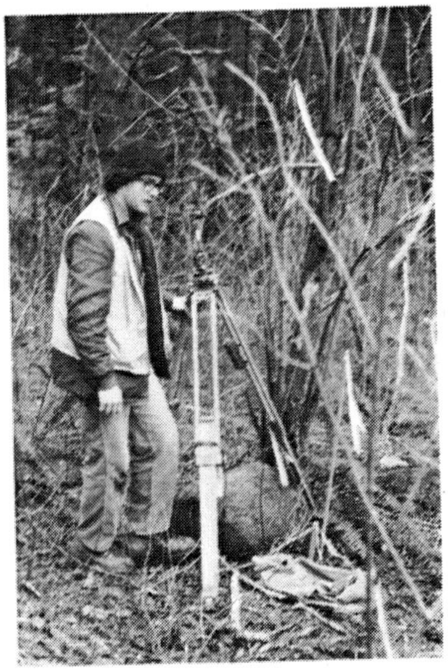

Fig. 31 Phil Costaggini 1978
Taking readings from atop Costaggini Rock.
Courtesy Jensen Collection 1978 ©

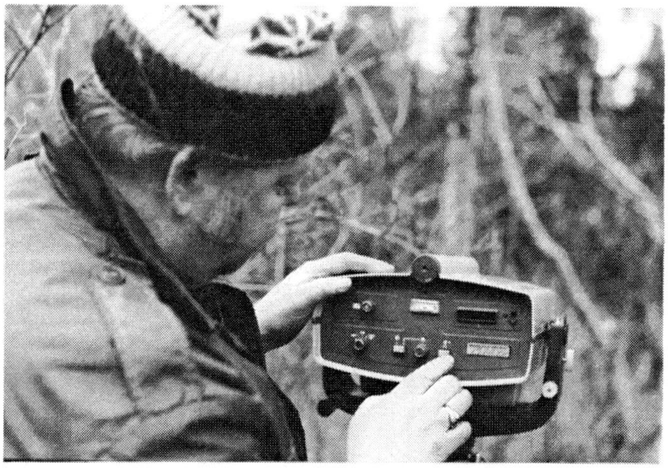

Fig. 32 Wayne Jensen 1978 checking equipment
Courtesy Jensen Collection 1978 ©

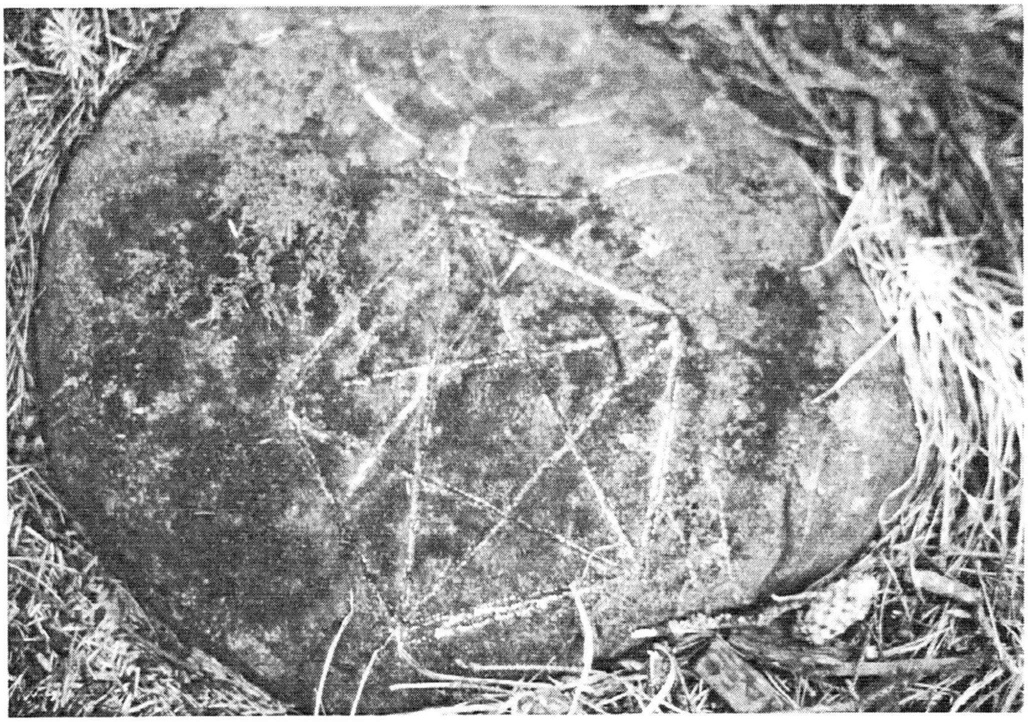

Fig. 33 Costaggini Rock - Pedro Nunes loxodrome is represented on top of rock in the photo.
Photo courtesy Jensen Collection 1978 ©

These symbols on the Costaggini Rock (see top of fig. 33) represent the rhumb lines. In navigation, a rhumb line or loxodrome is a line crossing all meridians at the same angle or a path of constant bearings. The idea of a loxodrome was invented by a Portuguese mathematician, Pedro Nunes, in the 1500's. The loxodrome demonstrated why a ship, which held a steady course, did not travel the shortest distance. Much of Nunes' work related to navigation. Nunes realized the shortest distance between two points on earth would require a ship to steer in a spiral course, i.e. the loxodrome (see fig. 34). In addition to his other teaching posts, in 1537 he founded the Instituto Pedro Nunes at the University of Coimbra to teach mathematics and science. He was appointed Royal Cosmographer in 1529, and served as Chief Royal cosmographer from 1547 until his death in 1578. In his *Treaty Defending the Sea Chart*, Nunes argued that a nautical chart should have its parallels and meridians shown as straight lines. Yet he was unsure of how to solve all the problems this caused, which lasted until Gerard Mercator, a globe maker, who worked with John Dee, developed the projection system which is still used today. [46]

Drake captured Portuguese pilot Nuno de Silva in Africa in 1578, and sailed with him for nearly a year before releasing him on the Pacific Coast in April of 1579. Drake would have had plenty of time to learn this rhumb method, if he had not already known about it previously.

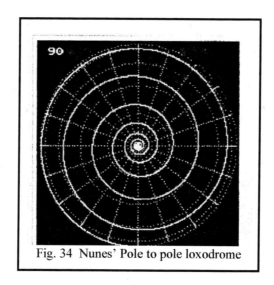

Fig. 34 Nunes' Pole to pole loxodrome

Gerard Mercator's projection map attempted to fit a curved surface onto a flat sheet which distorts the true layout of the Earth's surface. Mercator worked with Gemma Frisius and both had a friendship with John Dee. Dee brought two large globes back to England after studying with Frisius in 1547. [47] Here once again, we see the connection between the lessons of prominent 16th century mathematicians and the Neahkahnie Mountain survey.

Wendle's Rock.
PACIFIC OCEAN
1. AUGUR ROCK
2. TREASURE ROCKS, 1 & 2
3. NORTH MOUND
4. WENDLE'S ROCK
5. HIGH POINT
6. HIGH POINT
7. TRIANGULATION RAYS
8. LOST TO LOGGING

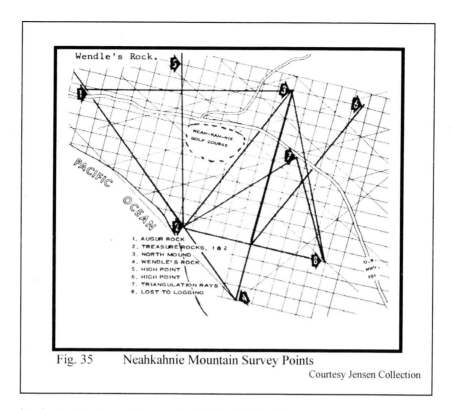

Fig. 35 Neahkahnie Mountain Survey Points
Courtesy Jensen Collection

The survey thesis by Costaggini concluded the following:

1. The survey was completed by early explorers of the 16th century.
2. The fact that the survey was in Latin and English pointed to an English explorer.

See Appendix I - Survey of Artifacts at Neahkahnie Mountain, Oregon, by Phillip A. Costagginiand Robert J. Schultz for the complete survey report.

Some Important Conclusions to be Drawn from the Neahkahnie Survey

Where the community of Neahkahnie is now located, Francis Drake's surveyors plotted and laid out a mile square piece of land and called it New Albion, or New England. The finding of Drake's survey and his Port of New Albion is extremely important to the history of the United States, and particularly the Pacific Northwest, for here, at Neahkahnie, Oregon, one finds:

◊ The first scientifically surveyed and measured piece of ground in North America,
◊ A monolith monument engraved with the first English unit of measurement used in North America,
◊ The first measurement of North America continent's width from the Pacific Northwest,
◊ The first latitude and longitude calculation of the Pacific Northwest,

◊ The Nehalem Bay Area on the North Oregon Coast is the first place England or any other European country claimed lands on the Pacific Northwest coast during the Age of Exploration. This occurred 41 years before the landing at Plymouth Rock, 197 years before the United States became a country, 209 years before the next English or American flag was flown by Captain John Meares and Captain Robert Gray, 226 years before Lewis and Clark's Voyage of Discovery.

Chapter 3 Hondius Map and Nehalem Bay

HONDIUS MAP BROADSIDES

Dutch cartographer Jodocus Hondius produced a world map (fig. 1) in 1590-95 that is considered one of the finest and most recognizable early copper plate maps and which contains the first image of Nehalem Bay. The map outlines both the Francis Drake and Thomas Cavendish paths, taken on their respective circumnavigation voyages. Hondius was in England in the early 1580's and met with Drake, a number of times, who would have had considerable input regarding the map's description and routes taken. There are four broadsides, as they are called, at each corner of the map (fig. 1), which depict Drake's circumnavigation scenes. The upper right broadside depicts a port on the coast of Java, and is considered by many historians an excellent representation. The bottom left is Drake's ship in the Moluccas, and is also recognized as an excellent representation. Our focus is the upper left depicting the "*Portus Nova Albionis*" which is a drawing of Nehalem Bay. (See fig. 36 Hondius Broadside)

Portus Novæ
Albionis
Fœda corporum laceratione & crebris in montibus sacrificijs, hujus
Novæ Albionis portus incolæ, Draci, jam bis coronati, decessum deflent.

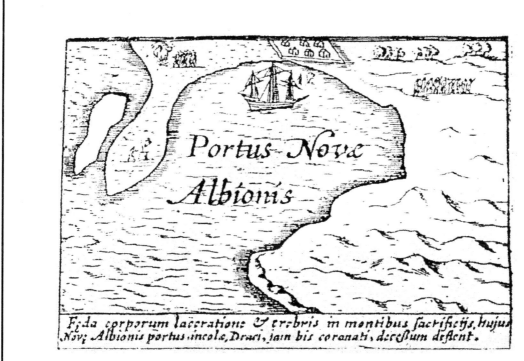

A drawing of Drake's "bay of fires" in the corner of the Hondius Broadside map

Fig. 36 Hondius Broadside map (HBM) circa 1590-95 Courtesy Maritime Museum, Rotterdam

Two prominent California bay theoreticians, Robert F. Heizer and Raymond Aker, have stated that the California bays do not match the Hondius Broadside. In their words, either the map is wrong or the theory of a California landing is wrong. Heizer, Anthropological Professor at the University of California at Berkeley, in 1974 wrote of the Hondius Map,

> "[is]...*something more than a mere product of the imagination of the map-maker, Jodocus Hondius"*,[1] [though] *"... until more is known of its* [fig. 36] *inspiration, it should not be classed as a "principal key".* [2]

Though Heizer agrees that the other three Hondius Broadsides are fine representations, his makes the statement "not be classed as a principal key" because the geography and anthropological record of Northern California bays does not match with the Hondius Broadside.

Raymond Aker, President of the Drake Navigators Guild from 1963 - 2003 said,

> *"Hondius' work was highly regarded, and he, ...was authorized by Elizabeth's privy council at the urging of Sir Christopher Hatton, one of Drake's principal sponsors for the voyage of circumnavigation." *[3]

These two learned men concur that the map of Nova Albion is a <u>correct representation</u> of the bay when Heizer states its more than product of imagination (but doesn't match California), and Aker recognizes the Hondius work as highly regarded. As we will see, the Hondius Broadside must be considered solid evidence that the Nehalem Bay map (Hondius Broadside) be thought of as one of the principal keys to Drake's landing site.

HONDIUS MAP AND NEHALEM BAY COMPARISONS

Professor of Archaeology, A. L. Kroeber, University of California, Berkeley known as the father of archaeology in California, theorized that there could have been two landings by Drake in the North Pacific, [4] which is another way of saying the California bays do not match the Hondius Broadside, and Drake may have landed somewhere other than California.

Notice the Hondius Broadside of the bay (fig. 36), which Drake called Portus Nova Albionis (Latin for Port of New England). Here we see a peninsula with a parallel sandbar island alongside to the west by northwest. Due to the catastrophic earthquake and tsunami of January 1700 in Nehalem Bay, the sandbar has been redistributed along the oceanfront in a different configuration and the pre-existing river channel is now closed off from sand build-up (See fig. 38 and Appendix III).

Dr. Thomas Newman, Professor of Archaeology at Oregon State, reported the ground along the coast sunk up to 1-1/2 meters on the Netarts Spit around 1700. Netarts is twenty miles south of Nehalem Bay. [5]

Additionally, a geological study in 2007 conducted by Dr. Curt Peterson, Geology Professor at Portland State University, is examining the rate of sand accretion in Nehalem Bay.[6] Dr. Peterson's study has recognized the oceanfront as being 10 feet below the current street levels on the south end of Manzanita, the town which borders Nehalem Bay to the north. Previous findings by Portland State University Geologist Leonard Palmer, Ph.D., and Anthropologist Daniel Scheans, Ph.D., resulted in the identification of a pre-existing river channel. [7] (see Appendix III).

The sand spit, a body of sand running perpendicular with the oceanfront altered the mouth of bay and river, (see fig. 38) was planted with trees by Oregon State Parks in the mid-1960's. The jetty system, built by the citizens of Nehalem and the Army Corps of Engineers between 1913 and 1918, extended the spit further south, causing the sand to accumulate up to ten feet or more, along the oceanfront as we see it today.[8]

The Nehalem Wetlands Review published by the Army Corps of Engineers in 1977 states,

> *"Prior to improvement* [the jetty system], *the River maintained bar depth from 12 to 14 feet at Mean Lower Low Water. Under original conditions, the entrance channel was 400 to 600 feet in width and was subject to great changes in position and direction as well as depth."*[9]

This would have been sufficient for the Golden Hinde to navigate as Fletcher said, *"…[we] needed 13 feet of water to make her fleet"*[10] fully loaded with spices and other goods since leaving Nova Albion.

Today, Nehalem Bay has experienced repeated "formation of wetlands which begins with the depositing of material along the margins of the estuary forming shallows…. When the tide flat becomes sufficiently stabilized for rooted vegetation to become established, a tidal marsh wetland is formed. The marsh itself is a dynamic community within which an orderly replacement of plants takes place through time, and eventually the process would produce an upland meadow or Sitka spruce woodland." [11] The Nehalem Wetlands Review described the consequences of this process in Nehalem Bay over the past century: Sedimentation in Nehalem Bay has resulted in a major expansion of the marshes into the mudflats. In 1961 it was estimated that the margin of the marsh expanded 1,200 feet across the Bay between 1875 and 1939 at a rate of 18 feet per year, and that since 1939, the rate has increased to 27 feet per year.[12] Prior to 1875, the Lewis and Clark Atlas map 85 drawn during their tour of discovery depicted the Nehalem Spit as insignificant by using three dots (See fig. 37).

Nehalem Bay Spit
Tillamook Bay Spit at high tide
Tillamook Bay exposed at low tide

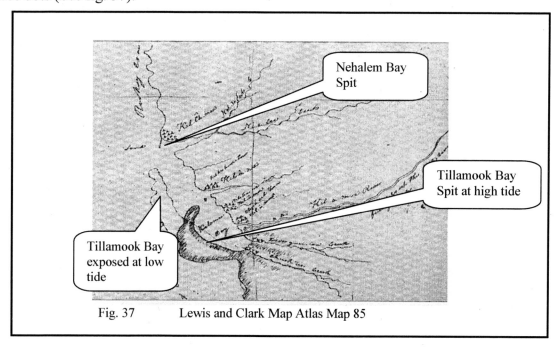

Fig. 37 Lewis and Clark Map Atlas Map 85

Figure 38 below shows sand accretion along the oceanfront from the City of Manzanita to the North and along the Nehalem Bay spit. Notice how the line of sand demarcation marks the original mouth opening of the bay (See fig. 36 Hondius Broadside).

Demarcation line showing sand accretion along ocean front and spit
Pre-1700 channel to ocean
Existing boat ramp
Original mouth of Nehalem Bay
Nehalem Bay spit
Jetties
PACIFIC OCEAN
NEHALEM
BAY
Nehalem Junction
Wheeler
Wheeler Heights
Brighton

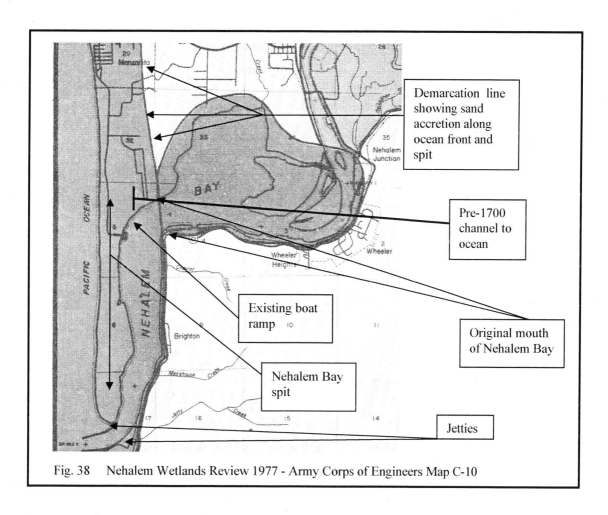

Fig. 38 Nehalem Wetlands Review 1977 - Army Corps of Engineers Map C-10

Compare figure 38 map with the figure 39 which was taken from the north looking to the south in 1914.

Notice figure 36 to the left of the peninsula and to the west is the island depicted in the Hondius Broadside compared with figure 39.

Existing 2008
boat ramp

Peninsula

Sand spit
running
to the
south

Island in
the
Hondius
Broadside

City of Manzanita

Fig. 39 Nehalem Bay Mouth 1914 - Near the top center is the peninsula running to the left. In the center of the picture is the island depicted in the Hondius Broadside and the sand surrounding was once ocean. Jetties were built and located to the south (not seen in photo circa 1930).   Courtesy Jensen Collection

There is no need to turn the Hondius Broadside map to fit the Nehalem Bay configuration, unlike the theorized California sites which must turn the Hondius Broadside up to 170 degrees to try and match up to their bays.

Hondius' Portus Nova Albionis and Nehalem Bay Overlay

Portus Nove
Albionis
OREGON
NEHALEM RIVER
6122
(Nehalem River)
C.&G.S. 6122

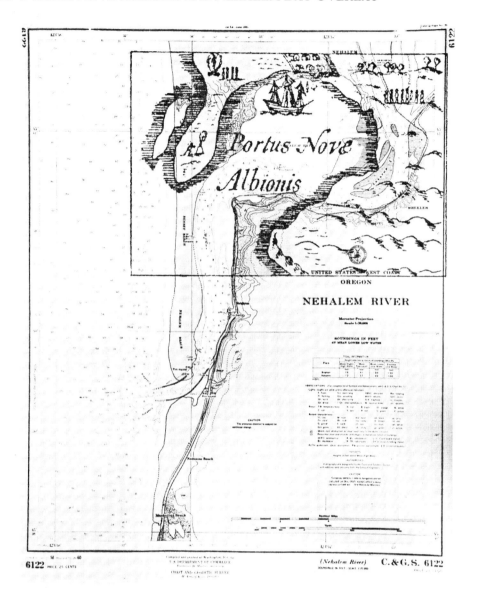

Fig. 40 U.S Survey map overlaid by the Hondius Broadside
Courtesy Jensen Collection © 1973

Now let us compare feature by feature of the Hondius map of *Portus Nova Albionis*. Note there are ten distinctive comparisons between fig. 41 and fig. 42 which are Nehalem Bay locations, plants, topography and documented archaeological sites. Natural ocean deposits and the planting of the spit by Oregon State Parks in the mid-1960's has extended the sand spit to the south but the original peninsula, in Drake's time, still existed.

Notice the southern entrance on both (fig. 41 and 42) maps by comparing them side by side. Sand can shift, but rock and clay points do not and we see the area known as Fisher's Point (item 3) on the South side of the bay has not changed since Drake was in Nehalem Bay.

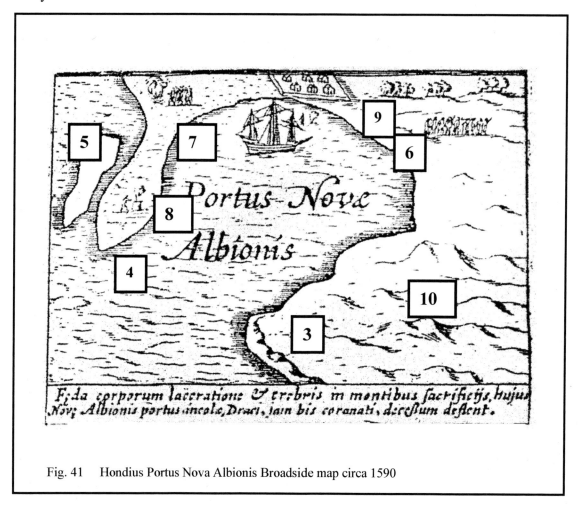

Fig. 41   Hondius Portus Nova Albionis Broadside map circa 1590

Where the Indians are depicted on fig. 41 item # 8 of the Hondius map, are known archaeological sites (see Appendix III). This area now lies inside Nehalem Bay State Park property.

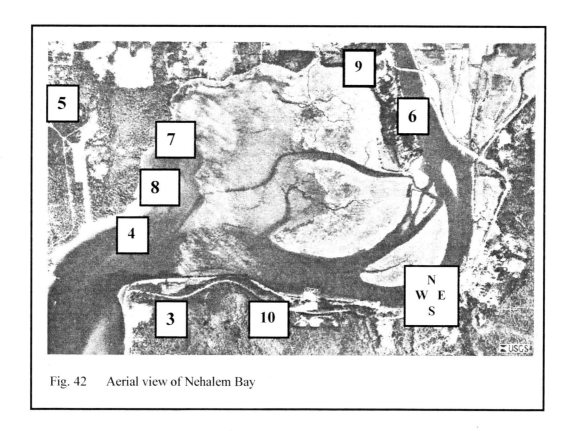

Fig. 42   Aerial view of Nehalem Bay

Now compare the geography and topography of the aerial fig. 42 with the fig. 41 Hondius Broadside map.

The ten distinctive items which describe the *Portus Nova Albionis*, fig. 41 are:

1. North and south orientation of the map with Nehalem Bay
2. East and west orientation of the map with Nehalem Bay
3. South point of the bay mouth is Fisher's Point.
4. Peninsula is the bay mouth to the north
5. Island located west of the peninsula
6. Three hills with trees
7. Indian site ¾ mile from fort location
8. Documented archaeological sites
9. Fort location alongside Alder Creek
10. Mountainous Area

Now we can examine each item in detail as to why the Nehalem Bay (fig. 42) matches the Hondius Broadside map (fig. 41).

Items 1 and 2 - It's easy to see the directional orientation of both the bay and the map.

Item 3 - Fisher's Point is named after the first pioneer to live at this point of the bay.

Item 4 - The peninsula at the north side of the bay mouth is a known archaeological site.

Item 5 - The island or sandbar located on the HBM (fig. 41) can be seen on the fig. 42. Curt Peterson Ph.D., Professor of Geology at Portland State University, performed an examination using 100 MHz ground penetrating radar during the summer of 2007. He found the sand surrounding the island (item 5) and along the Nehalem Bay State Park spit (fig. 38) as one of the only places on the North Oregon Coast which is acquiring large amounts of sand build-up. The findings by Portland State University Geologist Leonard Palmer, Ph.D. and Anthropologist Daniel Scheans, Ph.D., resulted in the identification of a pre-existing river channel[13] which placed the bay entrance just north of the existing boat ramp and the peninsula (see fig. 38). [14] Due to the earthquake and tsunami in January of 1700, the ground along the Nehalem Bay shifted causing the bay and river to flow in different directions. This catastrophic event, along with the building of the jetties by the Corps of Engineers along the north and south side of the existing river channel mouth in the early part of the 20th century, and the planting of trees on the spit by the Oregon Park System in the early 1960's, enhanced the build-up of sand, causing the shift of the river mouth to exit into the ocean at the current location and previously unnatural place. [15]

Item 6 - Notice the three hills of trees in the upper right corner of Hondius Broadside (also seen in fig. 43). The trees of the HBM are shaded on the eastern side, as was the practice for 16th century cartographers. Additionally, and most important, are the three hills themselves. The HBM appears to have been drawn from a perspective looking north from the mountainous areas of item 10. As we will see in Chapter 6, Francis Fletcher noted his description of Indians coming down the hill (Item 6), leaving their bows at the top. He describes the cries of Indian woman heard ¾ of a mile away. Fletcher also describes how after three days there was an assembly of Indians on top of the hills from inland.

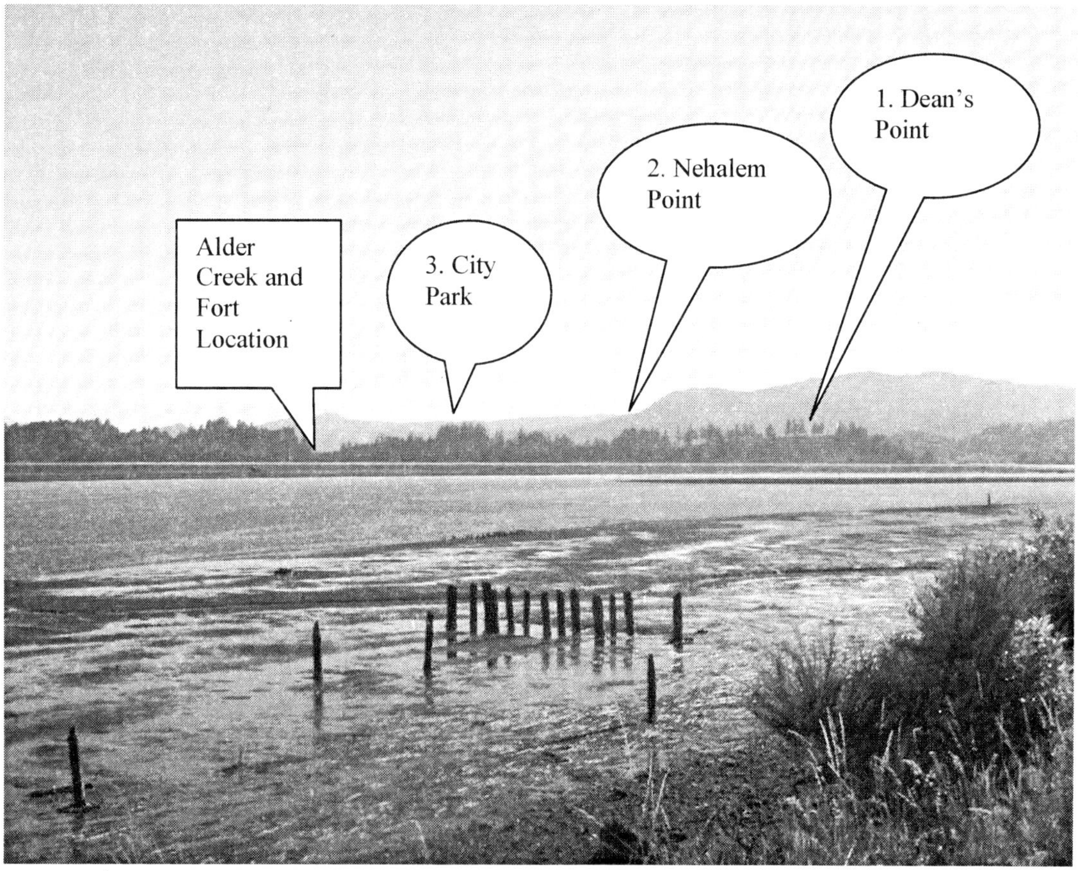
1. Dean's Point
2. Nehalem Point
Alder Creek and Fort Location
3. City Park

Fig. 43 Three Hills – The tree line in the center of the photo shows the three hills. From right to left the three hills end at Alder Creek which lies below the Nehalem City Park. Photo by author © 2007

Items 7 and 8 – These are known archaeological Indian sites (35T157 and 35T14B) which are documented in Appendix III and they are ¾ mile distance from the mouth of Alder Creek. Old-time Nehalem Bay residents have reported other archaeological sites located around and on the three hills.

Item 9 – This is the mouth of Alder Creek where Drake built his fort of stone. If you look at the top of the page of the Hondius map (fig. 41) you'll notice Drake's fort pictured at the back of the bay. This is where Drake logically would have built his fort of stone and repaired the *Golden Hinde* in the nearby shallows. On the Hondius map the water areas bordering are depicted by very thin lines. You will notice that these fine lines appear on the right side of the fort. At the base of these hills is Alder Creek and to the west of the creek is where the fort was located. It's reasonable to believe that Drake would have built his fort on the opposite side of the creek from the Indians for defensive reasons.[16] The stone would have been easily carried by Drake's crew of 80-some-odd men from Dean's Point, less than a few hundred yards, where a quarry is present today. Drake most likely would have built a fort similar to the one he built in Panama in 1571; [17] a five-sided stand with an opening to the water to bring in his pinnace at night.

In addition, we will see that Fletcher mentions the screaming and wailing of the women that could be heard from the fort even though it was three quarters of a mile away. [18] The 1992 archaeological dig conducted by Dr. John Woodward, Mt. Hood Community College was assisted by Wayne Jensen at Cronin Point (fig. 41 item 8) which is three quarters of a mile from the fort site at Alder Creek (fig. 41 item 9).

Hill top
Alder Creek
Old growth spruce tree roots
Area sunken and without vegetation

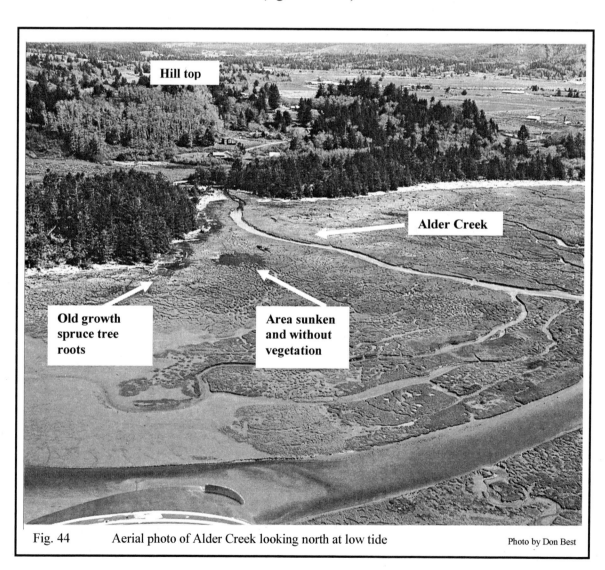

Fig. 44 Aerial photo of Alder Creek looking north at low tide Photo by Don Best

The aerial view of Alder Creek (photo 44) shows an approximately 60' x 60' area without vegetation to the west of the creek and 150 feet south of the present-day tree line. Approximately 100 feet from the site to the west by northwest are approximately five-hundred-year-old spruce tree roots which are exposed. Because of their slow growth and size of these tree roots, they are believed to be the pre-earthquake tree line of 1700. If this is the case, then the area without vegetation could hold the site of Drake's fort of stone, where his crew of 80 or so men would have unloaded the *Golden Hinde* to begin careening. They then began to blacksmith, caulk and tar the vessel during this time they were in the bay. Today, this land is owned by Tillamook County.

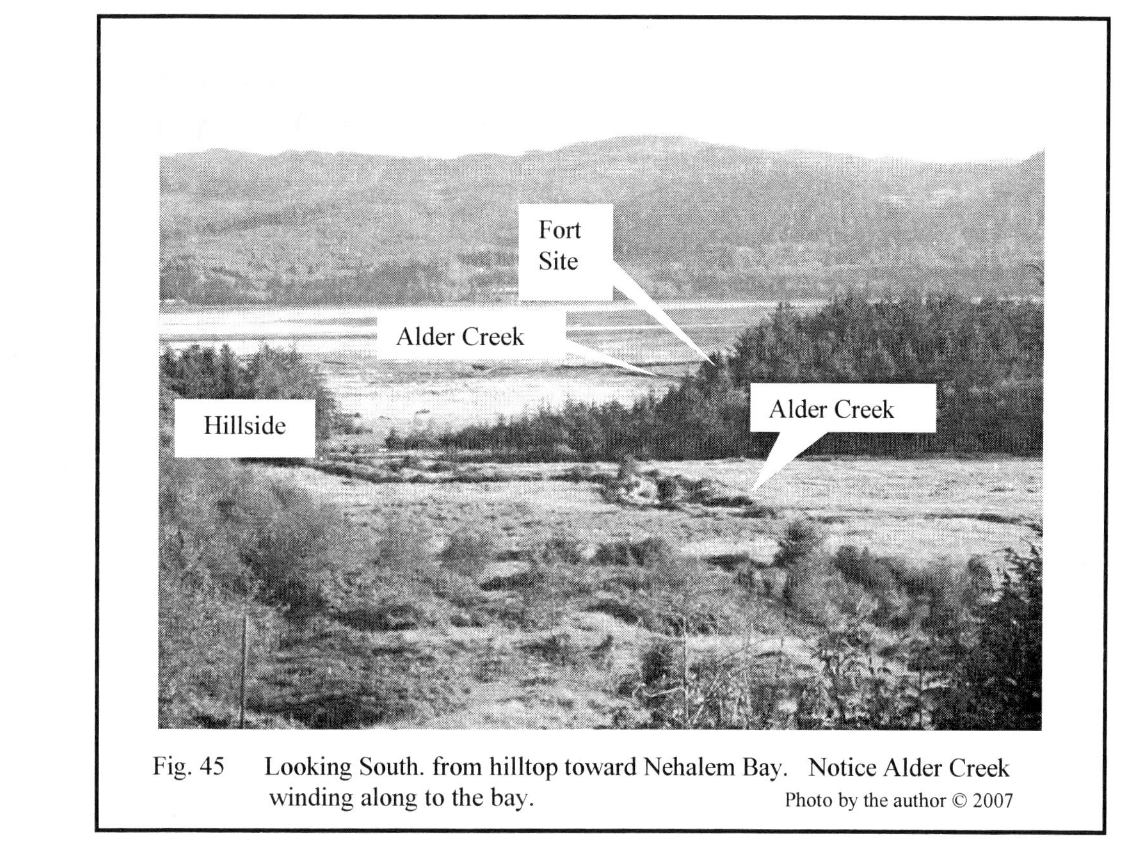
Fort
Site
Alder Creek
Hillside
Alder Creek

Fig. 45 Looking South. from hilltop toward Nehalem Bay. Notice Alder Creek winding along to the bay. Photo by the author © 2007

HONDIUS MAP COMPARED WITH CALIFORNIA DRAKE'S BAY AND POINT REYES

We will now compare the Hondius Broadside with the California bays of Raymond Aker, former President of the Drake Navigators Guild, *Sir Francis Drake at Drakes Bay, A summation of Evidence Relating to the Identification of Sir Francis Drake's Encampment at Drakes Bay, California.*[19]

1. The HBM must be turned 90 - 180 degrees in order for it to resemble Drake's Bay or Point Reyes.

2. Other than cliffs above the beach, none of the other geographical points match up when the HBM is compared with the California bays.

3. Comparing item 9 of the HBM (fig. 41) to Drake's Bay or Point Reyes, they do not have the three hills which resemble the map, nor do these bays have any trees.

4. There are claimed California Indian sites, but these are not documented archaeological sites and do not correspond to the distance of ¾ English miles away from the fort (an English mile in 1579 was 5,000 feet, changed by Queen Elizabeth in 1595 to match the rest of Europe).

5. Neither Drake's Bay nor Point Reyes has any creeks flowing into the bay although there are springs; again no match to the Hondius Broadside.

6. There cannot be a fort location alongside water or any of the other Hondius Broadside items which correspond with the California bays.

The California bays just do not measure up to the Hondius Broadside which is the reason there has never been an official State of California recognized landing site. I'm sorry, but the adventurous hypothetical cases for a California bay landing site could be applied to almost any bay with fog.

CERMENO'S DESCRIPTION OF POINT REYES IN 1595

Rodriguez Cermeno was a Spanish Captain of the *San Augustin* and was instructed to look for a port for galleons to anchor when returning from the Philippines. Cermeno's ship was wrecked in a storm while anchored at Point Reyes in 1595; he and his crew were the first Europeans to come in contact with the land of Northern California, as we know it today. Wagner describes the landing:

> *"About noon of the same day the sailors at the mast-head caught sight of Drake's Bay behind Point Reyes, whereupon the ship was steered in that direction and came to anchor in the bay. Rodriguez [Cermeno] named this*

port the "Bay of San Francisco", although he and his men also called it "Bahia Grande" [Great Bay]."[20]

The Great Bay is nothing like the bay described by Fletcher nor is it drawn as a great bay by Hondius. The bay was described by Fletcher as a bay of small ships because of its size was limited to small ships like Drake's *Golden Hinde* which drew a scant 13 feet of water to make her fleet,[21] which is comparable to Nehalem Bay's 12-14 foot depth of the channel.

Fig. 46   Neahkahnie Mountain circa 1936   Courtesy Jensen Collection

Cermeno said the country around Pt. Reyes reminded him of Castile, a region located within Spain's central plateau, or *meseta,* which accounts for approximately 60 percent of the country's total area. It is a region of hot, dry, windswept plains broken in places by chains of low mountains. There are few trees, and much of the terrain is covered by either *encinas,* which are similar to dwarf oaks, or scrub.[22] This is very unlike Fletcher's description and the Hondius drawing. To Drake the area was like his home port of Plymouth, hilly and green with trees and cliffs much like Dover, for Neahkahnie Mountain ends abruptly with cliffs plummeting into the ocean.[23]

Landscape Similarities of Plymouth and Neahkahnie Mountain

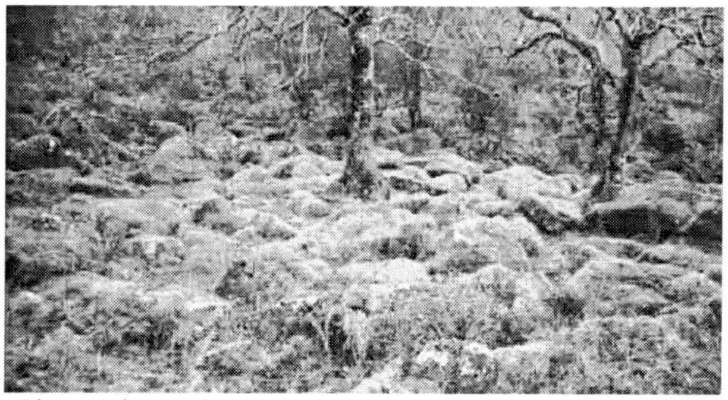

Plymouth Landscape

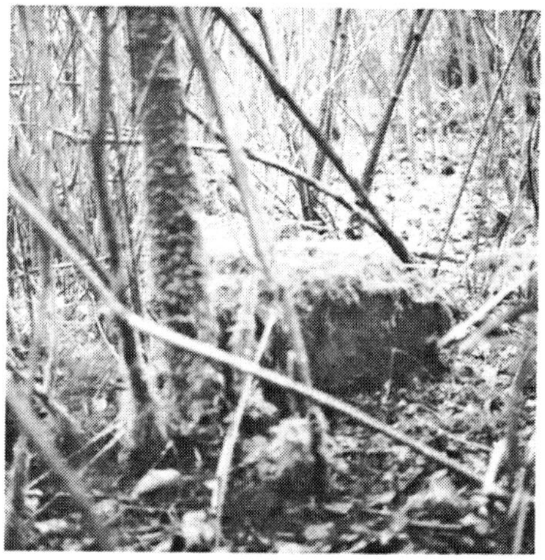

Neahkahnie Landscape

Photos: courtesy Jensen Collection

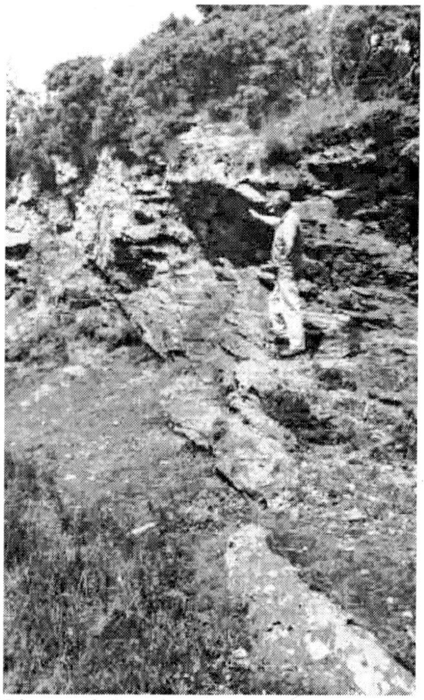

Plymouth Landscape

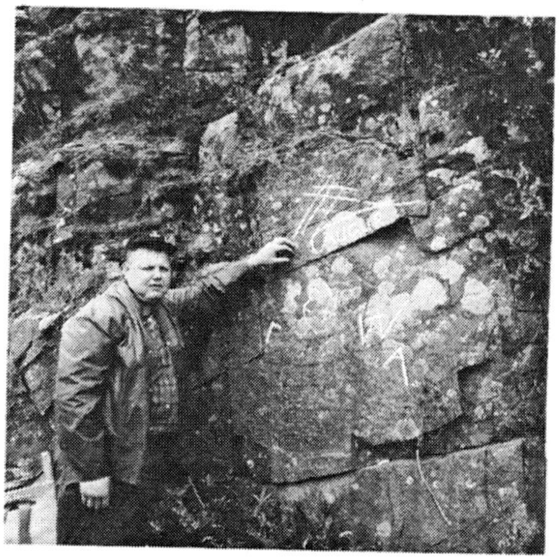

Neahkahnie Landscape

These photographs do not look anything like the Spanish Castile landscape which Cermeno described.

Chapter 4 Nehalem Indians and Francis Drake

FITTING DRAKE'S INDIAN DESCRIPTIONS

Professor A. L. Kroeber Ph.D., wrote in 1925,

> *"Documentary evidence has recently led to the theory that Drake's landing occurred some 10 degrees of latitude further north than (38°) has generally been believed. The question thus raised is for historians and geographers to solve. **Should their views be favorable to the new opinion, it would follow that an attempt would have to be made to fit Drake's Indian descriptions to the customs prevalent further north.**"* [1]

The information presented in this chapter is indeed "favorable to the new opinion" that Professor Kroeber mentioned. We will see that Francis Fletcher's descriptions of the Indians in *The World Encompassed* were describing long-established customs of the Pacific Northwest and Nehalem Bay aboriginal natives.

Kroeber admits that there isn't enough evidence to confirm Drake's landing along the Miwok/Pomo territory, *yet* he goes on to say,

> *"The Pomo-like baskets alone present an almost insuperable obstacle. If Drake's occupation of a more northerly portion of the coast is confirmed on other grounds, the interpretation of his voyage that will therefore almost necessarily follow is that he touched at two points..."* (see Chapter 6 for contemporary basket story).

Kroeber knew little of the Pacific Northwest Indians; he relied on information from Franz Boas and from another student of University of California at Berkeley, Homer G. Barnett.[2] Barnett's dissertation took the form of interviews with Louis Fuller, a Siletz Indian, in 1934. The Siletz are only 10 miles south of the Salish-speaking Indians, who inhabited Cascade Head, Oregon. The Nehalem/Tillamook Indians, 50 miles north, also spoke Salish and were related to the Cascade Head tribe through their common language. Barnett and Kroeber credited a good deal of their data as Miwok/Pomo ethnology which is 300 miles to the south, though the Siletz are more closely related to the Nehalem/Tillamook.

The Pacific Northwest Indian cultures and customs, as well as details of food, housing, tools and dress are recorded in a large body of ethnographic evidence which compares to Francis Fletcher's descriptions of the Natives and we will examine each. John Jewitt, James G. Swan, Clara Pearson, Robert Gray's first mate Haswell, and Astor members Franchére, Ross and Cox all wrote books or journals of their Indian adventures. These documents cover the contemporary period from 1788 to 1812. That was 30-plus years before acculturation began at limited seaports of the Pacific Northwest. It began with well-known Captains Cook and Vancouver, and the five Spanish voyages of exploration from 1774-1796. Other large bodies of archaeological, botanical and anthropological information develop a clear picture of the Indians who interacted with Drake and his crew while in Nehalem Bay.

LANGUAGE AND FOOD

There are a number of individual areas described by Fletcher in *The World Encompassed* which coordinate with the Nehalem Indians. A keystone item which tests Drake's landing with the Nehalem is language.

> In Kroeber's words, when he's writing about the "Problem of Identification" concerning the Indian language, *"The evidence on the final test - speech - is too scant to be conclusive"* (when trying to confirm California Indians meeting Drake).[3]

In *The World Encompasse*d, Fletcher writes the word "***Pet'ah***", the root Drake and crew were given by the natives to eat raw or roasted. This is the key to the "final test" as Kroeber puts it and appears to be one of the indisputable lynchpins establishing corroboration of Drake's presence in Nehalem Bay. The word ***wa-pato*** is in the Salish-speaking language of the Nehalem, and it is the same word Fletcher recorded in *The World Encompassed* as ***pet'ah.*** Fletcher did not hear a "Wa" in front of *pet'ah* because the Salish language is gruntal and pronounces words from down the throat. This gruntal sound was described by Elizabeth Jacobs who, in 1933-34, conducted fieldwork on the Nehalem Tillamook culture of northwestern Oregon. Working with her able Nehalem/Tillamook consultant Clara Pearson, one of the last Salish-speaking Nehalem Indians, Jacobs recorded extensive ethnographic and folkloric materials that far surpassed in quality and quantity the previous research investigators.[4] Fletcher, an untrained linguist and an

Englishman hearing wa-pato for the first time, from an Indian throat which grunted its words, could have easily heard and assumed it spelled as *Pet'ah*.

Kroeber, Heizer and others who continue to promote the Miwok/Pomo idea, have taken the word *pet'ah* and created or accepted it as the Miwok word *creed*. *Creed* neither sounds nor tastes anything like Fletcher's description or spelling of the word *pet'ah*. This author has eaten wapato raw, and they are quite palatable, much like a mild radish, unlike the California *creed* which is made of acorns, and is quite bitter to the taste (see Cermeno's description below).

One of the major food items of the Nehalem was a root called wa-pato which they ate raw or made into a bread. The root which Fletcher describes as pet'ah, *"whereof they make a kind of meal, and either bake it into bread, or eat it raw."* [5] There can be little doubt, that *pet'ah* is the same Salish language word - *wa-pato* and the root which Drake and his crew were given by the Indians.

Fig. 47   Wapato - common name Arrowhead
(Sagittarian latifolia)
Photo by author 2007

The wapato plant played an important part in the early history of the Columbia River Valley and the Northwest, and it is among the oldest flowering plants on earth. The characteristics of this plant have enabled it to survive millions of years and to adapt itself to harsh growing conditions.

Sagittaria latifolia (Arrowhead) is fundamentally a perennial marsh or aquatic herb and belongs to the Alixmaceae family. The arrowhead's leaves are narrow when they are growing under water and so are able to withstand the swift currents without being torn. However, the leaves growing above the water become flatter and are arrow-shaped, suited to absorbing or warding off too much sunlight, depending upon the need of the plant. [6]

Fig. 48   The Arrowhead plant which grows the Wapato bulb

The tubers growing in the soft mud are the edible part of the plant. Long before the white man visited the Northwest, the Indians called these bulbs by the name of "wapato", and they were a very important part of their regional food. Wapato is a name that reappears time and time again in the diaries or journals of the early travelers to the West. It is also mentioned in the journals of Lewis and Clark and was one of the staples of their diet during their winter in Oregon. Elk meat was provided by their hunters, but they purchased the wapato bulbs from the Indians.

Wapato saved many early travelers to the West from starvation, although eating too much of it caused pain in stomachs unaccustomed to it. David Douglas, the naturalist who named many Pacific Northwest plants, lived on little else during some of his trips in Oregon while studying botany. [6A]

"It is not possible to obtain these tubers by pulling the plant because they are borne at the end of the long, flabby root stocks and are sure to break off and be lost. The Indian [women] harvested them by entering the water, nearly shoulder deep, and pushing along a light canoe. Supporting themselves by hanging on to the canoes, they were able to separate the root of this bulb with their toes. As soon as the bulb was dislodged, it floated to the top of the water, and the [women] would toss them into the canoe. When the bulbs were washed and boiled, they resembled Irish potatoes, though with a sweetish flavor of chestnuts The boiled root was one of the staples of their diet."[7]

Roy F. Jones describes how Lewis and Clark named present-day Sauvies Island, located in the Columbia River a short distance west of Portland, as Wapato Island for the great quantities of food source once growing on the island. Because of the island's location, it was on a trade route of the Nehalem Indians who traveled to the Nehalem River headwaters which begin a short distance from the Columbia River and Wapato Island.

The word wapato comes from the Athasbascon Indian language, an Indian group along the Columbia River and to the east of Nehalem Bay.[8] Elizabeth Jacobs, based on her interviews with Clara Pearson in 1932 notes, "Most roots were roasted in hot ashes or boiled and then mashed and made into a loaf to be sliced for serving when cool. [Wapato], a mahogany-colored root about the size of a walnut, was eaten both cooked and raw although it was preferred raw when it appeared in the spring (see fig. 47 & 48). It tasted like a potato when cooked, though it was somewhat firmer."[9]

Species: *Sagittaria latifolia,* Wild Wapato, Arrowhead Family [10]

The plant is a marshy shoreline perennial which has distinctly arrowhead shaped leaves. Species has upright, emergent leaves and whorls of three petaled flowers on long stalks originating at the plant base. Large, round tubers are produced. *S. latifolia* grows to 1.5 m high.

Flower: Usually in whorls of three, each with 3 white petals and 3 green sepals (1-2 cm long). *S. latifolia:* flowers to 4 cm across. When in fruit the stalks spread outwards.

Fruit: Achenes approximately 2 mm long, crowded on globe-shaped heads. 0.5mm. *S. latifolia*: beak 1-2 mm, horizontal.

Root: Rhizomes with thick round tubers that may grow as large as chicken eggs.

Propagation: Tubers, rhizomes, seeds.

Importance of plant: Tubers were an important food source for Native Americans. Tubers also provide food for beavers and muskrats. Tubers and achenes provide food for waterfowl.

Distribution: *S. latifolia*: Common on Pacific coast, central, and eastern United States; in Washington, primarily west of Cascades and the Columbia River Gorge.

Habitat: Shorelines and marshy areas up to 1.5 m deep 10

Source: www.plants.usda.gov

Cermeno vs. Fletcher Food Descriptions

In early November of 1595 Rodriguez Cermeno, wrecked his Spanish Galleon, *San Augustin* at Point Reyes, California. He described the food obtained from the Indiansas acorns which are **bitter** and that they [Indians] made a type of acorn mush and **not a pleasant taste**. [11]

This is nothing like the word or taste of what Fletcher describes as **a root**, not an acorn from oak trees as Cermeno described, and which the Indians call _pet'ah_ whereof they make a kind of **meal**, not a mush, and either bake it into bread, or eat it raw.[12] There have been a number of pioneers who have eaten wapato and have described it as tasting pleasant, while Cermeno describes his acorns as bitter and not pleasant in taste. Alexander Ross, one of the original members of the Astoria Group of 1811,[13] describes wapato as pleasant to the taste when cooked.

After leaving Pt. Reyes on December 8th, 1595, 38°40' N. latitude, Cermeno sailed for four days after passing 37°; here the taste of acorns is again described: The natives, "very soon came back bringing a quantity of bitter acorns and some acorn mush in baskets shaped like medium-sized plates." [14]

On December 13, 1595 Cermeno again described the food he received previously at Pt. Reyes from the Indians, "... _as there was nothing to eat except a small quantity of bitter acorns which to be eaten had to be roasted._"[15] The only way to eat them was to roast them and even then they were of poor taste.

Here again, Cermeno's description of flat baskets like plates, mush and bitter tasting acorns does not match the example Fletcher gives of baskets (see Chapter 6) and pleasant tasting pet'ah which the Indians of Nehalem Bay provided for food.[16]

Concerning ethnographic information collected in the early 1930's on the Siletz by H.G. Barnett, a student of A. L. Kroeber[17] who says of Barnett's work:

> "_I believe that in the present work Barnett has probably assembled more new concrete information on the native cultures of the Oregon coast than was available in all previous sources put together. If this opinion is correct, it would seem to establish both Barnett's ethnographic competence and the value of the culture element distribution survey as a field method._"

Barnett lists acorns as <u>a **non important** food source of the Nehalem/Tillamook.</u> [18] This is because oak trees don't grow along the Oregon Coast.

Language and Food Conclusion

Because of the acorn's raw, bitter taste and the fact that acorns don't grow on the Oregon coast, one must conclude that Cermeno and Drake were eating different foods from different parts of the coast and meeting different Indians. Cermeno was meeting the Pt. Reyes Pomo/Miwok, while Drake was interacting with the Nehalem/Tillamook.

HOUSING

FLETCHER'S DESCRIPTION

Fletcher's *World Encompassed* describes the Indian houses as dug out or into the ground a couple of feet, round and entered through the roof. Ethnobotanist Douglas Deur, Ph.D., Ecosystem Research Coordinator at the University of Washington, believes that both long houses and round houses may have been common[19] (see fig. 49 and 50 below).

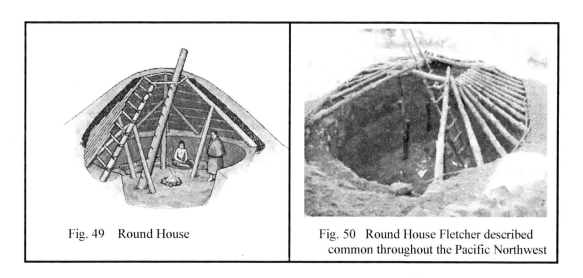

Fig. 49 Round House	Fig. 50 Round House Fletcher described common throughout the Pacific Northwest

Nehalem Clara Pearson remembered a number of Nehalem-type houses. One of them she described to Jacobs as,

> "...the dug-in-the-ground-house which was entered through a door in one end
> of the roof, and descended into by means of a ladder on the inside. Such a
> ladder was made by cutting foot-holes in a heavy plank." [This type of house]
> "...was considered a warm house for winter."[20]

The Royal British Columbia Museum in Victoria, British Columbia, has a round house which is described as a typical house for the Pacific Northwest and is the centerpiece of their aboriginal display. The house is dug into the ground two to four feet and ends in a steeple style in the center with the entrance at the top and a ladder descending down into the house. These types of houses were also typical in eastern Washington and Oregon as well. The description Fletcher gives of the native houses is clearly the type displayed in the Royal British Columbia Museum. Why and when the Indians of Nehalem Bay changed their house style to the long house, after Drake's visit, will need to be studied further. [21]

KROEBER WINTER HOUSE DESCRIPTION

Kroeber says, the Miwok [Northern California Indians] winter house was the earth-covered lodge, dug out three or four feet and entered through the roof by a ladder… Posts supported the roof beams. Over these were laid poles, then brush of some sort and mats, and a heavy coating of earth. The houses are said to have reached a diameter of 50 feet, with a height of nearly 20 feet from the roof entrance to the floor.

Kroeber goes on to say of these types of houses,

> *"This is the semi-subterranean house which extends with little modification from the center of California to British Columbia and beyond."* [22] [bold by author]

CERMENO'S HOUSE DESCRIPTION

Cermeno refers to Indian houses in this way:

> "[Cermeno] *went ashore with the Indians and landed on the beach of the port near some of their underground habitations, in which they live, resembling caves…"* [bold by author] [23]

HOUSING CONCLUSION

The descriptions of caves by Cermeno do not match Fletcher's description as round houses entered from the roof. Nor does the description A. L. Kroeber has given of a 50-foot round house entered through the front. Although, Kroeber's description of a semi-subterranean round house extending into the Pacific Northwest does resemble Fletcher's dugout style, which is round and entered through the roof. Because Cermeno describes "caves" entered through the front in which the Miwok Indians of Pt. Reyes, California were living, while the Indian houses in which Fletcher described were semi-subterranean, one must conclude that Drake and Cermeno were in different places, with Cermeno at Pt. Reyes and Drake in Nehalem Bay. Additionally, the fact that a sweat lodge could be described as a cave might be a legitimate claim, except that sweat lodges would not be built in large numbers as Cermeno described, but only built one or two at most in a village.

LONG HOUSES

Those who are familiar with Pacific Northwest Indians, are aware of the long houses in which they lived. There are numerous descriptions of these houses being up to 40 feet wide and 100 feet long which were entered through a front, ground-level opening. These houses also had an opening in the roof for smoke to escape and occupants slept on shelves along the edges. These structures are also semi-subterranean. Because of the housing similarities, additional research might suggest that these types of long houses could have been an adaptation from the type of fort or living structures Drake built in Nehalem Bay.

DRESS

The Indian men whom Drake met in the summer of 1579 were wearing fur garments down to the waist and the women wore rush skirts (see photos 51 - 55). Fletcher describes "shell necklaces" which are known as dentalia and found only in the off-shore waters of Puget Sound. They were of great value to the Indians and were used as a symbol of wealth.

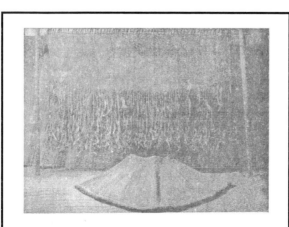

Fig. 51 Cedar Cape and hanging unfinished skirt
Edward Curtis Photo

Fig. 52   Chief with fur shoulder piece

Edward Curtis Photo

Voyage With Malaspina — 1791

Fig. 53   Tomas Suría[24] drawing 1791

Fig. 54   Women wore fringed, skirts.

Circa 1905 after acculturation.

Carolyn M. Buan & R. Lewis, Editors,

The First Oregonians, published by Oregon

Council for the Humanities, Portland, Or 1991

Cermeno described the Indians he met in November of 1595 at Pt. Reyes in this way,

> *"They go naked without covering and with their private parts exposed, but the women cover theirs with straw and skins of animals."* [25]

Cermeno wrecked in November, typically a much colder month of the year, while Drake's Indians were covered in fur in the middle of summer, yet Cermeno's Indians were naked in late fall. It may have been a colder than average year in 1579 when Drake was in Nehalem Bay, though current residents of the Oregon Coast are accustomed to often seeing visitors from the south bundled in their winter clothes while visiting in the summertime. In 1938 ethnologist Verne F. Ray reported a 50-year Mean Maximum Temperature [26] of 62.6 in August, whereas the southern people come from much warmer summer temperatures of 85-100 degrees. Drake's men wore their winter clothes because of the cold Oregon Coast summers.

DRESS CONCLUSION

One must conclude that Cermeno and Drake were in different locations and met different Indians accustomed to different climatic temperatures. The Pacific Northwest Indians needed to protect themselves with furs while the California Indians being 420 miles further south than Nehalem Bay, were accustomed to much warmer temperatures and needed little covering.

CANOES

Fletcher described the canoes of the Indians whom Drake met as being able to row away from the shore into ocean water and quick enough that, when Drake's men tried to get away, they were surrounded by canoes and could not row away in any direction. It was typical for the Pacific Northwest Indian to meet incoming visitors from the sea as described by Hugh Crockett's early telling of a rescue mission of the wreck *Georgiana* on Queen Charlotte's Island in the fall of 1851. He writes,

> *"I think I must say something about the Indians here. Fort Simpson is built at the main town of Simpshean's tribe, and they are one of the most numerous and powerful of the northern tribes. At Fort Simpson I saw more canoes at once*

than I have seen since. The people at the post said there were 700, many of them of the largest size. One hundred men could ride in some of them." [27] (see fig. 56 below).

Fig. 56   Greeting European ships in the 1700's
Painting by George Davidson 1792

Cermeno described the canoes he met in this way:

> "*...four other crafts like the first came out from land to the ship, and in each one was an Indian. A small craft which they employ, like a cacate of the lake of Mexico, a one-person craft.*" (*Cacate* usually means grass, hay or tule, the material was like the rushes of the lake of Mexico).

The craft was the Indian Rush *balsa*, in common use on the Northern California coast. (see fig. 57) Cermeno states that the Indian rowed it very swiftly with a <u>two-bladed oar,</u> much like a kayak paddle. [29]

H. G. Barnett said the Oregon Coast Indians never used double paddles while Cermeno describes the Indians using double paddles at Drake's Bay. [30]

Fig. 57 Tule Canoe as Cermeno described   Courtesy California Historical Society

Fig. 58   Typical Pacific Northwest hunting canoe

Edward Curtis photo

86

Cermeno described a one-man raft he encountered after two days sailing from Drake's Bay. "Nothing but **tule rafts** graced the waters of San Francisco Bay"[31] while Fletcher and Alexander Ross described the Pacific Northwest canoes as quite maneuverable and ocean going crafts capable of carrying upwards of 20 men (see fig. 58).

Professor Kroeber's comments concerning canoes were none too favorable for the pro-California Drake theorists when he wrote:

"Only the 'canoe' in which one man put out to meet the ship and in which others subsequently appear to have paddled when the English boats 'could row no way, but they would follow them,' presents a discrepancy. There is no authentic record of true ocean-going canoes on the whole Pacific coast from near Cape Mendocino to the vicinity of San Luis Obispo. Either custom changed after Drake's day or Fletcher's 'canoe' is a loose term for the tule balsa, which was often boat shaped, with raised sides, especially when intended for navigation." [32]

When describing other California watercraft, Kroeber says,

"The [California] *coast people used a raft of a few logs when needed to cross stream mouths and to visit mussel and sea-lion rocks offshore. A balsa, of course, is not practicable in the surf...This is not a Pomo peculiarity. All the coast tribes, from near Cape Mendocino to the vicinity of Point Concepcion, faced salt water all their lives without ever riding upon it except now and then on a few rude logs."* [33]

In contrast, the Pacific Northwest Indians were exceptional boat and canoe builders. They went everywhere by canoe. In August of 1788, John Hoskin's, 2nd mate, in the log of Robert Gray's *Lady Washington,* when entering Tillamook Bay, eight miles south of Nehalem Bay, described canoes coming from the ocean side,

"...at 11 AM there came alongside two Indians in a small canoe very differently formed from those we had seen to the Southward [California] it was sharp at the head and stern and extremely well built to paddle fast." [34]

Lewis and Clark give detailed descriptions and rough drawings of the canoes used by the Indians at the mouth of the Columbia River (see fig. 59). They say that these canoes were "remarkably neat, light, and well adapted for riding high waves." [35]

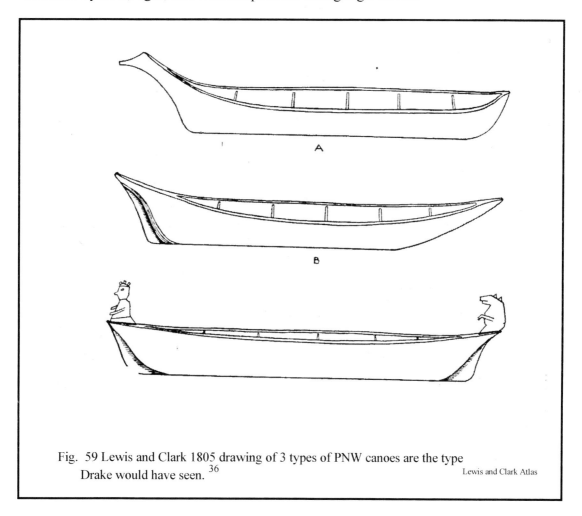

Fig. 59 Lewis and Clark 1805 drawing of 3 types of PNW canoes are the type Drake would have seen. [36]   Lewis and Clark Atlas

Nuno da Silva's deposition to the Spanish Inquisition in 1580, after Drake had released him from captivity, describes how Drake careened his ship off of South America in the south latitude of 49° on June 20th 1578,

> "There, out of fear of the Indians, they anchored at a small, sandy island, near the main land, **tarred the three vessels from top to bottom** [bold by author] and broke the other two so that the men could use them as fuel to cook their food and warm themselves, the country being extremely cold." [27A]

The Indians of the Pacific Northwest also blackened their canoes on the outside as well as painted them red on the inside. [28] Could this have been an imitation of Drake's tarring of his ship when he was in Nehalem Bay?

CANOE CONCLUSION

Cermeno and Drake described totally different types and materials of the Indian canoes which says they were in different locations along the coast. Drake was in Nehalem Bay, Oregon; Cermeno was at Pt. Reyes, California and each encountered different Indian tribes.

FLETCHER'S BLACK STAFF

Fletcher talks of a black staff of heavy wood measuring 4 to 4 ½ feet that was given to Drake (see Chapter 6). This black staff was called a power stick by the Nehalem Tribe (see fig. 60 & 61). Clara Pearson was raised by her grandmother and knew of the old ways, having grown up in Nehalem, and relayed to Elizabeth Jacobs,

> *"The power sticks carried by the shaman for doctoring were cedar or yew poles of four or five feet in length with carvings on one end which represented human faces. The eyes were of abalone shell and human hair was tucked tightly into holes around the top of the stick."* [37]

The heavy black staff carried by the Nehalem Chief was made from the yew tree, a slow-growing evergreen found throughout the Pacific Northwest coastal areas. The tree grows to its full height of 45 feet in about 75 years. The Indians used these trees for their bows, arrow shafts and hardwood utility items such as lances or pikes.

Tomas de Suría was the artist who sailed with Spanish Captain Alejandro Malaspina on his journey of discovery, mapping Alaska and Vancouver Island in 1791. Suría describes the Indians using a heavy black staff for their lances and says that they acquire the metal blades from the English.[38] Historian Henry Wagner describes these staffs as being made from yew; the wood is a natural reddish color which the Indians would burn to harden the wood and then make slurry of the ashes which produced the color.

Fig. 60 Power Stick carried by Shaman
Edward Curtis Photo

Fig. 61   Power Stick   Edward Curtis Photo

Anthropologist Franz Boas describes the power sticks in his discussion of Shamanism,

> *"He had two carved wands, called qelqaloxten, with a head at one end and a*
> *figure of two men at the other end.   These wands were said to belong to the*
> *salmon.   The head of a humming bird was tied to one end.   After he was through*
> *with these sticks, he took two others, which were painted with coal."* [39]

Ethnologist Verne Ray describes the yew as a favorite wood for the foreshaft of the arrows which were,

> *"...straightened with a perforated wooden straightener and polished with a*
> *scouring rush.   Feathering was double with tangential placement ... trimmed*
> *with the red-shafted woodpecker."* [40]

Yew Tree [41]

Common name: Pacific Yew; Western Yew

Scientific Name: *Taxus brevifolia*

Description: The Pacific Yew is an evergreen tree that grows 2-15m (6-45 feet) in height, with a trunk diameter of up to 30 cm (11 inches). Its branches tend to droop and its trunk and branches are often gnarly and twisted. The bark is reddish-brown and scaly, with some scales shedding to reveal a bright red under bark. The needles are dull- to dark-green, flat, alternate one another, and 1 inch (2-3 cm) long with a sharp tip. The bottom side of the needle is white with a light green central line running the length of the needle, (Pojar and Makinnon 1994). A bright red, fleshy fruit with a belly button-like hole on the tip surrounds the seeds of the Yew.

Geographical range: Found throughout the western region of northern California, Oregon, Washington, British Columbia, Canada, and Alaska. This tree is restricted to very western forests of northern British Columbia and Alaska, (Pojar and Makinnon 1994).

Habitat: This tree is found in low- to middle-elevation old-growth Douglas-fir/ Western hemlock forests which grow in abundance along the Pacific Northwest coast. It requires moist soil and a high shade environment with occasional sun flecks penetrating through the canopy, (Pojar and Makinnon 1994).

Use as a Human Resource: The hard and durable wood from the Yew tree was a primary resource for coastal Native American tribes. Tribes used this wood to make bows, wedges, clubs, paddles, digging sticks, adze handles, harpoon shafts, spears, sewing needles, awes, knives, dishes, spoons, boxes, drum frames, bark scrapers, combs and many other useful tools. Yew wood is still sought today by wood carvers, as its beautiful wood changes in color from yellow to deep-red the deeper it is carved into the heartwood.

Notes: The bright red berries are poisonous to humans. This tree is only found in old-growth forests as it takes numerous years to establish itself and grows incredibly slow.   Source: www.en.wikipedia.org/wiki/western_yew

MISINTERPRETATION OF BLACK STAFF

Professor A. L. Kroeber misinterprets these power sticks altogether and describes it as a royal mace that the California Indians carried. If this were the case, there would be some other mention of this type of stick in California ethnology, yet isn't any evidence of a heavy black scepter of this size or type used by California Indians. Only the shamans throughout the Pacific Northwest carried power sticks. Other proponents of the "Drake in California" theories have ignored the subject of the power stick altogether.

TAB'AH

Francis Drake has been credited by some historians for bringing smoking tobacco back to England in 1583. This was three years before Drake rescued inhabitants of the first English colony established by Walter Raleigh at Roanoke, VA, in 1586 before anyone from Roanoke had returned to England.

Some have suggested that the word Tab'ah could be a substitute for the word tobacco by Fletcher but it was, in fact, a Salish-language word describing their smoking of tobacco. *Tab'ah*[42] was the tobacco which grows wild in the Pacific Northwest. Verne F. Ray[43] also mentions that the natives smoked tobacco, as well as Kinnikinnick, a wild native plant which grows in the Pacific Northwest. He describes how the Chinook would go into the fields and add lime to sweeten the acid-loving natural plant (*Nicotina Occentalis*) which still grows naturally throughout the Pacific Northwest.[44]

The Nootka Indians of Vancouver Island cultivated natural tobacco by adding ash (which in fact is lime) that would invariably make the tobacco grow very large. This process is described in 1802 in John Jewitt's journal during his 2-1/2 years of living as a captive with Maquinna, the chief of the Nootka on Vancouver Island. Afterwards the plant was ground in large stone bowls[45] and it was either smoked or chewed.

There can be little doubt this is the same tab'ah herb which was given to Drake as described by Fletcher in *The World Encompassed*.

Fig. 62 Native tobacco plant
Nicotiana Occentalis

Fig. 63 Nicotiana Occentalis flower

BASKETS

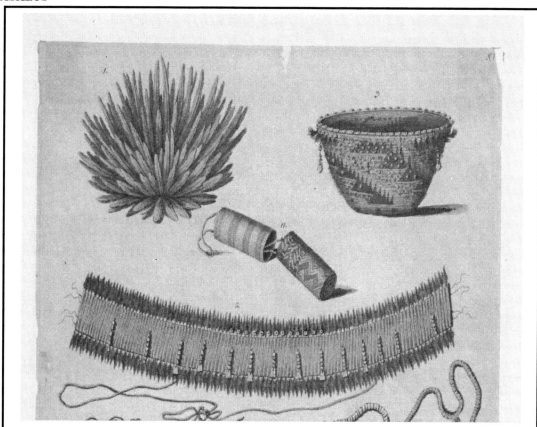

Fig. 64   Dated between1803 and 1807 Eleven numbered items including adornments, necklaces,
bow and arrows, and baskets. Pacific Northwest Artifacts; Travel sketches.   Bancroft Library

Decorative waterproof baskets were common among Pacific Northwest Indians as well as other wood and grass crafts. (See Chapter 6 for additional baskets.)

SOFT "DOWNE" FOR CLOTHING

Fletcher describes the Indians spinning the finest softest down he had ever seen,

> "...*His guard also had each coaets of the same shape, but of other skins: some having cawles [collars] likewise stuck with feathers, or covered over with a certain downe, which growth up in the country upon a herb much like our lettuce; which exceeds any other downe in the world for fineness....*"

The fireweed and lettuce plant look much alike when allowed to seed; tall thin plant stalks with sparse leaves and with seed tops as in photo 65. When seeding, instead of a <u>head</u> of lettuce, Fletcher correctly describes "much like our lettuce", this soft down from the fireweed plant (see Chapter 6 for additional fireweed descriptions and uses). Hard evidence has shown, that this plant, called fireweed, (*Augustifolium,* the summer plant) was steadily observed over a two-year period by the author and verified by ethnobotanist Douglas Deur, University of Washington, as fireweed from which down was gathered for clothing.

Fig. 65   Plant known as fireweed (*Augustifolium*) in full bloom going to seed
Photo by author

Fireweed is one of the plants which grow first in an area that has been burnt. The Nehalem Indians are known to have burned off the Neahkahnie Mountain face in order to make hunting easier (see fig. 46), since deer and elk will graze on open-field foliage rather than in the heavy forest. The mountain face would have large areas of fireweed for picking of the down by the Nehalem for use in collars, headdresses and other clothing items reserved for the chief and other tribe members of importance.

Even today, fireweed down is known as the finest plant material to be used in a mix with wool. Fireweed is harvested after it goes to seed in late summer. [46]

Finally, the open-minded reader should realize that the Indians who met Drake were well-dressed, well-fed, intelligent and bright enough to live off the land for at least 9,000 years before Drake arrived. However, the natives had never seen such a sight, such a large ship with clouds for sails, men with guns, cannon, metal and big medicine. Perhaps it's no wonder they treated Drake like a god and a supreme shaman.

INDIAN LEGENDS

Supreme Deity Legend

Reverend Joseph H. Frost was the first European descendent to document the stories of reverence for a supreme deity of the Nehalem/Tillamook Indians. In 1841, Frost was traveling by foot from Astoria via the ocean beaches on his way to Yamhill (a city 22 miles Southwest of Portland, OR) and was being led over Neahkahnie Mountain by a Tillamook Indian. Frost recorded in his journal,

> " in a meadow, overlooking the ocean was a large stone carved in the image of their supreme deity, Ne-Carney [Ekahnie], who they believed was a man who went up into the mountain and turned into stone and never returned." [47]

Due to spelling and pronunciation from various early authors, Ekahnie, Econe', Acone' and NeCarney all refer to the same supreme spirit of the Nehalem, Tillamook and Clatsop Indians along the Northwest Coast of Oregon. James G. Swan in *The Northwest Coast or Three Years' Residence in Washington* describes Econe' as the supreme spirit of the Clatsops, while today, E-kah-nie is the recognized local spelling and pronunciation. The research for this monograph has found no other references to a supreme spirit or deity among Pacific Northwest Indians, let alone, as Frost describes, <u>as a man</u> who went up to the mountain and turned into stone and never came back. Nehalem Indians had no written language, and when Drake inscribed stones with letters and other symbols, the natives might have believed only a god could perform such an act. And the fact that Drake, a man, departed and never returned, suggests him as the supreme deity. As we will see in Chapter 6, Drake and the crew were treated with awe and reverence during their stay. The large carved stone in the image of Ekahnie mentioned by Frost is in a meadow and at the western point of the Neahkahnie Mountain Survey performed by Drake. (see Chapter 2 Neahkahnie Survey for additional information).

COPPER CANOE LEGEND

Jose Mariano Mozino gave an account of an Indian legend in *Noticias de Nutka* in 1792 while in Nootka, B.C., he relates how the Creator came to their village on a copper canoe with oars of the same copper and the ship carried many handsome young men. Astonished by this spectacle, an Indian girl remained stunned at the foot of the tree, until one of the paddlers advised her *"that it was the All–Powerful who had had the goodness to visit that beach..."*, *Qua-utz,* who was their Creator deity, had the goodness to visit and thereby save her from misfortune.[48] This Nootka bay is where the Spanish ported their ships which the Indians called *Yuquatl*[49] At the time, Mozino's account documented that the Indians could remember their stories back 200 years . If we start with 1792 minus 200 years, making the Indian Creation Deity story back to 1592, just 13 years after Drake's time in the bay.

Fletcher mentions landing in a "bad bay" before their five-week stay in Nehalem Bay.[50] The "copper canoe" appears to resemble the *Golden Hinde* with its gilded monikers, and the "handsome young men" were the crew members whose average age was well under 30 years.

CONCLUSION

There are no California bays with Indian legends connected with a man or group of men who are referred to as gods or supreme deity. These two Pacific Northwest Indian legends are connected with Francis Drake's anchoring in Nehalem Bay, described in Fletcher's *World Encompassed.*

Chapter 5 Three Islands of Saint James

Upon leaving Nehalem Bay on July 23rd 1579, Fletcher's *World Encompassed* states,

> *"Not far without this harbor did lye certain Islands, we called them the Islands of Saint James, having on them plentiful and great store of seals and birds, with one of which we fell July 24, whereon we found such provision as might competently serve our turn for a while."* [1]

Fletcher described leaving Nehalem Bay and sailing to islands "not far" in which they took enough seals and birds to supply themselves on their voyage.

These islands can be easily seen from Neahkahnie Mountain on clear days and are known today as the Three Arch Rocks, a National Marine Game Reserve. As Fletcher stated in the *World Encompassed*, these nearby islands exibit hard evidence that Drake stopped there to take on food supplies before sailing to the Moluccas from the Pacific Northwest Coast on July 25th 1579.

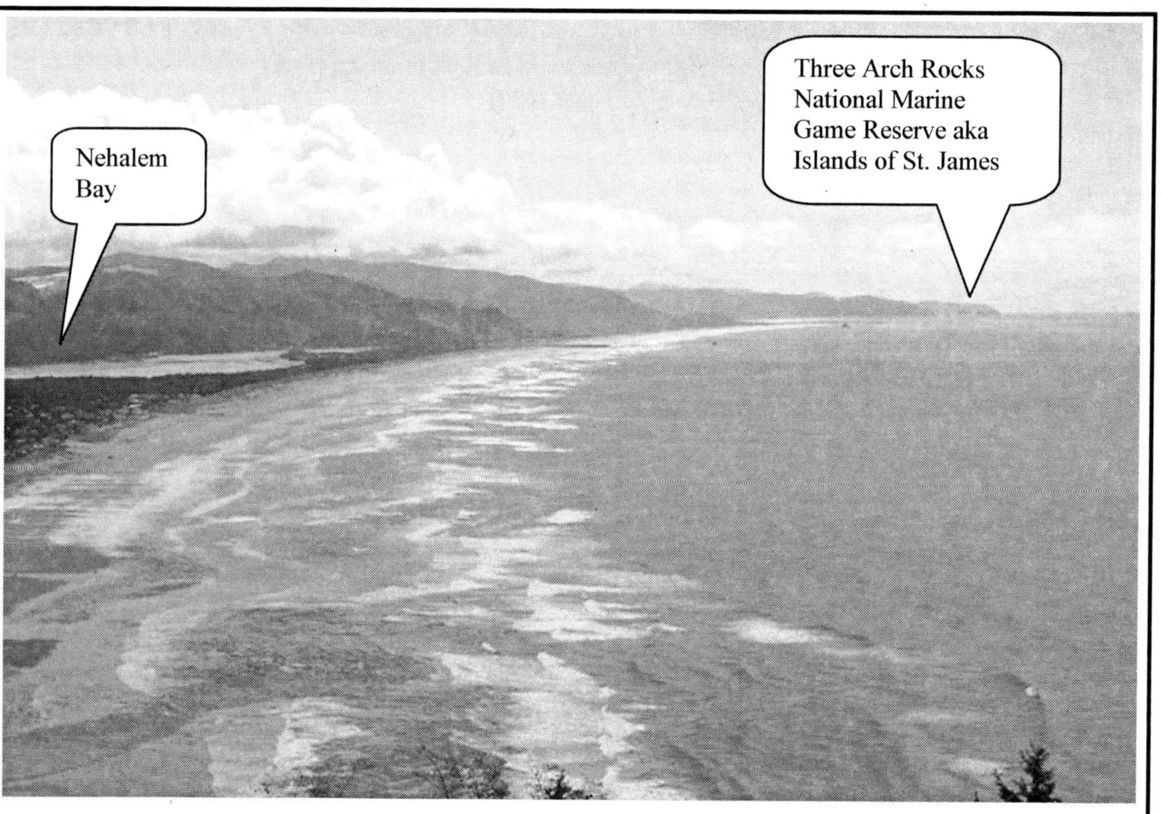
Nehalem Bay
Three Arch Rocks National Marine Game Reserve aka Islands of St. James

Fig. 66 View from Neahkahnie Mountain looking at the Islands of St. James known today as Three Arch Rocks National Marine Game Reserve. Photo Courtesy Don Best Photography

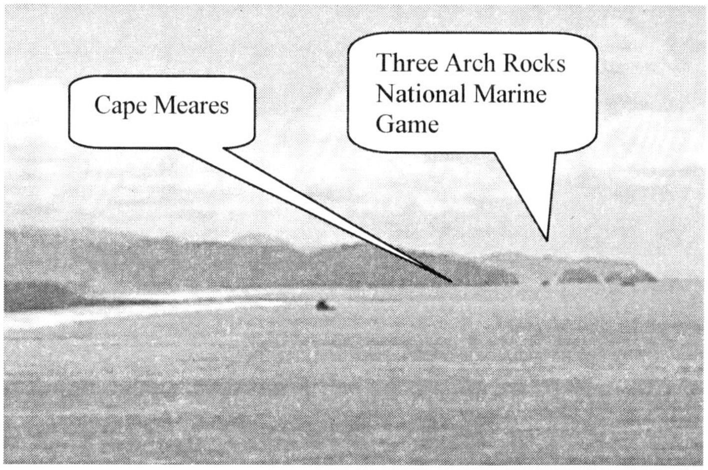
Cape Meares
Three Arch Rocks National Marine Game

Fig. 67 View from Neahkahnie Mountain (close-up)
Photo Courtesy Don Best Photography

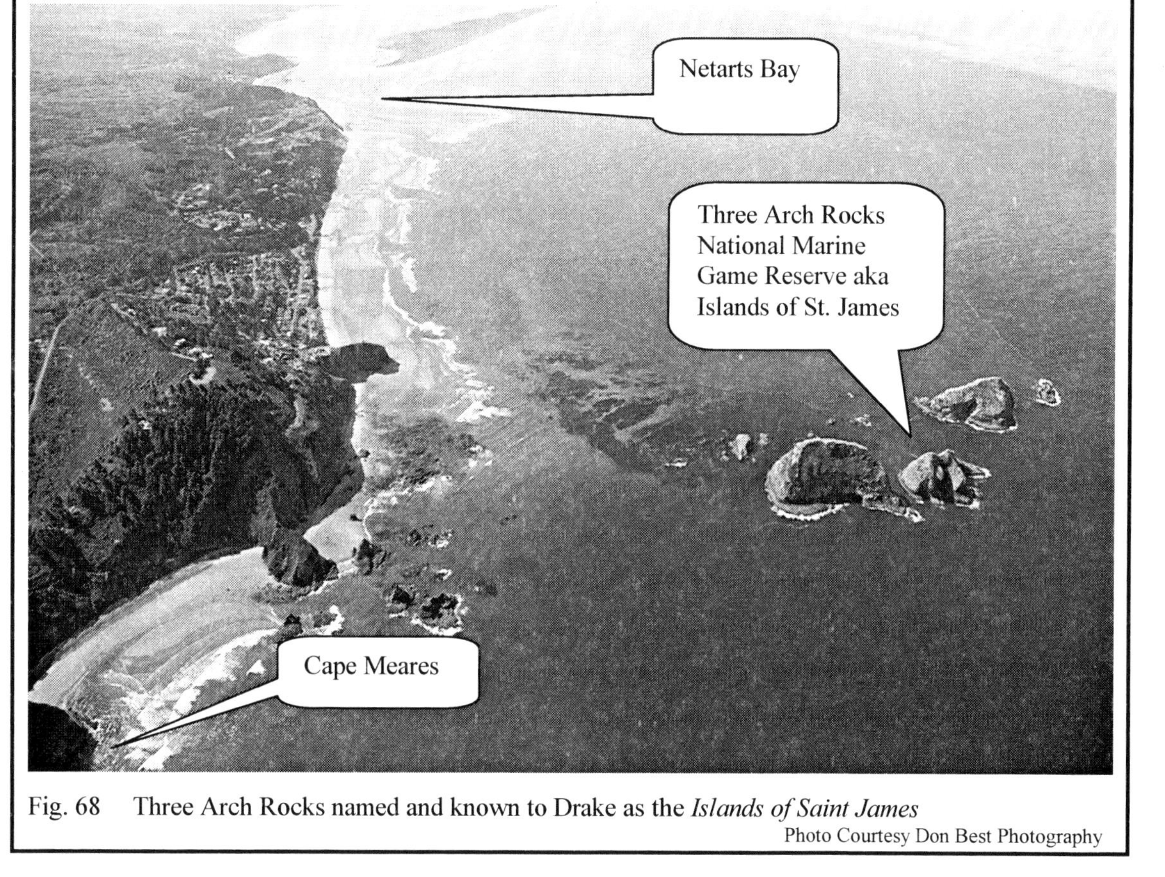
Netarts Bay
Three Arch Rocks National Marine Game Reserve aka Islands of St. James
Cape Meares

Fig. 68 Three Arch Rocks named and known to Drake as the *Islands of Saint James*
Photo Courtesy Don Best Photography

These islands can be easily seen on a clear day from Neahkahnie Mountain and beach. They are 11 minutes of a degree (approximately 16 miles) south of Nehalem Bay off of the Cape Meares headland.

Oregon State Park Cape Meares Monument reads:

Early Photographers Helped Preserve Islands for Wildlife

| Fig. 69 | William Finley and Herman Bohlman 1906 | Courtesy of Portland Audubon Society |

Site of Weekly Slaughter

Every Sunday in early 1900's, while circling in chartered boats, passengers shot and killed nesting seabirds on Three Arch Rocks. Photographers William Finley and Herman Bohlman observed the grisly scene in 1903; an influential naturalist, Finley helped pass legislation to halt the slaughter. With Finley's help, President Theodore Roosevelt declared Three Arch Rocks a National Wildlife Refuge in 1907.

Fig. 70   Murres Colony on Three Arch Rocks National Marine Reserve
Courtesy of Portland Audubon Society

An Important Site for Wildlife

Thanks to those early efforts, Three Arch Rocks now supports about 220,000 murres … some 2,000 to 4,000 Tufted Puffins also nest there, and seals and steller sea lions use the rocks as a breeding area.

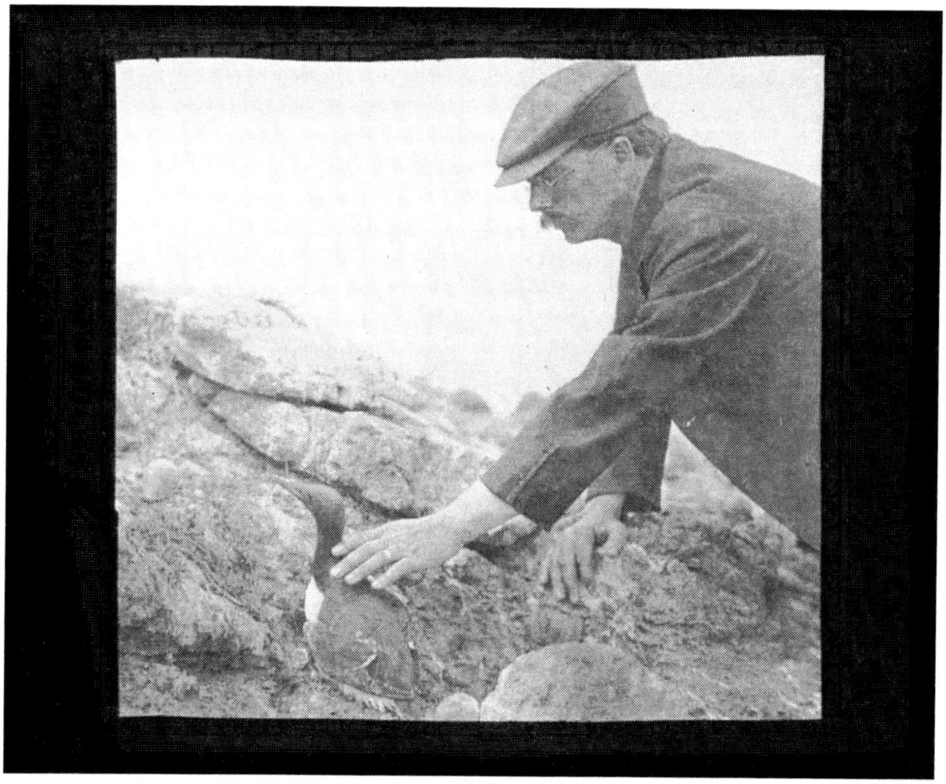

Fig. 71 William Finley at Three Arch Rocks National Marine Reserve
Courtesy of Portland Audubon Society

OTHER EXPLORERS AND SURVEYORS WHO ENCOUNTERED THESE ISLANDS

On August 18, 1775 Spanish Captain Bruno de Hezeta's diary states;

> *"I surveyed the Cabo Frandoso, which is situated with another cape that I named Falcon located in latitude 45° 43' [north], running through an angle of 22° of the third* [SW] *quadrant. Beyond this cape the coast continues through an angle of 5° of the second [SE] quadrant. This land is mountainous but not very elevated, nor as well forested as that from latitude 48° 30' down to 46°. In sounding I found considerable difference, for at a distance of seven leagues I sounded in 84 varas but as I approached the coast I sometimes found no bottom. This leads me to believe there are some reefs or sandbanks on this coast, which is also shown by the color of the water. In some places the coast ends in a beach, and in others in steep cliffs.*
>
> *A level mountain, which I named La Mesa {the table}* [Cape Meares], *will enable any navigator to be sure of the position of Cabo Falcon, even if it*

could not be observed, for it is in latitude 45° 28', and it can be seen at a
considerable distance, being fairly high.
In the latitude of 45° 30' *there are three rocky headlands or hillocks that I*
named Las Tres Marias" [the Three Marys which Drake had previously
named the Islands of St. James]. [2]

A report by George Davidson, the Superintendent of the Coast Survey made to the House
of Representatives of the United States, 37 Congress, 3rd Session, described what John
Meares stated when passing, what is now named Cape Meares in July 1788,

"The distant southerly headland we called Cape Lookout [present day Cape
Meares]. *This cape is very high and bluff and terminates abruptly in the sea.*
At about the distance of two miles from it there rose three large rocks, which
are very remarkable for the great resemblance they bear each other. The
middle one has an archway, perforated, as it were, in its center, through which
we plainly discover the distant sea. ***They more particularly attracted our***
notice as we had not observed between King George's sound and this place
any rocks so conspicuously situated near the land; [bold by author] *their*
distance from each other might be one-quarter of a mile, and we gave them the
name of the 'Three Brothers.' By eight in the evening we were three or four
leagues of[f] Cape Lookout [Cape Meares], *which we judged to lie in latitude*
45° 30' north, longitude 235° 50' east." [3]

(Note: Prior to 1857, Cape Meares was called Cape Lookout. Cape Lookout today,
is the next headland two miles to the south of Cape Meares.)

Davidson described these islands as "four" islands in his report of the <u>1850 U.S. coast</u>
<u>survey,</u> along Cape Meares.

"Four rocks [Drake called these islands St. James] *are laid down off the*
southwest face on the Coast Survey reconnaissance of 1850, and one on the
north. [4]

In the <u>1853 survey</u> he says,

"Three large rocks and one small one are laid down off the southwest face in,
the original sheets of the reconnaissance of 1853, the most distant being one
mile from shore, with several small ones between them and the shore, and two
or three others off the northwest face. [5]

Davidson continues reporting on the 1857 coast survey,

"In coming down this coast in the fall of 1857, we made a few notes upon some
objects, and find the following memorandum made whilst near this point [Cape
Meares]: *"Three high rocks (one arch) off point south* [present day Cape
Meares]*; one more on the north side. ... the northern part of this cape* [Cape
Meares] *is placed in latitude 45° 30', longitude 123° 58', and stretching*
southward two miles to the cluster of rocks above described. We applied the
name to this cape [Cape Meares] *in 1857."* [6]

CONCLUSION

The three (or sometimes four) rocks today are known as the Three Arch Rocks National
Marine Game Reserve, the first marine reserve in the United States. Despite their small
size, 15 acres, Three Arch Rocks Reserve is of enormous importance to nesting seabirds,
and to breeding and resting steller sea lions. With its monolithic proportions and
distinctive shapes, it is one of the best known landmarks on the Oregon Coast. These
islands are the very same islands which Drake landed on July 23, 1579 and named *Islands*
of St. James. [7]

Chapter 6   Fletcher's *World Encompassed*

Purpose of the Voyage

The first page of *The World Encompassed* by Reverend Francis Fletcher stated the purpose of the Drake voyage;

> *"Others not contented with school points* [book and classroom mathematics] *and such demonstrations... have added thereunto their own history and experience. All of them in reason have deserved great commendation of their own ages and purchased a just renowne with all posterity. For if a surveyor of some few Lordships, whereof the bounds and limits were before known, worthy deserves his reward for his work, not only for his travel but for his skill also measuring the whole and every part thereof did a good job measuring a few bits of land which was already delineated by fences, trees, houses, churches and towns: how much more, above comparison, are their famous travels by all means possible to be eternized, who have bestowed their studies and endeavor, to survey and measure this globe almost immeasurable? Neither is here that difference to be objected, which in private possessions is of value:* **Whose Land Survey you?** [bold added by author] *for as much as the Maine Ocean* [Pacific Ocean] *by right is the Lord's alone, and by nature left free, for all men to deal withal, as very sufficient for all men's use, and large enough for all men's industry."*

Francis Drake's primary purpose of his voyage was to lay claim the unclaimed world for England. His daily actions were to survey the globe which included the Maine Ocean [Pacific Ocean], and at the same time, what lay beyond the known Spanish land claims. Because he was to survey and map the world and claim unclaimed lands, Drake's first actions, after taking over a ship, were to take charts, break compasses and throw navigation instruments overboard. The charts recorded winds and latitudes the 16th century Spanish used to navigate from and to the Philippines, as well as other lands.

There were only a few Spanish maps which illustrated the Pacific Coast and they are as follows:

1. In April 1579 off the island of Cano, close to the port of Nicoya, Nicaragua, Drake could have determined how far the Spanish had explored by reading captured Spanish maps of Alonzo Sanchez Colchero, a pilot for the China trade who was captured on Don Francisco de Zarate's ship. [1] These maps would have shown eastern and western trade winds along with their latitudes.

2. Spaniards Juan Rodriguez Cabrillo and Bartolome Ferrelo sailed to the 42-1/2° north latitude in 1542-3, which is near the present day Oregon-California border. It is doubtful that maps captured by Drake reflected this, since even later maps do not reflect an Oregon location because they (Cabrillo and Ferrelo) did not land. The recorded maps only show Monterey Bay which lies at 36° 36' N latitude. [2]

3. The signed "Battista Agnese" map, dated May 14, 1542, is the earliest map of California and goes no further then 36° N. [3]

4. The *Bibliotheque National,* dated June 25, 1543 and signed by Battista Agnese, goes no further than 36° N. [4]

5. A map by Diego de Homem, dated 1568 shows the California coast to 36° N. [5]

6. The next Spanish map was made in 1603 by Sebastian Vizcaino which was after the Drake voyage of 1579.

Without any other known Spanish maps to show otherwise, it can be said with some certainty, that Drake must have known, from captured maps, that the Spanish had been as far as Monterey Bay's 36° 36' north latitude, but no further.

Henry R. Wagner's *Spanish Voyages to the Northwest Coast of America in the Sixteenth Century* offer this conclusion as to why the Spanish did not explore above 36° or claim the Upper California region above Monterey Bay, "At the time that Cabrillo and Vizcaino visited the territory, gold was the only resource that could have been exploited, and that lay too far from the coast to be discovered by any maritime expedition. The timber, grain, fruits, petroleum, and the multitudinous products which now bring wealth to this region were valueless or would have been had they been produced. One of the reasons why gold and silver occupied such a large share of attentions of the many adventures from the various European countries and were so eagerly sought, lay in the fact that by reason of their great value in small bulk they and they alone could be exported to purchase necessities or luxuries of life." [7]

Fig. 72 Neahkahnie Mountain 1936 with coast Highway 101 was under construction. Notice trees growing only on the mountain ridge line after years of burning by the Indians.   Photo Jensen Collection

THE WORLD ENCOMPASSED TIMELINE IN NEHALEM BAY AND NEAHKAHNIE MOUNTAIN

In order to provide a chronological historical picture of Drake's Nehalem Bay landing, a timeline analysis and point-by-point summary of Francis Fletcher's *The World Encompassed (WE)* will follow:

1. The Drake departure from England

2. Drake's time spent in Argentina at Port St. Julian

3. Departure from South America to find the Northwest Passage

4. The summer of 1579 in Nehalem Bay and Drake's departure from said bay.

DEPARTURE FROM PLYMOUTH, ENGLAND

December 13, 1577 (pg3 WE)

> *"Whence having in a few days supplied all defects with happier sails we once more put to sea December 13, 1577".*

After an initial shake-out cruise November 15th to the 28th, Drake set sail with five ships on the first English voyage to circumnavigate the globe on December 13, 1577.

MAGELLAN STRAIT

June 20 - August 17, 1578 (pg 25 WE)

> *"Thus the next day the 20 of June we entered Port Saint Julian [Argentina] which stranded in 49 deg. 30 min and hath on the Southside of the harbor picked rocks like towers, and within the harbor many Islands, which you may ride hard aboard off, but in going in you must borrow of the North Shore".*

Here Fletcher describes how Drake was able to sail among islands and rocks with the *Pelican*, renamed the *Golden Hinde*, after sailing through Magellan Strait. Port Saint Julian had also been the resting place for Magellan and his crew in 1520. We see that Drake knew his position, as he always did, barring storms or cloudy days, when he took readings by the sun, moon and stars to navigate.

June 22, 1578 (pg 25 WE)

> *"Being now June 22 come to anchor, and all things fitted and made safe aboard, our General with certain of his company, (viz. Thomas Drake, his brother, John Thomas, Robert Winter, Oliver the Master gunner, John Brewer, and Thomas Hood) rowed further in with a boat to find out some convenient place which might yield us fresh water, during the time of our abode there..."*

Drake rows in to determine a location for their encampment, as Fletcher writes later when describing Drake going up into the country. Drake, as any good captain, would explore a new bay and would have used a number of his best crew on his exploration into the Nehalem Bay in 1579.

(pg. 33 WE)

> *"In the land, as we digged to bury this gentleman* [Thomas Doughty had been causing other members of the crew to disobey and talk of mutiny. Drake had him executed by authority of the Queen], *we found a great grinding stone, broken in two parts, which we took and set fast in the ground, the one part at the head, the other at the feet, building up the middle space, with other stones and turfs of earth, and engraved in the stones, the names of parties buried there* [John Carthagene, a Magellan crewmember who advocated mutiny and Thomas Doughty], *with the time of their departure, and a memorial of our generals name in Latin, that it might better be understood, of all that should come after us."*
>
> [bold added by author]

This paragraph is one of the most telling with regard to Drake's actions pertaining to engraving stones in Latin. In Wagner's *Creation of Rights of Sovereignty Through Symbolic Acts, 1938,* he overlooked the engraving of stones as a symbolic act.

The name of Drake in stone - as a memorial – was left <u>so all should know, who come after them, that he was there</u> at Port St. Julian. Drake or a crewmember was the designated carver and the same person would have carved both the Neahkahnie Mountain Survey Rocks and the Port Saint Julian tombstone in Argentina. As of this writing, the Royal Maritime Museum in London has expressed an interest in obtaining any information about the tombstone inscribed by Drake. The Neahkahnie Mountain survey rocks are presently in Tillamook County Pioneer Museum, the M. Wayne Jensen Jr. estate, and in private collections.

DRAKE DEPARTS SOUTH AMERICA TO THE PACIFIC NORTHWEST
April 16, 1578 (pg 62 WE)

> *"From Guatulco we departed the day following…whereon we sailed 500 leagues in longitude, to get a wind: and between that and June 3, [we sailed] 1400 leagues in all, till we came into 42 deg. of North latitude, where in the night following, we found such alternation of heate, into extreame and nipping cold,*

that our men in generall, did grievously complaine thereof; some of them feeling
their health much impaired thereby, neither was it, that this chanced in the night
alone, but the day following carried with it, not only the markes, but the stings
and force of the night going before, for besides that the pinching and biting air,
was nothing altered; the very ropes of our ship were stiff, and the rain which fell,
was an unnatural congealed and frozen substance, so that we seemed rather to
be in the frozen Zone...".

After capturing Spanish maps and diverse supplies, Drake left Guatulco, South America and sailed NW and then NNE until he made landfall the following day.

JUNE 18, 1579 LANDFALL (Pg 67 WE)

"The next day after coming to anchor in the aforesaid harbor the people of the
country showed themselves; sending off a man with great expedition to us in a
canoe. Who being yet but a little from the shore, and great way from our ship,
spoke to us continually as he came rowing on. And at last at a reasonable
distance staying himself, he began more solemnly a long and tedious oration,
after his manner; using in the deliveries thereof, many gestures and signs,
moving his hands, turning his head and body many ways; and after his oration
ended with great show of reverence and submission, returned back to shore
again."

After exploring the area around Vancouver Island at 48° north to look for the Northwest Passage, Drake sailed south along the coast until he reached 45° 41' at Portus Nova Albionis, which is today's Nehalem Bay on the north Oregon coast. Drake spent nearly five weeks repairing his ship and doing surveys on Neahkahnie Mountain which has been referred to as his "Point of Position". [9] Thomas Blundevil(l)'s *New and Necessary Treatise of Navigation,* published in 1613 suggests that they came in at 44°, John Drake as well said they came in at 44°, but Blundevil(l) said Drake stopped in a bay (Nehalem Bay) and then part of the crew went north to find the Strait of Anain (Northwest Passage) and then returned to Nehalem Bay. Further research may be necessary.

The actions of the Indians related by Fletcher on this day are much like the descriptions made by John Jewitt and the first 18th century Spanish explorers during their first contacts with Pacific Northwest Indians at Nootka, Vancouver Island, B.C..

John R. Jewitt's story of capture and slavery at the hands of Chief Maquinna, the great chief of the Nootka people, began in 1802 when Maquinna, because of a previous insult by Spanish explorers, decided to annihilate the next ship he encountered. The *Boston* was the unlucky ship, and the entire crew was killed except for Jewitt, the ship's blacksmith and John Thompson, a sail maker who was represented to Maquinna, as Jewitt's father. Jewitt and Thompson were finally rescued after two-and-a-half years. While living with the natives, he had kept a journal, recognized as one of the earliest ethnological documents of its time.

Nootka is only slightly more than $3°$ north of Nehalem Bay unlike the California speculation, which cites the Oregon Siletz tribes for their ethnology comparisons and who were $6°$ north of where Drake is supposed to have landed in California. (Note: one degree of latitude is approximately 69 miles.)

(pg 67 WE continued)

> *"He* [the Indian] *shortly came again the second time in like manner, and so the third time; When he brought with him, as a present from the rest, a bunch of feathers, much like the feathers of a black crow, very neatly and artificially gathered upon a string, and drawn together into a round bundle; being very clean and finely cut and bearing in length an equal proportion one with another..."*

Headdresses were common among the natives. This was the headdress of raven or crow feathers, a bird revered by the Pacific Northwest Indians and recognizable as described by Fletcher.[10] Pearson described the headdress worn by warriors as a "buckskin crown, covered with abalone shells and with feathers sticking up. This crown was a leather headband with abalone decorations sewed on flatly and rimmed with feathers that stood up around the top of the head".

Fig. 73   Nootka Native   Curtis Photos

TAB'AH - TOBACCO

(pg 68 WE)

> *"With this (headdress) also he brought a little basket make of rushes, and filled with a herb which they called Tab'ah. Both which being tied to a short rod, and cast into our boat..."*

This type of tying on a rod or carrying their herbs was described by Clara Pearson, a native Nehalem-Tillamook Indian, in 1932 to entomologist Elizabeth D. Jacobs. This "Tabah" appears to be *Nicotiana Occentalis*, a native tobacco plant (see photo 62 and 63) grown inland, which the Indians cultivated by adding ash (lime), as described by John Jewitt. Jewitt described how the Indians travel inland to put ash on the tobacco plants so they will grow bigger. [11] Captain Vancouver first saw tobacco cultivated near Point Caution in 1783 and observed: "On each side of the entrance some new habitations were constructed and, for the first time during our intercourse with the Northwest American Indians, in the vicinity of these habitations were found some square patches of ground in a state of cultivation, producing a plant that appeared to be a species of tobacco, and which we understood is by no means uncommon amongst the inhabitants of Queen Charlotte's Island, who cultivate much of this plant."[12]

(pg 68 WE)

> *"Our General intended to have recompensed him immediately with many good things, he would have bestowed upon him: but entering into the boat to deliver the same, he could not be drawn to receive them by any means; save one hat, which being cast into the water out of the ship..."*

Jewitt, Vancouver, Cook and 18th century Spanish explorers and scribes described similar actions of first contact in their logs and journals.

(pg 68 WE)

> *"...After which time, our boat could row no way, but wondering at us as gods, they would follow the same with admiration"*

Here Fletcher is describing the many Indians surrounding them with their canoes in the bay. (see fig. 58 and 59) Since he referred to rowing, we understand that Drake sent an expedition into the bay to check the depth of the bay to secure a place to land the *Golden Hinde* and prepare the ship for repair.

Alexander Ross of the Astoria party in 1811 stated, "All the natives along the coast navigate in canoes, and so expert are they that the stormiest weather or roughest water never prevents them from cruising on their favorite element. The Chinook (Columbia River) and other war canoes are made like the Birman barge, out of a solid tree, and are from forty to fifty feet long, with a human face or a white-headed eagle, as large as life, carved on the prow, and raised high in front. The canoes of the natives inhabiting the lower portion of the Columbia River are made remarkably neat, light, and well-adapted for riding high waves. I have seen the natives near the coast riding waves with safety and apparently without concern where I should have thought it impossible for any vessel of the same size to have lived a minute."[13] Verne Ray notes, "Canoes on the sea coast, particularly, are waxed or oiled and pitched, painted and ornamented with curious images at bow and stern, those images sometimes rise to the height of five feet; the pedestals on which these images are fixed are sometimes cut out of solid stick with the canoe, and the imagery is formed of separate small pieces of timber firmly united with tenons and mortises."[14]

This ocean canoeing would not be possible with Northern California tule rafts which are used for lake and estuary travel (see Chapter 4 Nehalem Indians).

There is some speculation that European ships took their design from the Pacific Northwest Indian canoes,[15] but in retrospect, we might say it could be the opposite, since the Indian canoes look rather like the *Golden Hinde* with animal heads at each end of their war canoes. (this may be an area for further study). (See fig. 59)

COMING TO SHORE
Jan 21, 1579 - [June 21, 1579][16]
(Pg. 68 WE)

> *"The 3rd day following, was the 21st, our ship having received a leak at sea, was brought to anchor near the shore, that we were to prevent any danger, that might chance against our safety, our general first of all landed his men, with all necessary provision, to build tents and make a fort for the defense of our selves and goods..."*

Drake brought the *Golden Hinde* into Nehalem Bay on this day. Just one year prior, on June 22, 1578 at Port St. Julian, Drake performed the same sort of reconnaissance mission with his smaller boat to see if the natives were friendly, to look for fresh water, and to test the depth of the bay.[17] Additionally, Drake sounded (measured) the bay and river entrances a number of times when he was in the Caribbean on earlier voyages.[18]
It would seem reasonable that the Indians led Drake into the bay over any existing bar with their expert canoe-handling capabilities just as other Pacific Northwest explorers were led into other bays by the natives.

Fletcher goes on,

> *"...when the people of the country perceived us doing, as men set on fire to war, in defense of their country, in great haste and companies, with such weapons as they had, they came down unto us; and yet with no hostile meaning, or intent to hurt us; standing when they drew near, as men ravished in their minds, with the sight of such things as they never had seen, or heard of before that time; their*

errand being rather with submission and fear to worship us as Gods, than to

have any war with us as with mortal man."

The Indians were peaceful, awed, submissive and perceived Drake's men as gods, totally alien to them with weapons, tools, clothes, and a ship that was the most complex piece of machinery on the planet. All of this was totally different from their way of life for the prior 9,000 years of living in Nehalem Bay. This was the first European contact with Pacific Northwest Indians. Ross Cox of the 1811 Astor group described the Nehalem and surrounding Indian groups in this way, "During this period we made several excursions on pleasure or business to the villages of the various tribes, from one to three days journey from the fort [Fort Astoria/George at mouth of the Columbia] They differ little from each other in laws, manners, or customs, and were I to make a distinction, I would say the Cathlamahs are the most tranquil, the Killymucks [Tillamooks] the most roguish, the Clatsops [Nehalem are grouped with the Clatsops as officially recognized tribes as of 2007] the most honest, and the Chinooks the most incontinent." [19]

Drake began to clear the land and construct his fort as he had done on the east coast of Panama in 1573. [20]

The Hondius Broadside map (fig. 36) commemorates the first place where European and Indian religious services were performed in the Pacific Northwest. Fletcher would conduct services and at times Drake would read from the Bible[21] while the Indians were praying with hands held high, to their new supreme deity, Francis Drake. Research has shown there are no other instances of Pacific Northwest Indians which have a documented supreme spirit or deity. [22]

(Pg. 68-69 WE)

"Which things as it did partly show it self at that instant, so did it more and more

manifest it self afterwards, during the whole time of our abode amongst them. At

this time, being willed by signs to lay from them their bows and arrows, they did

as they were directed, and so did all the rest, as they came more and more by

companies unto them, growing in a little while, to a great number both of men

and woman."

Fletcher describes Indians coming from miles around to see these gods which had arrived in their country. It would have only taken two to five days round trip in Drake's time for the news to travel up and down the coast. The Indians would have come by foot; as described by Fletcher when they come to the top of the hill in greater numbers than Drake and crew could have imagined. The great population serves to illustrate that the land and waters of the Pacific Northwest were rich with food and plentiful, unlike the dry Castilian landscape of the Northern California which supported smaller populations.

Jose Mariano Mozino Suarez de Figueroa was the official botanist appointed by the viceroy of New Spain to accompany the expedition of Juan Francisco de la Bodega y Quadra to Nootka Sound in 1792. Mozino was in Nootka from April through September, 1792 and discusses almost every aspect of Nootka and its Indians at the time of their initial contact with European civilization. Mozino said that when the chief, Maquinna, prepared a feast for other *taises* [chiefs] when they came to visit him, "I counted up to thirty-six [dishes], a number I judge comes from the several kinds of fish, birds, and animals on which they ordinarily subsist." [23] (Philip Drucker's introduction to *Noticias De Nutka* states that Mozino's experience in the Pacific Northwest not only allowed the Spanish scientist rare insight into the reaction of these Indians but enabled him to describe their daily life with unique detail. Alberto M. Carreno, who edited the original narrative written in Mozino's own hand, describes Mozino as "one of the most conspicuous scientific personalities that New Spain produced in the eighteenth century." Dr Mozino was a graduate of the botanical institute founded by the Royal Botanical Garden in Mexico City.)

Although Fletcher does not mention flattening of the Indian heads, the Indians of Nootka Sound of Vancouver Island were related to the Nehalem Bay Indians. Both tribes spoke the Salish language, had many ethnographic items in common and used the head-flattening method (see fig. 74). To flatten the heads, they would wrap their newborns in a cradle and use a board pressing down on the front of the head to make a flat head with a pointed top. Only the tribe members were permitted to do this to enhance their looks.

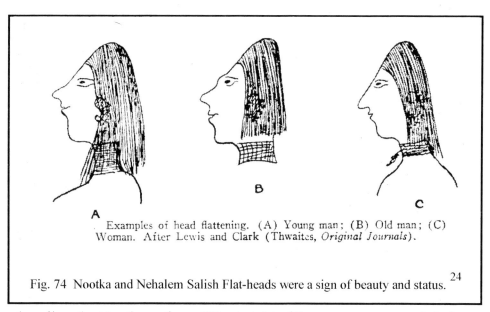

Examples of head flattening. (A) Young man; (B) Old man; (C) Woman. After Lewis and Clark (Thwaites, *Original Journals*).

Fig. 74 Nootka and Nehalem Salish Flat-heads were a sign of beauty and status. [24]

Mozino describes the Nootka natives, "The height of the common person is below average; that of the chiefs is medium; this difference may be due to the different occupations to which the former apply themselves from childhood. Their heads are elongated, not because of a natural defect but because from their birth they are placed in an oblong box which serves as a portable cradle. In this they are held with strong bindings so that they always remain with this deformed configuration: the forehead is raised up; the nose is flattened at the bridge and widened at the nostrils; the cheek-bones are raised and set wide apart, which makes the majority of them wide-faced; and almost all of them are round-faced". [25] Slaves which were taken during raiding parties from distant villages were not permitted to flatten the heads of their offspring.

As we have related, Clara Pearson, born in the 1870's, was one of the last Nehalem/Tillamook survivors who could speak the native Salish language, and she was interviewed at length by Elizabeth D. Jacobs in 1933. Mrs. Pearson had the reputation among all others who had been interviewed to be the most knowledgeable about the ancient culture, myths and traditions. Jacobs relates "The Nehalem mother attended to the head flattening of the baby. The head presser was put on when the child was about ten days old. Heads were flattened only in front. A board was not used; rather, a solidly wrapped bundle of buckskin was strapped across the forehead of the child and around the cradle. The child was removed from the cradle twice a day to have its bedding changed. At this time the head presser was also removed and the forehead massaged to rest it. A veil of cloth or very soft skin called {nesweiqu-d^{z}i-ten} hung from the head presser over the baby's face to keep insects and dust from the baby's eyes and face." [26]

DRAKE TREATED AS A GOD
(Pg. 69 WE)

Fletcher continues, *"To the intent therefore, that this peace which they themselves so willing sought...Not with standing nothing could persuade them, ... that we should be Gods."*

The Indians were dove-like in their actions toward Drake and his men. Surely they had never seen anything like these huge canoes with clouds for sailing and many good looking young men (see Chapter 4 Indian Legends).

INDIAN GIFTS

"In recompense of those things which they received of us as shirts linen cloth, & c. they bestowed upon our general, and diverse of our company, diverse things, as feathers, cawles [collars] of network, the quivers of their arrows, made of fawn-skins, and the very skins beasts that their women wore upon their bodies."

This reciprocal gift-giving was quite common among the Pacific Northwest natives. There is an annual gathering called a potlatch hosted by the richest tribal leader, in which he gives away everything he owns of value. The tribe members would return equal or more of the blanket, bow, food or other utilitarian items received as a gift. It was assumed, or perhaps was required so as not to lose face or status to give gifts in return.[27] Ultimately, the more the giver of the potlatch could give away, the more status he obtained. There were a number of other reasons for giving a potlatch besides birth and death of a clan member.

Clara Pearson also described deer skins and cawles [collars] of network from woven cedar bark for clothing as seen in Chapter 4.

INDIAN HOUSES

(Pg. 69 WE)

"Having thus had their fill of this time visiting and beholding of us, they departed with joy to their houses, which houses are digged round within the earth, and have from the uppermost brimmes of the circle, clefts of wood set up and joined close together at the top, like our spires on the steeple of a Church; which being covered with earth, suffer no weather to enter, and are very warm, the door in the most part of them, performs the office also of a chimney, to let out the smoke; its made in bigness and fashion, like an ordinary scuttle in a ship, and standing slope wise; their beds are the ground, only with rushes strewed up it, and lying round about the house, have their fire in the middle, which by reason that the house is but low vaulted, round and close, given a marvelous reflexion to their bodies to heat the same."

The Royal British Columbia Museum in Victoria, B.C. has reconstructed one of these round houses, and states that these dwellings covered with earth (bark growing wild moss and ferns) were quite common in the Pacific Northwest. (see Chapter 4)

As to why Meriwether Lewis & William Clark only saw longhouses traveling down the Columbia River to the Pacific, one can speculate that the documented earthquake of January 1700 along the Oregon Coast either caused the natives to move out of the immediate area into Eastern or Southern Oregon where these types of houses are also quite common of the Chinook Indians who populated the river, chose longhouses instead of the round house. Or it could be that the first longhouse (rectangular houses some 40 x 100 feet with pitched roofs) began after the Indians observed and imitated Drake's building in Nehalem Bay.

The Hondius map depicts tents with the opening at the long narrow end just as longhouses are built. Adaptation and exposure to new ideas and cultures has always changed the world. After all, Drake was in Nehalem Bay 209 years before the next Englishman, John Meares, exposed the Nehalem to the European culture.

Acculturation began in 1788 with Meares and Robert Gray. By 1840 there were only ten percent remaining aboriginals from those recorded in 1805 by Lewis & Clark's journal, which estimated over 2,000 Indians living between Tillamook Bay (eight miles south) and the Nehalem Bay.

During his stay, Fletcher would have visited the Indian houses. During the day the chests which store blankets and other utilitarian items were set on shelves around the edges. At night the chests were placed under the shelves or platforms and the Indians would sleep on what Fletcher described as shelves and on the floor which would be protected from the ground by a heavy layer of ferns. [28]

A fire in the center with the smoke going through the roof was the common practice among most Indians. The fires, "were somewhat boxed-off from the rest of the room. They were surrounded by boards laid on edge which stood about one and a half feet high and were three or four inches thick. There was plenty of space between the fires and the bunks." [29]

Finally, rush mats were an everyday item used for bedding and wall dividers in the temporary houses sometimes erected at seasonal fishing or food gathering locations by the Nehalem Bay Indians. [30]

INDIAN DRESS

(pg 70 WE)

Regarding the native garments, Fletcher said,

> *"Their men for the most part go naked, the women take a kind of bulrushes and combing it after the manner of hemp, make themselves thereof a loose garment, which being knitted about their middles, hangs down about the hips ... which nature teaches should be hidden. About their shoulders they wear also the skin of a deer, with the hair on it."*

Clara Pearson, in speaking with Elizabeth Jacobs, told of clothing in which, "The women wore skirts of cedar bark or grass for everyday purposes while their dress skirts were made of braided rushes and were called 'rope skirts'. The upper part of the woman's body was covered with a cedar bark or 'skin cape' in cold weather. Beaver fur was made into capes that hung hip length and wrapped around the shoulders in shawl fashion." [31] This skirt was made of pounded inner bark of the cedar, which became as soft as cotton, which was then woven into a network of clothing. In 1811, Alexander Ross of the Astor group described this type of dress in this way, "...the women wear a kind of fringed petticoat suspended from the waist down to the knees, make of the inner rind of the cedar bark, and twisted into threads, which hang loose and keep flapping and twisting about with every motion of the body, giving them a waddle or duck gait. (see Chapter 4 Indians) This garment might deserve praise for its simplicity, or rather for its oddity, but it does not screen nature from the prying eye; yet it is remarkably convenient on many occasions. In calm the sails lie close to the mast, metaphorically speaking, but when the wind blows the bare poles are seen. They were most uncouth-looking objects; and not strongly calculated to impress us with a favorable opinion of aboriginal beauty, or the purity of Indian manners." [32]

INDIAN SHRIEKING AND CRYING
(Pg. 70 WE)

"As soon as they returned to their houses, they began among themselves a kind of most lamentable weeping & crying out; which they continued also a great while together, in such sort, that the place where they left us (being near about 3 quarters of an English mile distant.... in a most miserable and doleful manner of shrieking."

The shrieking and crying described by Fletcher was typical of the Pacific Northwest Indians mourning. Some have theorized that the Indians thought Drake was "from the dead". A more plausible theory is the Indians were mourning one of their own who had died recently or had been take hostage. When Maquinna was taken hostage by a rescuing ship's captain, it caused Maquinna's tribe to weep and cry in the same mourning manner which Fletcher described.[33]

The distance from the fort where Fletcher describes the Indians being 3/4 of an English mile (3/4 x 5000 feet) [34] coincides with archaeological Indian site TNB1 (see Hondius Broadside map and Appendix III, IAS map). This documented archaeological Indian site measures 3/4 of a mile from Alder Creek which coincides with Hondius map of the tent encampment (see Chapter 3).

FORT WITH WALLS OF STONE

"Not with standing this humble manner perfecting themselves, and awful demeanor used towards us, we thought it no wisdom to far to trust them (our experience of former infidels dealing with us before, make us careful to provide against an alteration of their affections, or breach of peace if it should happen) and therefore with all expediation we set up our tents, and entrenched ourselves with walls of stone; that so being fortified within ourselves, we might be ... about our other business."

A fort of stone was built along Alder Creek in Nehalem Bay protecting Drake and crew from any surprise attacks by the Indians before they could repair the ship and claim these lands for England.

(pg 70-71 WE)

"Against the end of two days ...there was gathered together a great assembly of men, women, and children ... bringing with them as before had been done, feathers and bags of Tab'ah for presents or rather indeed for sacrifices, upon the persuasion that we were Gods."

As discussed earlier, Oregon Coast tribes and the Chinook on the Columbia River sowed little plots of tobacco for smoking. [35] Verne Ray wrote, "A native species of tobacco [Nicotiana Occentalis] was planted and cultivated by the Chinook, who live at the mouth of the Columbia River which is forty miles to the north of Nehalem along the coast. [36]
Botanist David Douglas wrote, "The *Nicotiana* is never sowed by the Indians near the villages lest it should be pulled and used before it comes to perfect maturity; they select for its cultivation an open place in the wood, where they burn a dead tree or stump, and strewing ashes over the ground, plant the tobacco there. An informant explained to him [Douglas] that the wood ashes invariably made the tobacco grow very large." [37]

(Pg. 71 WE)

"When they came to the top of the hill, at the bottom where of we had built our fort..."

See Hondius map of the fort with the three hills in the background (of the map) and compare the photo from Fisher's Point (see fig. 43). This shows the fort alongside present day Alder Creek which flows into Nehalem Bay. Notice also the finely drawn lines which depict the waters edge all around the bay. Pay particular attention to the fine lines adjacent to the fort which means water at the east side of the fort where Alder Creek is located.

INDIAN GOOD TALKER
(Pg. 71 WE)

> "...at the bottom where we had built our fort, they make a stand; where one appointed as their chief speaker wearied both us hearers, and himself too, with a long and tedious oration; delivered with strange and violent gestures, his voice being extended to uttermost strength of nature and his words falling so thick one in the neck of another, that he could hardly fetch his breath again..."

This was a typical Pacific Northwest long talker or "good talker" described by both Jewitt and Pearson. The long talker was the best orator and would be able to talk for hours to present a case. "Good talkers were used if there was a dispute or a killing amongst tribe members," related Mrs. Pearson when describing how disputes are settled amongst her people. "In village government sanctions of heredity did not confer power upon an individual. I heard of no headman who pronounced or imposed rules, orders or fines … I heard often about wealthy people rather than headmen. Custom, village opinion, precedents, family decisions, and heads of families controlled conduct. Most often families resorted to monetary payments to resolve difficulties with other families. For example, when a person had been killed by a co-villager, the matter of settlement was as follows: One of the murdered man's relatives who was a "good talker" went outside early in the morning [surrounded by his family group] and yelled as loud as he could so the whole town could hear him. He would say, this makes me feel awful bad in my heart and there's lots of powerful doctors around here. That is, he addressed with flattery all the people, and especially the shamans, who were the residents of highest social status. Then he proceeded to outline the circumstances of the death of his relative in a manner that would perhaps resemble a cross between an obituary and a prosecuting attorney's address. When he finished speaking, a relative of the murderer or some "good talker" who had been asked to represent the murderer's side would reply from the opposite end of the village. Then a formal offer of payment was made. When the aggrieved family expressed satisfaction with the payment offered, the amount was presented on the spot. After the good talker was finished and in the event of a peaceful outcome, which was by far the more usual occurrence, the visiting group was invited into the village and entertained. They went into one of the big houses and had a feast and a fun dance." [38] Fletcher described this exact type of event; after the good talker finished his speech a fun dance with the Indians was performed in the fort.

INDIAN WOMEN TEARING THEIR FLESH
(Pg. 71-72 WE)

> Fletcher goes on, *"In the mean time the women, as if they had been desperate, used unnatural violence against themselves, crying and shrieking piteously, tearing their flesh with their nails from their cheeks…they would with sure cast themselves upon the ground, never respecting whether it were clean or soft, but dashed themselves…some nine or ten times each, and others holding out until 15 or 16 times: A thing more grievous for us to see, or suffer could we have hoped it, then trouble to them as it seemed to do it."*

In this description by Fletcher we see the same actions Jewitt recorded in his journal of 1802. Jewitt details an example of self-mutilation which occurred during his rescue in which he tricked Maquinna to carry a note (Maquinna couldn't read), to the rescuing ship's captain. Jewitt told of his captivity by Maquinna and subsequently, Maquinna was held prisoner and, the Salish-speaking Indians begin to howl and scratch their faces which Jewitt describes as, "When, on its arrival, they were told that the captain had made Chief Maquinna a prisoner and that John Jewitt had spoke bad about him in a letter, they all, both men and women, set up a loud howl and ran backwards and forwards upon the shore like so many lunatics, scratching their faces and tearing the hair in handfuls from their heads. …Maquinna's wives and the rest of the women came around me, [Jewitt] and throwing themselves on their knees, begged me with tears to spare his life" [40]

There has been no documented self-mutilation by any California tribes.

June 26, 1579 (pg 73 WE)

> *"Before his coming, were sent two Ambassadors or messengers to our General, to signify that their Hy'oh, that is, their king was coming and at hand. They in the delivery of their message, the one spoke with a soft and low voice, prompting his fellow; the other pronounced the same word by word after him, with a voice more audible; continuing their proclamation for such it was about half an hour.*
>
> *... before their king (making a princely a show as possibly he could) with all his train came forward."*

The word *Hy'oh* is spoken and sung throughout many Indian songs of many tribes. Jacobs made sound recordings of Mrs. Clara Pearson in 1934 where *Hy'oh* is repeated many times in a number of different songs, one of which is a "grief" song (Tape 41, RCA Disc 14627 B, Part 3, Duration 0:25). [41] The California theory of *Hy'oh* being an exclusive Modoc/Pomo language word is without merit because Pearson has demonstrated in her singing, *Hy'oh* being common Indian word or cry.

INDIAN CHIEF
(Pg. 73 WE)

> *"In the forefront came a man of a large body and a goodly aspect, bearing a Scepter or royal mace (made of a certain kind of black wood, and in length about a yard and a half) before the king. Where upon hanged two crowns, a bigger and a less, with three chains of a marvelous length, and often doubled; besides a bag of the herb Tabah."*

Here Drake, Fletcher and crew are seeing the Shaman of the tribe for the first time. As stated in Chapter 4, Mrs. Pearson related to Elizabeth Jacobs a description of the staff which Fletcher also described as a 4-to-4 ½ foot black wood; "The power sticks carried by the shaman for doctoring the sick were cedar or yew poles [Wagner also describes the power stick as yew tree] of four or five feet in length with carvings on one end which represented human faces. The eyes were of abalone shell and human hair was tucked tightly into holes around the top of the stick. These poles were called [galg'al-'uxten]." [42] The yew tree that grows in the Pacific Northwest, is a hard, yet flexible wood which the Indians used for their bows. The black color was made by burning the stick and then making a slurry with the black ashes which was used as a stain. (See Chapter 4) The Royal British Columbia Museum in Victoria, B.C. has power sticks in its collections.

SHELL NECKLACES
(Pg. 73-74 WE)

"The crowns were made of knit work, wrought upon most curiously with feathers of divers colors, very artificially placed, and of a formal fashion. The chains seemed of a bony substance; every link or part thereof being very little, tiny, most finely burnished, with a hole pierced through the middle. The number of links going to make one chain, is in a manner infinite; but of such estimation it is amongst them, that few be the persons that are admitted to wear the same; and even they to whom its lawful to use them, yet are stinted what number they shall use; as some ten, some twelve, some twenty, and as they exceed in number of chains, so are they thereby known to be the more honorable personages."

Chains of shells were quite common among the Pacific Northwest Indians. They were used as ornamentation, currency and traded for goods. Lewis and Clark tried to trade blankets for these types of shell chains but were refused.

Fig. 75   Dentalia Necklace exhibited by Siletz Indians ca. 1900

Photo Oregon Historical Society

125

When describing these chains of shells, Jewitt wrote, "…the king or principal chiefs, [wear] bracelets and necklaces consisting of a number of strings of *I-whaw* (dentalia shells), an article much prized by them, and which makes a very handsome appearance. The *I-whaw*, as they term it, is a kind of shell of a dazzling whiteness, and as smooth as ivory. It is of a cylindrical form, in a slight degree curved, about the size of a goose quill, hollow, three inches in length and gradually tapering to a point, which is broken off by the natives as it is taken from the water. This they afterwards string upon threads of bark and sell it by the fathom. It forms a kind of circulating medium among these nations, five fathoms being considered as the price of a slave, their most valuable species of property. It is principally obtained from the Ai-tiz-zarts, a people living about 30 or 40 miles to northward [from Nootka Sound, British Columbia], who collect it from the reefs and sunken rocks with which their coast abounds, though it is also brought in considerable quantity from the south." [43]

Alexander Ross wrote, "The circulating medium in use among these people is a small white shell called higua (dentalia), about 2 inches long, of a convex form, and hollow in the heart, resembling in appearance the small end of a smoking pipe. The higua (dentalia) is thin, light, and durable, and may be found in all lengths, between 3 inches down to 1/4 of an inch, and increases or decreases in value according to the number required to make a fathom, by which measure they are invariably sold". [44]

Downe Soft as Silk
(pg 74 WE)

> *"Next to him that bare this Scepter, was the king himself with his guard about him; His attire upon his head was a cawles [collar] of knit work, wrought upon somewhat like the crowns, but differing much both in fashion and perfections of work; upon his shoulders he had a coat of the skins of conies [English rabbit], reaching to his waist; His guard also had each coats of the same shape, but of other skins: some having cawles [collars] likewise stuck with feathers, or covered over with a certain downe, which growth up in the country upon a herb much like our lettuce; which exceeds any other downe in the world for fineness,*

and being layer upon their cawles [collars] *by no winds can be removed: of*
such estimation is this herb among them, that the downe thereof is not lawful to
be worn, but of such persons as are about the king (to whom also it is permitted
to wear a plume of feathers on their heads, in sign of honor) and the seeds are
not used but only in sacrifice to their gods. After these in their order, did
follow the naked sort of common peoples; whose hair being long was gathered
into a bunch behind, in which stuck plumes of feathers, but in the forepart only
single feathers like horns, every one pleasing himself in his own device."

The down and sacrificial seeds reported by Fletcher are from what is known today as fireweed (*Augustilum*). When Fletcher describes a plant, "like our lettuce" he is describing the lettuce plant which has been allowed to go to seed. These seed stalks will grow to a height of 2 to 5', bearing the flowers, down and seeds (see Chapter 4; Fireweed). The fireweed seeds are extremely fine as are the tiny lettuce seeds, and it takes many plumes of the fireweed to collect a supply of the seeds. The down was spun by hand into a yarn and then woven into garment collars or headdresses.

Fig. 76 Fireweed Headdress of PNW Tlingit Chief
Case and Draper Photo, Bancroft Library

Fig. 77   Fireweed woven into woven cedar bark coat of PNW Kwakiult
Edward Curtis Photo

As previously stated, fireweed derived its name because it is one of the first plants to grow after the ground is burned. It's been documented that the Nehalem Indians would burn off the mountain and the fireweed would grow, thus providing them with the finest down known and with their sacrificial seeds. Without trees and underbrush the elk would graze along the face of the mountain, making it easer for the hunters.

There are numerous descriptions by Ray, Jewitt and Pearson, of Pacific Northwest Indians using feathers to decorate themselves

The Indians at the time of Jose Mariano Mozino had a ceremony in which the high priest fasts many days and leads in song to honor their *Quautz* (creator) and in which the *tais* (chief) shows honor by his sacrifice of throwing whale oil into the flames and scatters feathers into the wind [45]

The ritual of throwing things into the wind and sacrifice of the seeds or feathers into the fire, sounds much like the ceremonies the Indians performed when honoring Drake.

There are no recorded descriptions of California tribes performing any of the above types of ceremonies.

(Pg. 74 WE)

"This one thing was observed to be general amongst them all; that every one
had his face painted, some with white, some black, and some with other colors,
every man also bringing in his hand one thing or other for a gift or present:..."

Face painting, was quite common among Native Americans. Clara Pearson described
these same colors which Fletcher reported among the Nehalem. [46]

John Jewitt described face painting of the Nootka in this way, "They place their principal
pride in decorating their heads and faces, and none of our most fashionable beaus, when
preparing for a grand ball, can be more particular. I have known Maquinna [Nootka
Chief], after having been employed for more than an hour in painting his face, rub the
whole off and recommence the operation anew when it did not entirely please him.
The manner in which they paint themselves frequently varies according to the occasion,
but it oftener is the mere dictate of whim. The most usual method is to paint the eyebrows
black, in form of a half moon, and the face red in small squares, with the arms and legs and
part of the body red. Sometimes one half of the face is painted red in squares, and the
other black: at others, dotted with red spots, or red and black instead of squares, with a
variety of other devices, such as painting one half of the face and body red, and the other
black. These red and black painting materials and other minerals are brought to them in
bags by the Newchemass, a very savage nation who live way to the north. They provide a
superior kind of very fine and rich ochre, and a fine black shining powder procured from
some mineral rock called *pelpelth* (mica), which they hold in much estimation." [47]

PET'AH – WAPATO ROOT
(Pg. 74-75 WE)

" ...Their train or last part of their company consisted of women and children
each woman bearing against her breast a round basket or two, having within
them divers things, as bags of Tab'ah , a root which they call Pet'ah , whereof
they make a kind of meal, and either bake it into bread, or eat it raw; broiled fish
like a pilchard; the seed and downe forenamed, with such like:...Their baskets"

As discussed in Chapter 4, *Pet'ah* is one of the four most specific items, along with the Neahkahnie Survey, Hondius map, and Islands - which authenticate Drake's stay in Nehalem Bay. *Pet'ah* is wa-pa-to, and it was the prime aquatic plant food source of the Nehalem Bay Indians.

The Nehalem Indians at the time of the Lewis and Clark Expedition called this root wapato, 223 years after Drake. Lewis and Clark traded for wapato during their stay at Fort Clatsop. It's stated in their journal that on their expedition to find whale blubber for food and for lamp fuel in January of 1805, on one occasion they could acquire only a little wapato because it was of such value. While traveling on their journey to the Pacific coast they even named an island in the lower Columbia River as Wapato Island because of the great abundance of this aquatic plant. "A few miles below the cascades, a large river, called the Willamette (called the Multnomah by Lewis and Clark), enters the Columbia from the south by two mouths, between which an extensive island is named Wapato Island, from an edible root [*Saggitafolia*] so called, [48] found growing upon it in abundance." Alexander Ross in 1811 described the wapato during his stay at Fort Astoria, "a perennial root, of the size, shape, and taste of the common potato, is a favorite article of food at all times of the year. This esculent is highly esteemed by the whites; many other roots and berries are to be had, all of which grow spontaneously in the low marshy ground." [49] Nehalem Bay is less than forty miles south of the Columbia River where Fort Astoria was located. This writer has eaten wapato both raw and boiled, and it is quite palatable. (See Chapter 4 Wapato photos) As stated previously, there is no "wa" in front of *pet'ah* due to the gruntal nature of speech coming from the throat in Salish language [50] as described to Jacobs. A person unfamiliar with the language and hearing wapato coming from the throat and grunted would understand it to be *Pet'ah*. This food source, described by Fletcher as "pet'ah", in the way it's found, prepared and eaten can only be wapato.

Today's bay has changed, but in Drake's time Wapato Island (Sauvies Island) and the backwaters of the Nehalem Bay were full of wapato. Wapato could be grown today if it were not for current dike roads blocking the backwaters built in the mid 20th century, and other necessary uses of the land.

The boiled fish Fletcher describes as a pilchard is an old English description of a sardine family known by the Nehalem as a candle fish or as the Indians called it *Eulachon*. These fish are so plentiful and rich in oil that they were used as candles as well as a food source. "Oil was highly prized. Foods were dipped into it and formed a favorite sauce. Trade in candle fish was extensive. Long trails known as grease trails led into the interior where the coast people traded with the Athasbascon speaking peoples. The oil does not deteriorate with time and could be stored a year or two." [51]

Fig. 78   Candle fish (Eulachon) drying   Portland Historical Society

Alexander Ross describes these fish in this way, "There is a small fish resembling the smelt or herring, known by the name of ulichan (candle fish), which enters the river in immense shoals, in the spring of the year. The ulichans are generally an article of trade with the distant tribes, as they are caught only at the entrance of large rivers. To prepare them for a distant market, they are laid side to side, head and tail alternately, and then a thread run through both extremities links them together, in which state they are dried, smoked, and sold by the fathom, hence they have obtained the name of fathom-fish". [52]

WATERPROOF BASKETS

(pg 75 WE)

> *"Their baskets were made in fashion like a deep bowl, and though the matter were rushes, or such other kind of stuff, yet was it so cunningly handled, that the most part of them would hold water, about the brims they were hanged with pieces of the shells of pearls, and in some places with two or three links at a place, of the chains forenamed: thereby signifying that they were vessels wholly dedicated to the only use of the gods they worshipped: and besides this, they were wrought upon with the matted downe of red feathers, distinguished into divers works and forms."*

A. L Kroeber has said that for anyone to prove Drake met Indians other than the Miwok or Pomo, they would need to show the water-tightness of those Indian's baskets. The Pacific Northwest Indians are well-known for their baskets which hold water, and into which they would drop hot fired rocks to cook their foodstuffs. Elizabeth Jacobs recorded, "Water buckets might be carved of wood, although tightly woven spruce root baskets were often used for this purpose. Sea shells, abalone and red feathers of the humming bird were collected and used by shaman for decoration [53] to ward off evil spirits and promoting good health."

According to Alexander Ross, "The women when not employed at their domestic labor, are generally occupied in curing fish, collecting roots, and making mats and baskets; the latter, of various sizes and different shapes, are made of the roots of certain shrubs, which are flexible and strong, and they are capable of containing any liquid. In this branch of industry they excel among Indian tribes" [54]

Mrs. Pearson described to Elizabeth Jacobs a very ingenious method of preserving. Jacobs writes, "Some women boiled berries and put them in cedar-bark baskets lined with maple leaves. A cedar-bark cover was sewn over the top of the basket to render the container waterproof. They then deflected the course of a small stream, dug deeply into the creek bed and put the basket of berries into the hole, which was then covered with many rocks, leaves and sticks. The stream was then redirected into its old course... tightly woven spruce root baskets were as often used for this purpose." [55] These baskets are second to none in their methods and skill of construction for cooking and food storage.

Robert Heizer's examples of decorative baskets used in his Miwok Pomo thesis to support the theory of the California Indian were not aboriginal baskets; they were in fact, contemporary art pieces, made by a William Ralganal Benson, circa 1916. [56]

(Pg. 75-76 WE)

"In the mean time our General having assembled his men together (as forecasting the danger, and worst that might fall out) prepared himself to stand upon sure ground, that we might at all times be ready in our own defense, if anything should chance otherwise then was looked for or expected. Wherefore every man being in a warlike readiness, he marched within his fenced place, making against their approach a most warlike show (as he did also at all other times of their resort) whereby if they had been desperate enemies, they could not have chosen but have conceived terror and fear, with discouragement to attempt any thing against us, in beholding of the same. When they came some what near unto us, trooping together, they gave us a common or a general salutation: observing in the mean time a general silence. Whereupon he [shaman] who bare the Scepter before the king, being prompted to another whom the king assigned to that office, pronounced with an audible and manly voice, what the other spoke to him in secret; continuing, whether it were his oration or proclamation, at the least half an hour. At the close whereof, there was a common Amen, in sign of approbation given by every person; And the king himself with the whole number of men and women **came further down the hill** [bold by author] *and as they came set themselves again in their former order. And being now come to the **foot of the hill** [bold by author] and near our fort..."*

After the Long Talker finished, the Indians proceeded down the hill above the fort until they were at the foot of the hill. In Chapter 3 the Hondius map shows the hills are behind the fort and shadowing of the trees on the east side. This was the accepted method of drawing maps in the 16th century. By putting the shading on the east side, the Hondius map corresponds to Nehalem Bay where there are hills directly above Alder Creek to the east. The location of Alder Creek and the fort correspond with the known archaeological Indian site which is three quarters of a mile from the fort.

(Pg. 76 WE)

> *"...the Scepter bearer with a composed countenance and stately carriage began a song, and answerable thereunto, observed a kind of measures in a dance; whom the king with his guard and every other sort of person following, did in like manner sing and dance, saving only the women who danced but kept silent. As they danced they still came on; and our General perceiving their plain and simple meaning, gave order that they might freely enter without interruption within our **bulwark** [bold by author]: Where after they had entered they yet continued their song and dance a reasonable time; their women also following them with their wassail bowls in their hands, their bodies bruised, their faces torn, their dugges [teats], breasts, and other parts be spotted with blood, trickling down from the wounds, which with their nails they had made before their coming."*

This is the first mention of kings, shamans and others engaged in tribal ceremonial dancing and drinking. This was the prelude to the natives being let into the bulwark or fort for purpose of socializing or conducting a ceremony (see fig. 60 & 61).

Mrs. Pearson related to Elizabeth Jacobs, "The shaman wore a belt made of braided human hair when he sang at his winter dance festival. The hair was bought from a long-haired woman and braided by himself. Sometimes he tied eagle claws on the ends of the belt, which hung down his back like a tail. This girdle was a symbol of special supernatural power and only a shaman could wear it. Sometimes shamans wore headdresses of hummingbird skins sewed together. Only skins of the male birds with their beautiful red coloring were used. A shaman who was ambitious to possess such a headdress hired boys to obtain the skins for him. The boys caught hummingbirds by means of a snail slime layered on salmonberry bushes. When the tiny bird lighted in a patch of this slime it caught and held him. These headdresses were as rare as they were difficult to obtain." [57]

DRAKE CROWNED SUPREME BEING

(Pg. 76 WE)

> " After they had satisfied or rather tired themselves in this manner, they make
> signs to our General to have him sit down; Unto whom both the king and divers
> others made several orators, or rather indeed if we had understood them,
> supplications, that he would take the Province and kingdom into his hand, and
> become their king and patron: making signs that they would resign unto him
> their right and title in the whole land, and become his vassals in themselves and
> their posterities: Which that they might make us indeed believe that it was their
> true meaning and intent; the king himself with all the rest with one consent, and
> with great reverence, joyfully singing a song, set the crown upon his head;
> enriched his neck withal their chains; and offering unto him many other things,
> honored him by the name of Hyoh. Adding thereunto (as it might seem) a song
> and dance of triumph: because they were not only unified of the gods (for so they
> still judged us to be) but the great and chief god was now become their god, their
> king and patron, and themselves were become the only happier and blessed
> people in all the world"

Here we witness Drake being crowned king, mightiest shaman and supreme god all in one being. The Nehalem, Chinooks of the Columbia River, Clatsop and Killimux (Tillamook) had a supreme spirit, spelled Econe' or Ekahnie or Ecarney. They believed that Ec'one [58] was the supreme deity, who at one time was a man, who went up to the mountain one day and never returned because he turned into stone. This stone, overlooking the ocean in a meadow, as described in an 1841 journal by Reverend Joseph Frost, is in the 'image' of their supreme deity, Francis Drake, keeping in mind that the Indians had no writing. (see Chapter 4 Indian Legends). The Chinooks, Clatsop and Tillamook are the tribes who came to the top of the three hills to see these 16th century Europeans.

(Pg. 77 WE)

> "Where fore in the name and to the use of her most excellent majesty, he took the
> scepter crown and dignity, of the said country into his hand .."

The scepter refers to the shaman's Power Stick, (see fig. 60 & 61) designating those who carried it as a shaman. The shaman was one of the most powerful men in the village and had power to heal and to inflict bad spirits on anyone who displeased him. The shaman was, by today's measurement, one of the richest men in the tribe. When Drake was passing out ointments and other healing miracles, the Indians experienced Drake's 'magic' as no other shaman had demonstrated. As far as his becoming the king, he had been treated with reverence and with such big ships, guns, silks, clothing and other goods, it appears that he became king because of his riches greatly exceeded those of the Indians.[59]

(Pg. 77 WE)

> "The ceremonies of this resigning, and receiving of the kingdom being thus performed, the common sort both of men and women, leaving the king and his guard about him, with our general, dispersed themselves among our people, taking a diligent view or survey of every man; and finding such as pleased their fancies, which commonly were the youngest of us, they presently enclosing them about, offered their sacrifices unto them, crying out with lamentable shrieks and moans, weeping, and scratching, and tearing their very flesh off their faces with their nails, neither were it the women alone which did this, but even old men, roaring and crying out, were as violent as the women were."

Here again, the Indians were paying homage to their new shaman in their traditional way so they could be on his good side for his special favors of healing and good spirits.

DRAKE HEALING INDIANS

(pg 78 WE)

> "After that time had a little qualified their madness, they then began to show and make known unto us their grief's and diseases which they carried about them, some of them having old aches, some shrunk sinews, some old sores and cankered ulcers, some wounds more lately received, and the like, in most lamentable manner craving help and cure thereof from us: making signs, that if we did but blow upon their grief's, or but touched the diseased places, they would be whole."

Supreme shaman, cure me, asked the Indians, blow on me or touch me and I will receive your cure. No wonder the Indians thought Drake was a god. The following Fletcher paragraph shows how Drake offered his medicines to cure them.

(Pg. 78 WE)

"Their grief's we could not but take pity on them, and to our power desire to help them: but that (if it pleased God to open their eyes) they might understand we were but men and not gods, we used ordinary means, as lotions, emplaisters and unguents most fitly (as far as our skills could guess) agreeing to the natures of their grief's, beseeching God, if it made for this glory, to give cure to their diseases by these means. The like we did from time to time as they resorted to us."

Here Fletcher describes not only treating the Indians of their ailments but also praying. Because Drake's men were teaching the Indians to pray to God the Indians seem to have taken this to mean this was how Drake cured them. After Drake left the bay, if an Indian wanted to be cured, it would seem a natural thing to pray for healing to Drake, their supreme shaman spirit and deity known as Ekahnie.

(Pg. 78-79 WE)

"Few were the days, where in they were absent from us, during the whole time of our abode in that place: and ordinarily every third day, they brought their sacrifices, till such time as they certainly understood our meaning, that we took no pleasure, but were displeased with them: whereupon their zeal abated, and their sacrificing, for a season, to our good liking ceased; not withstanding they continued still to make their resort unto us in great abundance, and in such sort, they often time forgot, to provide meat for their own sustenance…they fought to recompense us, with such things as they had, which they willing enforced upon us, though it were never so necessary or needful for themselves to keep."

It is the Indian custom to pay the shaman for his healing powers and this is what the Indians were doing by providing food in great abundance. Meat was a premium with

Indian tribes, whereas fish, which they presented to Drake and his crew, is available in great abundance in summer.

The sacrifices Fletcher speaks of would have been their slaves and women for the pleasure of Drake's men. Fletcher and Drake would not have approved of these actions for humanitarian reasons and because it could have created problems amongst the men with discipline or potential problems with the Indians. Also, fornication without marriage would have been a sin in Reverend Fletcher's eyes.

According to Hoskins, *Voyages of the "Columbia" to the Northwest Coast 1787*, "That these people are Cannibals is beyond a doubt, not from anything we saw but from their own confession and much credit is due to them for their diffidence in making it known for it was not until after they were frequently questioned and an acknowledgement made on our part that it was the case with us that they would own it and when again they were told we only said so to know if it was their custom they appeared to be much abashed but with a modest firmness would not deny what they had before asserted. This inhuman custom is only practiced on those whom the fortune of war throws into their hands and is conducted in the following manner; the men people are collected at the Chief's house for the purpose of music and dancing [with] a number of those unhappy prisoners [who] are at the same time present, joining in the sport not knowing whom fate has decreed to be the victim on this occasion each possibly consoling himself with the vain hope it is not his lot or mayhap with the more pleasing idea than the time is come which will put an end to all his misery in the midst of the music, several Chiefs[60] enter dancing after taking a few turns."

"We understood from the natives that they sometime made human sacrifices, and shocking to relate, that they eat the flesh of such poor victims. However I do not believe that this custom is very common and only happens on some very particular occasion. A prisoner of war [slave] is the person selected for this savage feast."[61]

Mutilation was not uncommon among Pacific Northwest Indians.

Jewitt asks Chief Maquinna, "…on my [Jewitt] enquiring the reason of this display [religious celebration], informed me that it was an ancient custom of his nation to sacrifice a man at the close of this solemnity in honor of their God, but that his father had abolished it and substituted this [ritual of bayonets run into small boys flesh without manifesting any symptoms of pain] in place." (footnote[39])

These descriptions of sacrifices relates closely to the wording of Fletcher's narrative when describing Nehalem Indian actions.

BUILDING SURVEY CAIRNS
(pg 79 WE)

"They are a people of a traceable, free, and loving nature, without guile or treachery; their bows and arrows (their only weapons and almost all their wealth) they use very skillfully, but yet not to do any great harm with them, being by reason of their weakness, more fit for children than for men, sending the arrow neither far off, nor with any great force: and yet are the men commonly so strong of body, that, which 2 or 3 of our men could hardly bear, one of them would take upon his back, and without grudging carry it easily away, up hill and down hill an English mile together: they are also exceeding swift in running and of long continuance; the use whereof is so familiar with them, that they seldom go, but for the most part run. One thing we observed in them with admiration: that if at any time, they chanced to see a fish, so near the shore, that they might reach the place without swimming, they would never, or very seldom miss to take it."

Up hill and down hill an English mile is a definite reference to the monument markers and cairns which they built with Drake's men in surveying Neahkahnie Mountain. When walking from the base of Neahkahnie Mountain near the beach to the top of Neahkahnie Mountain is an English mile of 5,000 feet (changed to 5,280 feet by Queen Elizabeth in 1595 to conform to the rest of Europe). Stone cairns were laid out around the entire mountain, though stones were not readily available; some had to be carried from nearby ravines to cairns many yards away. Neahkahnie Mountain is the highest point on the ocean from British Columbia to Northern California. It was burned off by the Indians to create a grazing area for the elk so as not have to chase or hunt them in the woods. In other words, an open area for game to be hunted and a good survey site.

The reference to fishing near the shore indicates the great numbers of salmon that once swam through the Nehalem Bay which the Indians could spear, now greatly diminished.

ENGLISH CONIE OR LAND OTTER
(Pg. 79-80 WE)

"After that our necessary business were well dispatched [careening of the *Golden Hinde*], *our general with his gentlemen, and many of his company, make a journey up into the land, ... The inland we found to be far different from the shore, a goodly country, and fruitful soil stored with many blessings for the use of man: infinite was the company of very large and fat Deer* [Roosevelt Elk], *which there we saw by thousands, as we supposed, in a herd: besides a multitude of a strange kind of Conies* [rabbits], *by far exceeding them in number: their heads and bodies, in which they resemble other Conies* [rabbits], *are but small; his tail like the tail of a rat, exceeding long; and his feet like the paws of a Want or Mole* [webbed] *under his chin, on either side, he hath a bag, into which he gathers his meat, when he hath filled his belly abroad, that he may with it, either feed his young, or feed himself, when he lifts not to travel from his borough: the people eat their bodies, and make great account of their skins, for their king's holidays was made of them."*

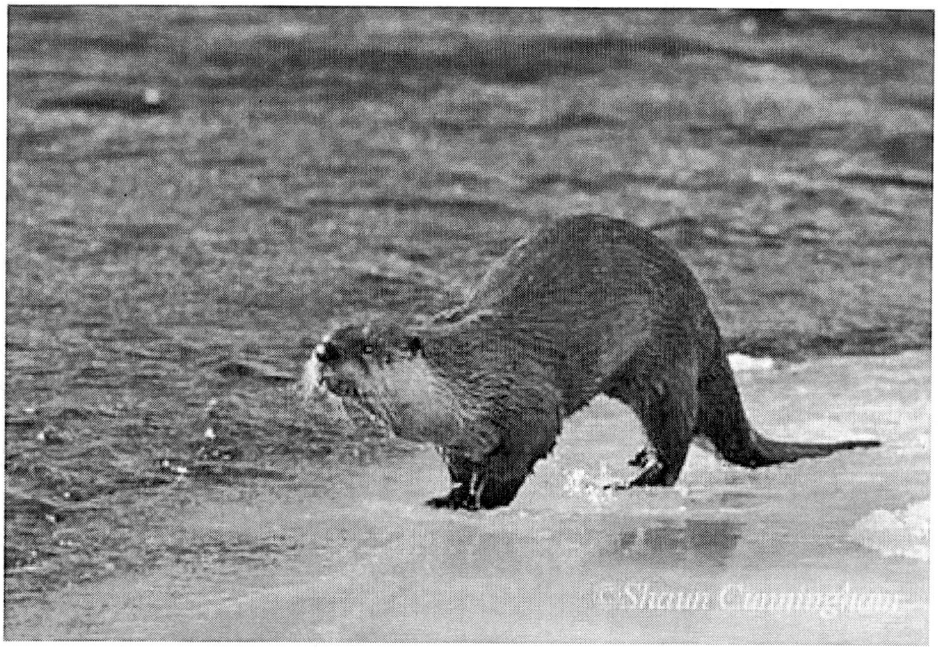
©Shawn Cunningham

Fig. 79 Land Otter with a small face like a rabbit, tail like a rat, webbed feet and beautiful fur described by Fletcher as a conie.
Shawn Cunningham Photo

Fletcher's description of the conies, or New World rabbits, can only be a land otter which was once plentiful and are now near extinction in Nehalem Bay. The land otter has webbed feet and rat-like tail. Fletcher, who would have been unfamiliar with the land otter, causing him to compare its face with the English rabbit, its webbed feet like a mole. Fletcher, a man of God and the soul, was not a naturalist and these New World animals could only be compared with animals in England of which he had knowledge. He shows the same inexperience as a naturalist when describing elk as "fat deer", fireweed much like our "lettuce" and in his descriptions of housing and canoe types, although his descriptions are quite accurate.

James Swan describes the land otter: "...breed in holes either under some old stump or in the side of a hill, always being sure to have such ready access to the water..." [62] giving credence to Fletchers description of web feet and returning to his borough with food for its young.

The sea otters and land otters were valued in China for their fur which was the reason trapping was established in the late 1700's along the Pacific Northwest coast. Gray, Meares and the Astor group were the primary trading capitalists between the Pacific

Northwest and Canton, China. Robert Haswell, the first mate on Gray's voyage in 1792 said, "The ship during the cruise had collected upwards of 700 sea otter skins and 15 thousand skins of various other species."[63] Fletcher mentions boroughs, the dens where land otters live and have their young.

In Wolfgang G. Jilek's, *Indian Healing Shamanic Ceremonialism in the Pacific Northwest* he states, "Barnett (1955)[64] lists some spirits who gave power almost exclusively to shamans among the Coast Salish of British Columbia, such as the double-headed snake, the thunder-bird, the fire, and the land otter.[65] The land otter had a special value among the Pacific Northwest Indian for its meat and fur.

There are no land otters in Northern California because of the lack of rivers and habitat.

The Neahkahnie Mountain Survey was performed (see Chapter 2) during the times when Drake and members of his crew went up into the land.

NAMING OF NEW ALBION AND WHITE CLIFFS
(Pg. 80 WE)

> *"This country our general named Albion, and that for two causes; the one in respect of the white banks and cliffs, which lie toward the sea: the other, that it might have some affinity, even in name also, with our own country, which was sometime so called."*

Fig. 80   Neahkahnie Mountain cliffs at 45° 43' N latitude, circa 1932   Photo Jensen Collection

In July 1774 the white cliffs were mentioned by Fray Tomas de la Peña who was one of the recorders of the Don Juan Perez voyage on the *Santiago*. He describes the ships position along the Oregon Coast between the latitudes of 46° 8' and 44° 35' -- "All morning we ran along the land, about three leagues from it; during the afternoon our course was the same and the coast was very clearly visible because the land was not so obscured by vapor as it had been in the morning. This land is thickly covered with timber, apparently pine, not only on the summit but along the flanks of the hills. Immediately on the coast we saw some level land where there is no timber but heavy growth of grass, **and there were several white cliffs close by the sea."** [bold by author] [66] These white cliffs mentioned by Peña are the same cliffs Drake saw, which was one of the reasons he named the area Nova Albion. In addition, it reminded him of Plymouth, England, with its topography of green rolling hills and mountains, trees and waterways.

Fray Juan Crespi was also a recorder of the voyage of the *Santiago* and his description of the Oregon Coast also mentions white cliffs; "We saw some tableland where there was no timber, but seemingly a great deal of grass. **We saw several white cliffs near to the sea,** [bold by author] and some ravines, or openings, which ran northwest and southeast." [67] These ravines and openings running northwest and southeast are openings of the Nehalem Valley which one would observe from the ocean. The Nehalem Bay sits at the mouth of the Nehalem Valley into which the Nehalem River drains 667 square miles of watershed and ravines which Crespi noted. [68]

(Pg. 80 WE)

> *"Before we went from thence, our general caused to be set up, a monument of our being there; as also of her majesties, and successors right and title to the kingdom, namely, a plate of brass, fast nailed to a great and firm post; whereon is engraved her graces name, and the day and year of our arrival there, and of the free giving up, of the province and kingdom, both by the king and people, into her majesties hands; together with her highness picture, and arms in a piece of sixpence current English money, showing it self by a hole made of purpose through the plate: underneath was likewise engraved the name of our general & c. The Spaniards never had any dealing, or so much as set a foot in this country; the utmost of their discoveries, reaching only to many degrees Southward of this place."*

A firm post with a brass plaque has not yet been found. Lead was commonly referred to as 'brass' in the 16th century.

The survey monument rocks inscribed on Neahkahnie Mountain show title for England and a monument to Drake's stay in Nehalem Bay.

Because Drake was in Nehalem Bay it has now become obvious that, when the Spanish having been referred to as "many degrees southward", refers to their being to 36.7° at Monterey Bay as their furthest point north. [69]

Cabrillo and Ferrelo were as far north as the present-day Oregon border in 1542-43 but did not land or claim any lands. They landed much further south than Monterey Bay. Other Spanish maps (see Chapter 1) only show to 37° North, therefore, because no other explorer had been any further north than Monterey Bay. Drake claimed New Albion from 38° North to 48° North.

Additionally, Drake did not need to be in any particular spot to claim the east or west coast of North America nor did he need to be at 38°, only that he had claimed the area which was one of his prime objectives -- to claim and record unclaimed lands.

The Silver Map, dated 1589, was created by Michael Mercator to show the track of Drake's famous voyage and has Nova Albion inscribed over the entire North American continent which also compares with the Van Sype map, (fig. 2) which was seen and corrected by Drake.

In the 1700's, when Spain again began exploring, they were only interested in land below 38° north (California) and above 48° (Canada and Alaska) north latitude. The lands in between 38° and 48° north latitude having been claimed by Drake and reflected on numerous maps made in the late 16th century and throughout the 17th century reflecting his claim of these lands as *Nova Albion* and this was acknowledged by Spain in its actions.

DEPARTURE TO THE ISLANDS OF ST. JAMES
(pg 80-81 WE)

> *"And now, as the time of our departure was perceived by them to draw nigh, so did the sorrows and miseries of this people, seem to themselves to increase upon them... How be it seeing they could not still enjoy our presence, they (supposing us to be gods indeed) thought it their duties to entreat us that being absent, we would yet be mindful of them, and making signs of their desires, that in time to come we would see them again, they stole upon us a sacrifice, and set it on fire erre we were aware; burning therein a chain and a bunch of feathers... they fell a lifting up their eyes and hands to heaven as they saw us do."*

Here the Indians were mimicking Drake and his crew in prayer. In what other ways might they have adopted mannerisms and ideas from Drake and the crew after their departure?

Their ships/canoes, tents/longhouses, weapons/pikes are all areas of similarity with early English designs which surfaced in the Pacific Northwest Indian ethnology. We see no English designs in any of the California bay Indians.

July 23, 1579 (Pg. 81 WE)

"The 23 of July they took a sorrowful farewell to us, but being loath to leave us, they presently ran to the tips of the hills to keep us in their sight as long as they could, making fires before and behind, and on each side of them, burning therein (as is to be supposed) sacrifices at our departure.

"Not far without this harbor did lye certain Islands (we called them the Islands of Saint James) having on them plentiful and great store of Seals and birds, with one of which we fell July 24 whereon we found such provision as might completely serve our turn for a while. We departed again the day next following, was July 25 And our General now considering that the extremity of the cold not only continued but increased the Sun being gone further from us, and that the wind blowing still (as it did at first) from the Northwest, cut off all hope of finding a passage through the Northern parts, thought it necessary to lose no time; and therefore with general consent of all, bent his course directly to run with the Islands of the Moluccas."

"*Not far without this harbor did lye certain Islands*" refers to the Three Arch Rocks National Game Reserve (see Chapter 5). Since Three Arch Rock National Game Reserve is sixteen miles due south of Nehalem Bay and with the prevailing Northwest wind in the summer, Drake would not have needed to tack or sail into the wind to land on these islands. [70]

CONCLUSION

After Drake left Nehalem Bay on July 23, 1579 (August 3rd according to the new Christian calendar, to which England converted in 1782 from the Julian calendar), he sailed south, *"Not far without this harbor did lye certain islands, we called them the Islands of Saint James,"* to three islands, off of what is now Cape Meares, now called Three Arch Rocks (see Chapter 5) where they took birds, seals and where, *"we found such provision as might competently serve our turn for a while."*

SUMMARY

The hard facts are:

1. The Hondius Broadside map coincides with Nehalem Bay
    a. Shape of the bay
    b. Documented archaeological Indian sites 3/4 mile from the fort
    c. The fort being alongside today's Alder Creek
    d. The openings of the bay to the north and south match the Hondius map
2. The 16th century survey of Neahkahnie Mountain
    a. The William Bourne triangulation
    b. The sun, moon and star survey
    c. The height of Neahkahnie Mountain
3. The pet'ah which Fletcher describes as a food source being wapato
4. The finest downe Fletcher had ever seen much like our lettuce being the local fireweed plant (*Augustilium*)
5. The three islands which we know as Three Arch Rocks National Game Reserve

These are all facts, without relying on conjecture.

Additionally, the fact that after the careening of the *Golden Hinde* was completed, Fletcher says they are on a direct course to the Moluccas, which means Francis Drake was never in California as we know it today. His land claim of the North American continent was from the Pacific Coast to the Atlantic Coast from 48° north latitude to the 38° north latitude.

The firsts:

◊   In 1579, the first land claim by Europeans on the Pacific Coast above 38° N. Latitude.

◊   The oldest monolith monument engraved with the first English measurement in North America.

◊   The first contact with Pacific Northwest aboriginals, predating previous first claims by almost 200 years.

Here ends my humble attempt to convince the scholar and layperson that Nehalem Bay was indeed the primary point of careening Francis Drake's ship for five weeks in the summer of 1579. This endeavor has put me in the position of disputing what many others have written. At times, I may not have been so subtle and would have much preferred to have written the facts of Nehalem Bay and let them stand on their own. However, in order to overturn this false identification of Northern California and other Oregon locations as the site of these events and with the myth-making having gone on for so many years, I've had no choice but to support my case in the most active and forcefully-convincing manner. Nehalem Bay, Oregon is the true and only harbor at which Francis Drake spent five weeks in the summer of 1579. Drake never set foot nor sailed the *Golden Hinde* upon any California bay.

FOOTNOTES

Chapter 1

1. *The California Historical Quarterly*, The California Historical Society, San Francisco, Volume LIII 1974
2. *Lost Harbor, The Controversy over Drake's California Anchorage*, Warren L. Hanna, University of California Press, Berkeley 1979
3. *The Discovery of a Gaping Gulf*, by John Stubbs, London 1579, Pg. xxvii
4. *The Geometrical Seaman*, Taylor, E.G.R. and Richey, M.W., Hollis & Carter for the Institute of Navigation 1962, Pg.34-36
5. *The Art of Navigation in England in Elizabethan and Early Stuart Times*, D.W. Waters, Yale University Press New Haven 1958, Appendix 12, pg. 535
6. *Art of Navigation*, D.W. Waters, pg 78
7. *Art of Navigation*, Appendix 10A, pg. 528
8. *Art of Navigation*, pg. 113-114
9. *New Light on Drake*, Zelia Nuttall, Hakluyt Society, London 1914, pg. 296
10. Library of Congress; www.loc.gov/rr/rarebook/catalog/drake-4-famourvoy.html
11. Nuttall, *New Light on Drake*, pg lvi – lv
12. ibid
13. *The World Encompassed By Sir Francis Drake*, Master Francis Fletcher, Preacher, Printed for Nicholas Bourne, London 1628, pg 80
14. *Principal Navigations, Voyages and Discoveries*, Richard Hakluyt, 1972. See *Anonymous Narrative* which many scholars have credited to Fletcher.
15. Nuttall pg. 296-320
16. See Appendix IV Depositions
17. *The World Encompassed*. Francis Fletcher, pg 80
18. http://en.wikipedia.org/wiki/Drake%27s_Plate_of_Brass
19. *The Plate of Brass Reexamined 1977, A Report Issued by The Bancroft Library*, University of California, Berkeley, pg. 24
20. *Drake's Plate of Brass Authenticated, Report on the Plate of Brass*, Colin Fink and E. P. Polushkin, Calif. Historical Society, San Francisco MCMXXXVIII, pg 25–27
21. *The Plate of Brass Reexamined* 1977, pg 25
22. *Elizabethan California*, Robert F. Heizer, Ballena Press, Ramona, California 1974, pg 70 and http://en.wikipedia.org/wiki/Drake%27s_Plate_of_Brass
23. ibid pg 31
24. ibid pg 75

Chapter 2

1. *Creation of Rights of Sovereignty Through Symbolic Acts*, Henry R., Wagner, The Pacific Historical Review 1938, pg 10
2. Ibid pg 3
3. Ibid pg 4
4. Ibid pg 6

5. *Creation of Rights of Sovereignty through Symbolic Acts 1400 - 1800*, Arthur S. Keller, Oliver J. Lisitzyn, and Frederick J. Mann, Columbia Univ. Press, NY 1938

6. *The Principal Navigations, Voyages, Traffiques & Discoveries of the English Nation*, Hakluyt, *The second voyage of Master Martin Frobisher... 1577*, VII, 219.

7. *A Report of the Voyage and Successes Thereof Attempted in the Yeere of Oure Lord 1583*, by Sir Humphrey Gilbert Knight, by Edward Haie, Genteelman, pp 53-54.

8. *The Discoverie Made by M. Arthur Pet and M. Charles Jackman, of the Northeast parts, beyond the Island of Vaigatz, with two Barkes: the one called the George, the other the William, in the year 1580*, Written by Huge Smith," online: www.ebooks.adelaide.edu.au/h/hakluyt/voyages/v40/chapter32.html#note246

9. *World Encompassed*, pg 33

10. Wagner, *Symbolic Acts*, pg. 63

11. *Real Treasure Discovered on Neahkahnie Mountain, The Secret Voyage of Sir Francis Drake to the North Oregon Coast*, Garry Gitzen, Wheeler, Oregon 2003

12 *Sir Francis Drake's Secret Voyage to the Northwest Coast of America, AD 1579*, by Samuel Bawlf, Sir Francis Drake Publications, Salt Spring Island, BC 2001, pg 147 Chapter 7 – footnote #17)

13. *North America's Hidden Legacy at Neah-Kah-Nie Mountain 1579*, Don Viles, North America Historiography, Garibaldi, Oregon 1982

14. *Certified Copy of Field Notes of Township No. 2. North, Range No. 10 West of the Willamette Meridian, Oregon* , Survey by C.J. Hadley under Contract 183 dated Feb. 26, 1873, "General Description, In the surveyed part of this township south of the Nehalem River the soil is nearly 1st rate; the level part ncar the beach is, however, swampy; the balance mountainous and broken. The timber, 1st rate, consisting of spruce, hemlock, cedar, alder, fir, maple, dogwood etc. North of the Nehalem nothing but barren sand destitute of vegetation. At the mouth of the Nehalem there are 2 or 3 Indian lodges. The Indians have a tradition of a vessel being cast away long ago and the crew burying gold there. They have shown petrified beeswax as evidence of the wreck. The unsurveyed part of this township is mountainous and very broken and covered with dense timber and it must be worth settlement".

15. *The Elements of Geometxia of the most Ancient Philosopher Euclide of Megara*, John Dee, London 1570

16. *The Geometrical Seaman*, Taylor, E.G.R. and Richey, M.W., pg 88

17. Ibid pg 56

18. Ibid pg 70

19. Ibid pg 44

20. Ibid pg 18

21. Ibid pg 35-36

22. Ibid pg 38-39

23. *World Encompassed*, pg 64

24. *Real Treasure Discovered n Neahkahnie Mountain*, Garry Gitzen

25. *Certified Copy of Field Notes of Township No. 2. North, Range No. 10 West of the Willamette Meridian, Oregon Survey,* by C.J. Hadley under Contract 183 dated Feb. 26, 1873

26. Oregon Native Son and Historical Magazine, *Legend of Nehalem*, Samuel A. Clark,

Vol. II, No. 1, Native Son Publishing, Portland, Oregon May 1900, pg 36-40

27. Oregon Native Son and Historical Magazine, *Wrecked Beeswax and Buried Treasure*, Samuel A. Clark, Vol. I, Native Son Publishing, Portland, Oregon, September 1899, pg 245-249

28. Oregon Native Son and Historical Magazine, *Legend of Nehalem*, Samuel A. Clark, pg 36-40

29. Speech Titled: *Sir Francis Drake Colony Found Neah-Kah-Nie Mountain*, Don Viles Neah-Kah-Nie Community Club Jan. 1971, Jensen Collection

30. Letter from University of Georgia to Wayne Jensen, Jensen Collection

31. Some have theorized the crosses are of a religious meaning because the Spanish always used crosses in their symbolic acts of possession. Notwithstanding religion, Drake may have used the cross in depicting a 90° angle on the survey.

32. *Gemma Frisius, his method of determining differences of longitude by transporting timepieces (1530), and his treatise on triangulation (1533)*, by A. Pogo, Harvard

33. Nuttall, *New Light on Drake,* Part VIII, Documents relating to Nuno Da Silva's trial by the inquisition 1579, pg 296

34. *John Dee: the World of an Elizabethan Magus*, Peter J. French, London 1972. If you want to know more, to paraphrase Gemma Frisius when asked to provide proof of triangulation by using the stars, he said, come see me.

35. *Drake Cermeno Vizcaino*, M. Wayne Jensen and Donald M. Viles 1971

36. Wagner, pg 16

37. *Cook's Log*, Volume 7, number 4, 1984, pg 290

38. *The Art of Navigation*, D.W., Waters, pg 517-518

39. *The Astrolabe: its Uses and Derivative*, Dr. R. T. Gunther, Scottish Geo Magazine, vol. 43, no. 1, May 1927, pg 135-147

40. Ibid pg 138

41. Ibid pg 140

42. *A Book Called the Treasure for Traveilers*, William Bourne, London 1578

43. Waters, pg xxii

44. *English Land Measuring to 1800: Instruments and Practices*, by A. W. Richeson, Published by The Society for History of Technology and M.I.T. Press 1966, pg 44 #3

45. ibid pg 49

46. www.en.wikipedia.org/wiki/rhumb_line

47. Waters, pg 481-4, figs. 42, 43

Chapter 3

1. *Elizabethan California*, Robert F. Heizer, Ballena Press, Ramona California 1974, pg 25

2. ibid pg 25

3. *Sir Francis Drake at Drakes Bay, A Summation of Evidence Relating to the Identification of Sir Francis Drake's Encampment at Drakes Bay, California, Based on the Research of the Drake Navigators Guild.*, by Raymond Aker, Copyright 1978 by Drake Navigators Guild

4. *Handbook of the Indians of California*, A. L. Kroeber, Dover Publications, NY, 1925 1976, pg 278

5. *Thomas A. Newman Dig 1955, Tillamook Prehistory and its Relation to the Northwest Coast Culture Area*, by Thomas A. Newman, University of Oregon, Thesis 1959

6. www. Captainrick.com

7. Letter from Allison Stenger, Ph.D., Research Director to Leland Gilsen, Ph.D., Historic Preservation Office State Parks and Recreation State of Oregon, Jensen Collection, Oct 15, 1989

8. *Nehalem Wetlands Review*, U.S. Army Engineer District, Portland 1977, pg C-49,

9. Ibid pg C-47

10. *World Encompassed*, pg 102

11. *Nehalem Wetlands Review*, pg D-30

12. *Nehalem Wetlands Review*, pg D-31

13. *Oregon Geology*, Volume 52, May 3, 1990, pg 57-60

14. Institute for Archaeological Studies letter dated October 15, 1989 to Leland Gilsen, Ph.D., Oregon State Parks Historic Preservation Office, Jensen Library Collection

15. *Oregon Geology*, pg 57

16. *World Encompassed*, pg 70

17. *Francis Drake Revived*, by Phillip Nichols, London 1626

18. *World Encompassed*, pg 70

19. *Sir Francis Drake at Drakes Bay, A Summation of Evidence Relating to the Identification of Sir Francis Drake's Encampment at Drakes Bay, California*, Raymond Aker, Based on the Research of the Drake Navigators Guild., Copyright 1978 by Drake Navigators Guild pp 32-34 photo by Robert Allen, pg 62

20. *Spanish Voyages to the Northwest Coast of America in the Sixteenth Century*, Henry R. Wagner, San Francisco, California Historical Society 1929, pg 154

21. *World Encompassed*, pg 102

22. www.everyculture.com/wc/Rwanda-to-Syria/Castilians.html

23. *A History of California - The Spanish Period*, by Charles E. Chapman, Ph. D., Macmillan Company 1921 1939

Chapter 4

1. *Handbook of the Indians of California*, A. L. Kroeber, Dover Publications, NY, 1925 1976

2. *The Nehalem Tillamook Ethnography*, by Elizabeth D. Jacobs, edited by William R. Seaburg, Oregon State University Press, Corvallis, Oregon 2003. pg 33

3. *Handbook of the Indians of California*, A. L. Kroeber, pg 277

4. *Nehalem Tillamook Ethnography*, by Elizabeth D. Jacobs

5. World Encompassed, pg 74

6. www.plants.usda.gov

6A. *Lower Chinook Ethnographic Notes*, Verne F. Ray, University of WA 1938, pg 36

7. *Wappato, Ancient Food from the Marsh*, by Neva Mae Harvey, Northwest Magazine, May 30, 1971

8. *Lower Chinook Ethnographic Notes*, Verne F. Ray, pg 36

9. *Nehalem Tillamook Ethnography*, pg 81

10. www.plants.usda.gov

11. *Spanish Voyages to the Northwest Coast of America in the Sixteenth Century*, Henry R. Wagner, San Francisco, California Historical Society 1929, pg 160

12. *World Encompassed*, pg 74

13. *Adventures of the First Settlers on the Columbia River*, Alexander Ross, Published by Smith, Elder and Co., Cornhill, London 1849

14. Wagner, Spanish Voyages, pg 160

15. Wagner, Spanish Voyages, pg 161

16. *World Encompassed*, pg 74

17. *Culture Element Distributions: VII Oregon Coast,* by H.G. Barnett, Anthropological Records, Volume 1, No.3, pp. 155-205, 2 figures in text, 1 map, University of California Press, Berkeley, California 1937, pg 203

18. ibid pg 203

19. Conversation with Douglas Deur, Ph.D., Research Coordinator, University of Washington, June 21, 2007

20. *Nehalem Tillamook*, pg 70

21. Royal British Columbia Museum, Victoria, B.C.

22. *Handbook of the Indians of California*, pg 327

23. *Spanish Voyages to the Northwest Coast of America in the Sixteenth Century*, Henry R. Wagner, San Francisco, California Historical Society 1929, pg 158

24. *Journal of Tomas de Suría of His voyage with Malaspina to the Northwest Coast of America in 1791*, Donald C. Cutter, Ye Galleon Press, WA1980

25. *Spanish Voyages*, Henry R. Wagner, pg 158

26. *Lower Chinook*, Verne F. Ray, pg 47

27. *A Small World of Our Own, The Wreck of the ship Georgiana*, edited by Robert A. Bennett; Hugh Crockett 1892, Pioneer Press Books, Walla Walla, WA 1985, pg 98

27A. Nuttall pg 296

28. *Lower Chinook Ethnographic Notes*, Verne F. Ray, University of WA 1938, pg 105

29. *Spanish Voyages*, Henry R. Wagner, pg 158

30. Barnett, Homer G., pp. 155-205, 2 figures in text, 1 map,

31. *A History of California - The Spanish Period,* by Charles E. Chapman, Ph. D., Macmillan Company 1921 1939, pg 15

32. *Handbook of the Indians of California*, pg 277

33. ibid pg 243

34. *Voyages of the "Columbia" to the Northwest Coast 1787-1790 and 1790-1793*, edited by Frederic W. Howay, Oregon Historical Society Press 1941, 1990, pg 32

35. Ibid pg 32

36. Ray, pg 102

37. Nehalem Tillamook, pg 89

38. *Journal of Tomas de Suri'a*, Donald C. Cutter, pg 46

39. *Notes on the Tillamook*, by Franz Boas, University of California Publications in Am. Arch, Vol. 20, Kraus Reprint 1965 1923

40. Ray, pg 117

41. www.en.wikipedia.org/wiki/western_yew

42. *World Encompassed*, pg 68

43. Verne Ray, pg 97

44. Ibid pg 97

45. *Aboriginal Use of Tobacco in British Columbia and its Origin Areas to the South*, MS Grant Keddie, Curator of Archaeology, Royal B.C. Museum, May 1, 2005

46. *Coast Salish Weaving*, By Kathy Duncan, *Jamestown S'Klallam Tribe*, 1033 Old Blyn Highway, Sequim, WA

47. *Joseph H. Frost's diary of 1841*, MSS, Oregon Historical Society Collection also see Oregon Historical Society & Oregon Geographical Names

48. *Noticias De Nutka, An Account of Nootka Sound in 1792*, Jose Mariano Mozino, University of Washington Press Seattle 1970, pg 26-27

49. ibid Mozino, pg 26

50. *World Encompassed*, pg 63-64

Chapter 5

1. *World Encompassed*, pg 81

2. *For Honor & Country, The Diary of Bruno de Hezeta*, Translation and annotation by Herbert K. Beals, Western Imprints, Press of the Oregon Historical Society 1985

3. *Report of the Superintendent of the Coast Survey, Showing the Progress of the Survey During the Year 1862*, by George Davidson, Assistant United States Coast Survey, Washington Government Printing Office 1864, pg 355 and Byram, R. Scott, The Work of a Nation-Richard D. Cutts and the Coast Survey Map of Fort Clatsop, Oregon Historical Quarterly, Vol. 106, No. 2 Summer 2005, pp 254-271

4. ibid Davidson pg 354

5. ibid Davidson pg 355

6. ibid Davidson pg 354

7. World Encompassed, pg 81

Chapter 6

1. Nuttall, pg 193-195

2. *Flood Tide of Empire, Spain and the Pacific Northwest, 1543-1819*, Warren L. Cook, New Haven and London: Yale University Press 1973, pg 25, "The expedition in 1542 led by Juan Rodrigues Cabrillo, in which Bartolome Ferrelo reached the high water mark of the sixteenth-century expeditions northward..."

3. *Spanish Voyages to the Northwest Coast of America in the Sixteenth Century*, Henry R. Wagner, San Francisco, California Historical Society 1929, pg 300

4. Ibid, pg 301

5. Ibid, pg 303

6. Ibid, pg 302-3

7. Ibid, pg 284-5

8. *Peoples of the Northwest Coast: Their Archaeology and Prehistory*, Ames, K.M., and H.D.G. Maschner, Thames and Hudson Ltd., London, New York, 1999. "Controlled burning was regularly practiced, possibly as early as 5,000 years ago in the Willamette Valley, by many groups to maintain plant food product and nut-producing areas and improve hunting grounds without trees along the heavily forested coast and

in some interior areas…"

9. *Sir Francis Drake's Secret Voyage to the Northwest Coast of America, AD 1579*, by Samuel Bawlf, Sir Francis Drake Publications, Salt Spring Island, BC 2001, pg 61, 111,116
10. *Nehalem Tillamook Ethnography*, pg 90
11. *Aboriginal Use of Tobacco in British Columbia and its Origin Areas to the South*, by Grant Keddie MS May 1, 2005
12. ibid, "The Tlingit [Vancouver Island Tribe] held a smoking feast in which tobacco was offered via the fire to all the dead of the clan hosting the feast. At these events clan mourning songs were sung and the clan history recalled."
13. *Adventures of the First Settlers on the Columbia River*, Alexander Ross, pg 97-98
14. *Lower Chinook Ethnographic Notes*, Verne F. Ray, University of WA 1938, pg 103
15. Conversations with Douglas Deur, PhD. University of Washington
16. World Encompassed the heading date as "Jan. 21 [1579]. We must assume either a misprint in the printing process or that the journal was at some time edited and the sequences of the events are out of order., pg 68
17. *World Encompassed*, pg 25
18. *Sir Francis Drake Revived*, by Philip Nichols London 1626
19. *The Columbia River*, by Ross Cox, London 1831, University of Okalahoma Press 1957, pg 164
20. *Sir Francis Drake Revived*, by Philip Nichols 1626
21. *World Encompassed*, Drake praying with John Doughty in Patagonia, pg 33
22. *Joseph Frost Journal*
23. *Noticias De Nutka, An Account of Nootka Sound in 1792*, by Jose Mariano Mozino, University of Washington Press Seattle 1970, pg 20
24. Ray, pg 69
25. Mozino, pg 9
26. *Nehalem Tillamook*, pg 128
27. Ray, pg 93
28. *Nehalem Tillamook*, pg 72
29. *Nehalem Tillamook*, pg 72
30. *Nehalem Tillamook*, pg 72
31. *Nehalem Tillamook*, pg 87-88
32. Ross, *The Columbia River*, pg 91
33. *White Slaves of Maquinna*, John R. Jewitt, Heritage House Publishing, B.C., 1815, 2000
34. Queen Elizabeth I changed the mile from 5000 feet to 5280 in 1596
35. *Aboriginal Use of Tobacco*, Grant Keddie, Curator of Archaeology, Royal B.C. Museum. May 1, 2005
36. Ray, pg 97
37. Ray, pg 97 # 7 Ray and David Douglas, pp 269-278
38. *Nehalem Tillamook*, pg 102-103
39. Jewitt Journal, pg 148
40. Jewitt Journal, pg 167
41. *Nehalem Tillamook*, Appendix 3 pg 229-232 Jacobs recorded 38 songs by Pearson of which Tape 41, RCA Disc 4627 B, Part 1, Duration: 0:30, An "*Iha*" spirit power

song. This and the next song are accompanied by drumming and Tape 41, RCA Disc 14627 B, Part 3, Duration 0:25, A "*grief*" song.

42. *Nehalem Tillamook*, pg 89
43. Jewitt, pg 75-76
44. Alexander Ross, *Adventures of the First Settlers on the Columbia River*, pg 95
45. Mozino, pg 26
46. *Nehalem Tillamook*, pg 165
47. Jewitt, pg 77
48. *The Northwest Coast or Three Years' Residence in Washington Territory*, James G. Swan, Harper 1857, 3rd printing 1977 University of Washington press, pg 124
49. *Adventures of the First Settlers on the Columbia River*, Alexander Ross, Published by Smith, Elder and Co.. Cornhill, London 1849
50. *Nehalem Tillamook*, pg 233
51. *Indian Art and Culture of the Northwest Coast*, by Della Kew and P.E. Goddard, Hancock House Publishing 1974
52. Ross, pg 94
53. *Nehalem Tillamook*, pg 89
54. Ross, pg 92
55. *Nehalem Tillamook*, pg 78-79
56. *Surviving Through the Days*, by Herbert W. Luthin, University of California Berkeley 2002, pg 262 and Elizabethan California, Heizer, pg 95, plate 2.
57. *Nehalem Tillamook*, pg 89
58. Ross, pg 87- 96 and Joseph Frost Journal
59. Ray, pg 93
60. *Voyages of the "Columbia" to the Northwest Coast 1787-1790 and 1790-1793*, edited by Frederic W. Howay, Oregon Historical Society Press 1941 1990, Hoskins's Narrative, pg 288
61. Ibid, Boit's Log mentions the same topic of sacrifice at 49 deg. 9" N, Long. 125 deg 30' W, pg 387
62. *Three years Washington Territory*, James G. Swan, pg 92
63. *Columbia's River The Voyages of Robert Gray, 1787-1793*, J. Richard Nokes, published by Washington State Historical Society, 1991
64. *The Coast Salish of British Columbia,* Barnett, Homer G. 1955,
65. *Indian Healing Shamanic Ceremonialism in the Pacific Northwest*, Wolfgang G. Jilek, Hancock House Publishing Ltd., Washington, Fifth printing 1997, pg 11
66. *The California Coast, A Bilingual Edition of Documents from the Sutro Collection*, edited by Donald C. Cutter, pg 187-189
67. Ibid, pg 267
68. *Nehalem Wetlands Review*, pg C-31
69. *The European Discovery of America The Southern Voyages 1492-1616*, by Samuel Eliot Morison, Oxford University Press NY 1974) , see photo of Castillo's map of California 1541, From Lorenzana, *Historia de Nueva Espana* 1770, pg 626
70. *Captain James Cook,* by Alan Villers, 1967 Scribner's Sons, N.Y., pg 47) Villers' autobiography states, "I (he) may well be the last man on earth who has sailed a ship like Captain Cook's around the world with the power of the free wind, taking and using what comes." He was born in Melbourne, Australia in 1903 and at the age of fifteen he

sailed away on a square-rigger. Except for a brief period spent whaling in the Antarctic he never left sailing ships, and in 1935 he started his trip around the world as commander of the *Joseph Conrad*, the last full-rigged ship to round Cape Horn. Discussing Portuguese Captain Luis Vaez de Torres on his voyage of discovery for Australia in 1603, Villers described how square-rigging ships limit them the way they could be sailed. "This little ship…unfit to beat back to windward if she must. Small square-riggers - or large - with rope rigging and lint wooden yards could not stand up to the endless slogging strains of constant tacking, especially on long open-sea voyages"

Appendix I   Costaggini Survey

(THIS PAGE INTENDED TO ACCOMPANY THE PAPER, "SURVEY OF ARTIFACTS AT NEAHKAHNIE MOUNTAIN, OREGON," BY P.A. COSTAGGINI AND R.J. SCHULTZ)

CIVIL ENGINEERING ABSTRACT:

A survey to find the interrelation of rock mounds (cairns), rocks with carvings and other artifacts was made in the vicinity of Neahkahnie Mountain (Tillamook County) Oregon, concluding in that the artifacts are remains of ancient surveys, most probably authored by the early explorers to the New World.

KEY WORDS: Ancient surveys; Archeology; Cairns; Explorers; History; Historical artifacts; Land claims; Maps; Neahkahnie Mountain; Oregon history; Rocks; Surveys; Symbolic possession; Topography; Triangulation; West coast

ABSTRACT: Acting upon a request to A.S.C.E. by the Director of the Tillamook County Pioneer Museum, a survey was performed to find the interrelation of surface rock mounds (cairns) and other surface artifacts located in the vicinity of Neahkahnie Mountain. The survey was performed to 3rd Order Survey Specifications (horizontal) of N.O.A.A. and included a tie to 2nd Order N.G.S. monuments at the top of the mountain. The mapped and adjusted data show similarities with a Sixteenth Century survey and provide insight into certain marks grooved into several large rocks. The conclusions are that the artifacts are remains of ancient surveys, or areacts of possession (or both), performed most probably by early explorers, of whom the English and Francis Drake are leading candidates for responsibility. The usefulness of the conclusions is that the data explain the artifacts better than other, locally published theories, and shed some additional light on the controversy of the location of Drake's three month landing. Additional survey work could be none north and west of the survey area.

SURVEY OF ARTIFACTS AT NEAHKAHNIE MOUNTAIN, OREGON

By Phillip A. Costaggini[1] and Robert J. Schultz,[2] A.S.C.E.

Introduction

Surface rock mounds, or cairns, and rocks with carvings,
located on Neahkahnie Mountain (Tillamook County) Oregon suggest
ancient surveys and/or acts of possession by European explorers.
In response to the Tillamook County Pioneer Museum Director's
request for A.S.C.E. assistance, the author traversed the locations in accordance with N.O.A.A. Third Order survey standards
for horizontal work, adjusted and platted the data, and analyzed
the results. The data show similarities with an English Sixteenth Century survey, and may explain certain marks on a stone
found in the Nineteenth Century. Certain hypotheses are generated concerning orientation of key points in the traverse net.

[1]Masters Candidate in Civil Engineering, Oregon State
University, Corvallis, Oregon.

[2]Professor of Civil Engineering, Oregon State University,

General Discussion

In September, 1976, M. Wayne Jensen, Jr., Director of the
Tillamook County Pioneer Museum in Tillamook, Oregon, contacted
the American Society of Civil Engineers in hopes of securing financial assistance to conduct a survey. His motivation was to
determine the interrelation of large rock mounds and carved stones
found on the slopes of Neahkahnie Mountain, a prominent Coast
Range peak between Nehalem Bay and Short Sands Beach. Mr. Jensen
reasoned that the monuments, not yielding information about buried
treasure, Indian artifacts or U.S. Public or private land surveys,
might be the remains of ancient surveys.

The request was in turn passed to the A.S.C.E.'s Oregon
Section, the National Committee on the History and the Heritage,
and finally to Professor Robert J. Schultz at Oregon State University. In consultation with Professor Schultz, Mr. Costaggini
accepted the task of conducting the research and survey.

The Neahkahnie Mountain Survey

Figure 1 is a U.S.G.S. 15 minute quadrangle map showing
the survey area. Table 1 lists the key stations with brief descriptions of each.

Survey Type and Description

The method of random traverse was selected because it

SURVEY AREA
Neahkahnie Mtn
OSWALD WEST STATE PARK
Neahkahnie Beach
Neahkahnie Lake
Nehalem
Manzanita
Bobs Creek
Alder Creek
NEHALEM
Dean Point
Mud
BAY
Fishery Point
Wheeler Heights
Cheyint
PACIFIC HIGHWAY
Brighton
Messhouse
Jetty
OCEAN
NEHALEM
SOUTHERN
Nedonna Beach
Neahkahnie School
McMillan
Crescent Lake
Manhattan Beach
Lake Lytle

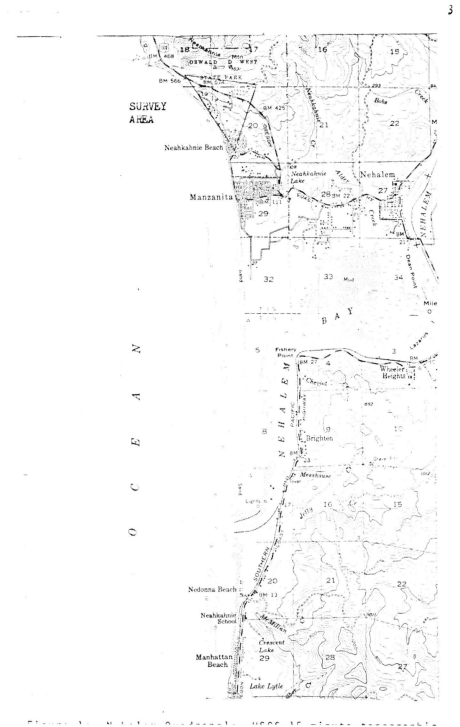

Figure 1. Nehalem Quadrangle, USGS 15 minute topographic

Table 1: List of Key Survey Stations, Neahkahnie

Station Name	Survey Name	Description
North Cairn	A	Cairn
Triangle	B	Stones in a pattern of an equilateral triangle, 6 ft. (1.82 m.) on a side; 2 ft. (0.61 m.) high
North Mound Two	C	Stones in a small stack
North Mound Three	D	Stones in a small stack
South Cairn	E	Cairn
Augur	F	Face of a cliff with carvings
Rock Rays	RR-2--RR-5	Small stones in a "V" alignment
Triangulation Points	H-1--H-3	Several rocks with carvings
Center Rock One	L	Large stone whose flat top is nearly horizontal; carved lines in a radial pattern
Highway 101 Rocks	37-A--37-B	Wall of stones 6 ft. (1.82 m.) wide, 3 ft. (0.91 m.) high, intersected by a 2nd row of stones.
Center Rock Two	0	Stone with carvings
North Mound Five	4B	Stones in a small stack
North Mound Six	4C	Stone with carvings
North Mound Seven	4D	Stones in a small stack
Wentz Stone	P	Large stone with carved figures, numbers and crisscrossing lines.
East Rock Mound	ER-4	Stones with carvings

afforded the opportunity of achieving relatively good accuracy as well as tying into the two local National Geodetic Survey Second Order Stations. Three closed, horizontal control loops were run (see Figure 2). Horizontal Loop One contained 40 stations and tied the two cairns (A and E) together. Horizontal Loop Two contained 7 stations and tied the point Augur (F) to the Loop One. Horizontal Loop Three contained 5 stations and tied the previous loops to the government stations. The purpose of horizontal Loop Three was to provide an independent check upon azimuth as

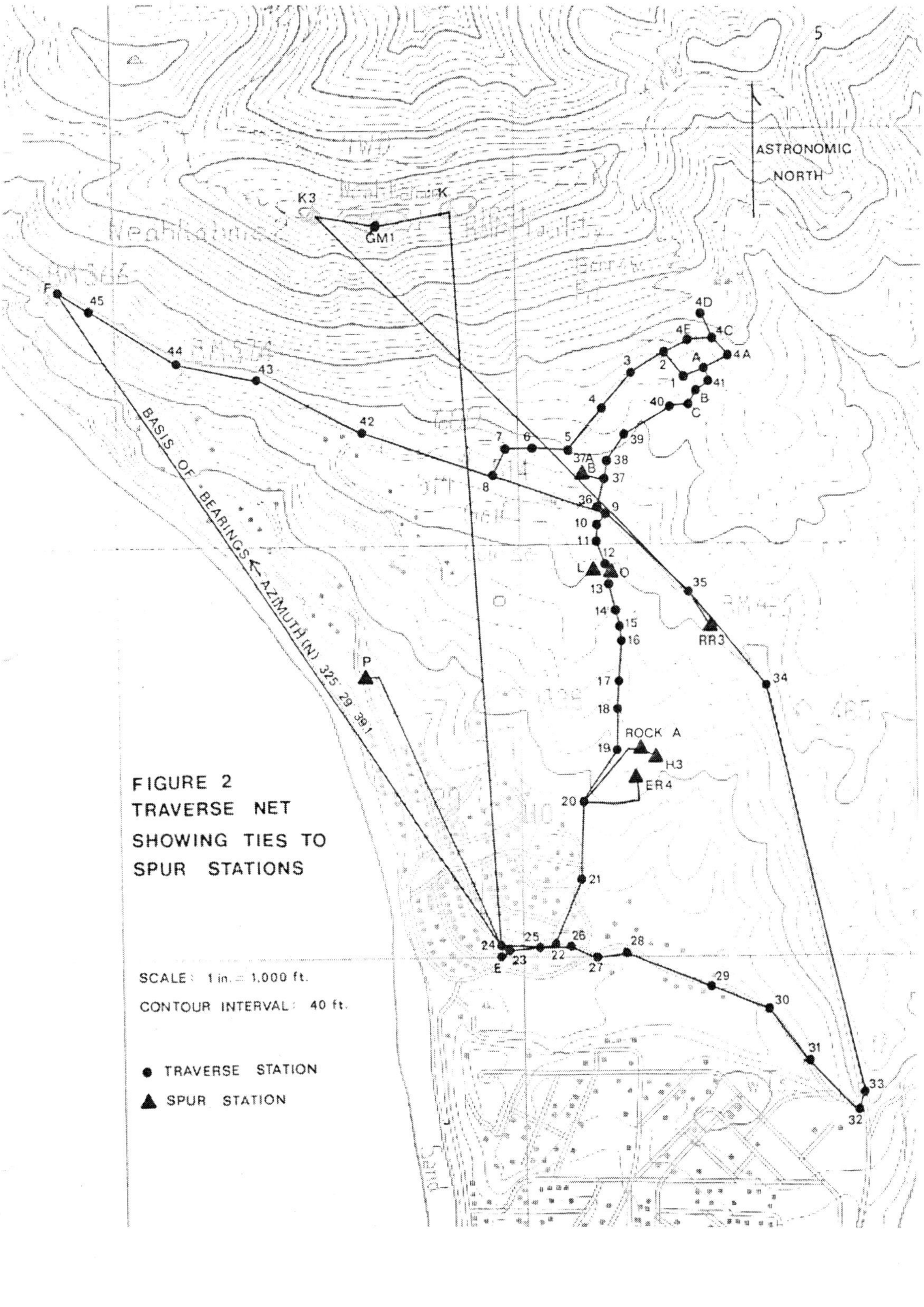

ASTRONOMIC NORTH
FIGURE 2
TRAVERSE NET
SHOWING TIES TO
SPUR STATIONS
SCALE: 1 in. = 1,000 ft.
CONTOUR INTERVAL: 40 ft.
TRAVERSE STATION
SPUR STATION
BASIS OF BEARINGS ← AZIMUTH (N) 325° 29' 39.1"
ROCK A

well as distance. The basis of bearings was obtained for the line 24 to F by Polaris observations. A closed vertical loop of direct levels was run between two Oregon State Highway Department bench marks, establishing the elevations of 8 traverse stations. The remaining elevations were computed from zenith angles and slope distances of the traverse work. The data was reduced to mean sea level for computer adjustment by least squares.

Instrumentation for the horizontal data collection was a Wild T-2 optical theodolite and a Hewlett-Packard 3805 distance meter with two single prism glass reflectors.

Traverse Results

Table 2 lists the results of the traverse field data. Table 3 lists the leveling results.

Tie to N.G.S. Monuments

Horizontal traverse Loop Three is described in Figure 2. N.G.S. Triangulation Station Neahkahnie is located on the eastern most of the three peaks which form the mountain. Station GM-1 was a traverse station located on the center peak, at which no N.G.S. stations or marks were found (which is in agreement with the Government Recovery Notes for the center peak stations). Station GM-1 was necessary because the outside two peaks were not intervisible due to the presence of trees. On the western peak, N.G.S. Triangulation Station Neahkahnie 2 is obliterated, but its

6

Table 2: N.G.S. Third Order Horizontal Specifications and Traverse Results

Classification	Third Order, Class II	Neahkahnie Results and Additional Explanations
1. Recommended spacing of stations	As required for other (than metropolitan area) surveys	As required. The traverses were performed in a rural area without regard to station spacing. Dense woods precluded obtaining 328 ft. (0.1km.) minimum sight lengths.
2. Horizontal directions or angles		
a. Instrument	1"0	1"0
b. Number of observations	2	2
c. Rejection limit from mean	5"0	5"0
3. Length measurements		
a. Standard error	1:30,000	1:225,000 or greater. All lines were measured by EDM equipment, corrected for temperature and humidity at the time and place of observation. The standard error was obtained through the repeatability of the instrument.
4. Reciprocal vertical angle observations		
a. Number of and spread between observations	2 Direct, 2 Reverse 2 Direct, 2 Reverse 20"	2 Direct, 2 Reverse 20"
b. Number of stations between known elevations	15-20	25-30. Known elevations were obtained by leveling over 8 traverse stations on Hwy. 101.
5. Astro Azimuths		
a. Number of courses between azi. cks.	30-40	40
b. No. of observations	4	6
c. No. of nights	1	1

7

Table 2: Continued

Classification	Third Order, Class II	Neahkahnie Results and Additional Explanations
d. Standard error	8".0	3".2
6. Azimuth Closure	8".0 per station or 30" (N)$^{\frac{1}{2}}$	Horiz. Loop One: +20".0 total (+0".5 per station) or 189" Horiz. Loop Two: + 3".9 total (+0".6 ½er station) or 79" Horiz. Loop Three: -20".0 total (-4".0 per station) 67"
7. Position Closure after azi. closure	2.62 ft.(0.62Mi)$^{\frac{1}{2}}$ (0.8m (K)$^{\frac{1}{2}}$) or 1:5,000	Horiz. Loop One: 1:22,000 Horiz. Loop Two: 1:31,000 Horiz. Loop Three: 1:21,000

Table 3: N.G.S. Third Order Vertical Specifications and Leveling Results

Classification	Third Order, Class II	Neahkahnie Results and Additional Explanations
1. Principal uses; min. stds; higher accuracies may be used for special purposes	Misc. Local control; may not be adjusted to Natl. Net.; small engr. projects	Project as defined in Table 2.
2. Recommended spacing of stations	As needed	As required to complete level loop.
3. Spacing of marks along lines	Not more than 1.86 mi (3 km.)	All less than 1.86 mi. (3 km.)

Table 3: Continued

Classification	Third Order, Class II	Neahkahnie Results and Additional Explanations
4. Gravity requirement	Not applicable	Not applicable
5. Instrument standards	Geodetic levels and rods	Zeiss level and Philadelphia rod
6. Field procedures	Double or single run	Double run
a. Section length	0.62-1.86 mi. (1-3 km.) for dbl.	1.15 mi. (1.85 km.)
b. Maximum length of sight	295 ft. (90 m.)	104 ft. (31.7 m.)
7. Field procedures a. Maximum difference in lengths, forward and backwd. sights/set up	33 ft. (10 m.)	11 ft.(3.35 m.) forward run 13 ft.(3.96 m.) backward run
b. Per section (cum.)	33 ft. (10 m.)	115 ft. (35.05 m.) forward run 100 ft. (30.48 m.) backward run
c. Maximum length of line between connections	15.53 mi. (25 km.) double run	2.29 mi. (3.70 km.) double run
8. Maximum closures a. Section; forward and backward, loop or line	$0.05 \text{ ft.}(\text{mi.})^{\frac{1}{2}}$ $(12 \text{ mm.}(\text{km.})^{\frac{1}{2}})$ Section: 0.05 ft. (0.015m.) Loop: 0.08 ft. (0.024 m.)	Closure forward: -0.01 ft. (-0.003 m.) Closure backward: +0.15 ft. (+0.046 m.) Closure loop: +0.14 ft. (+0.043 m.)

position was computed from traverse ties made to the station's two existing Reference Marks, as shown in Figure 3. N.G.S. Station Neahkahnie 2 was not re-established because higher than Third Order methods were required. Table 4 compares the computed and published distances and azimuths of the line Neahkahnie to Neahkahnie 2.

Polaris Observations

The astronomic azimuths from traverse station 24 (instrument) to traverse station F (target) for six horizontal circle positions are listed in Table 5. Though Third Order specifications call for 4 positions, time and weather permitted the collection of two extra positions.

Analysis of Results

A survey was conducted to locate horizontal positions of historical interest for M. Wayne Jensen. Figure 4 gives the results of the survey. The several theories attempting to explain the Neahkahnie Mountain Artifacts may be examined in the light of these survey results.

In his archeological work, Mr. Jensen discovered the cairns at A and E, as well as the several collections of rocks with man-made carvings (see Table 1 and Figure 4). Mr. Jensen accumulated the following observations:

1. There were no precious metals or stones of value found

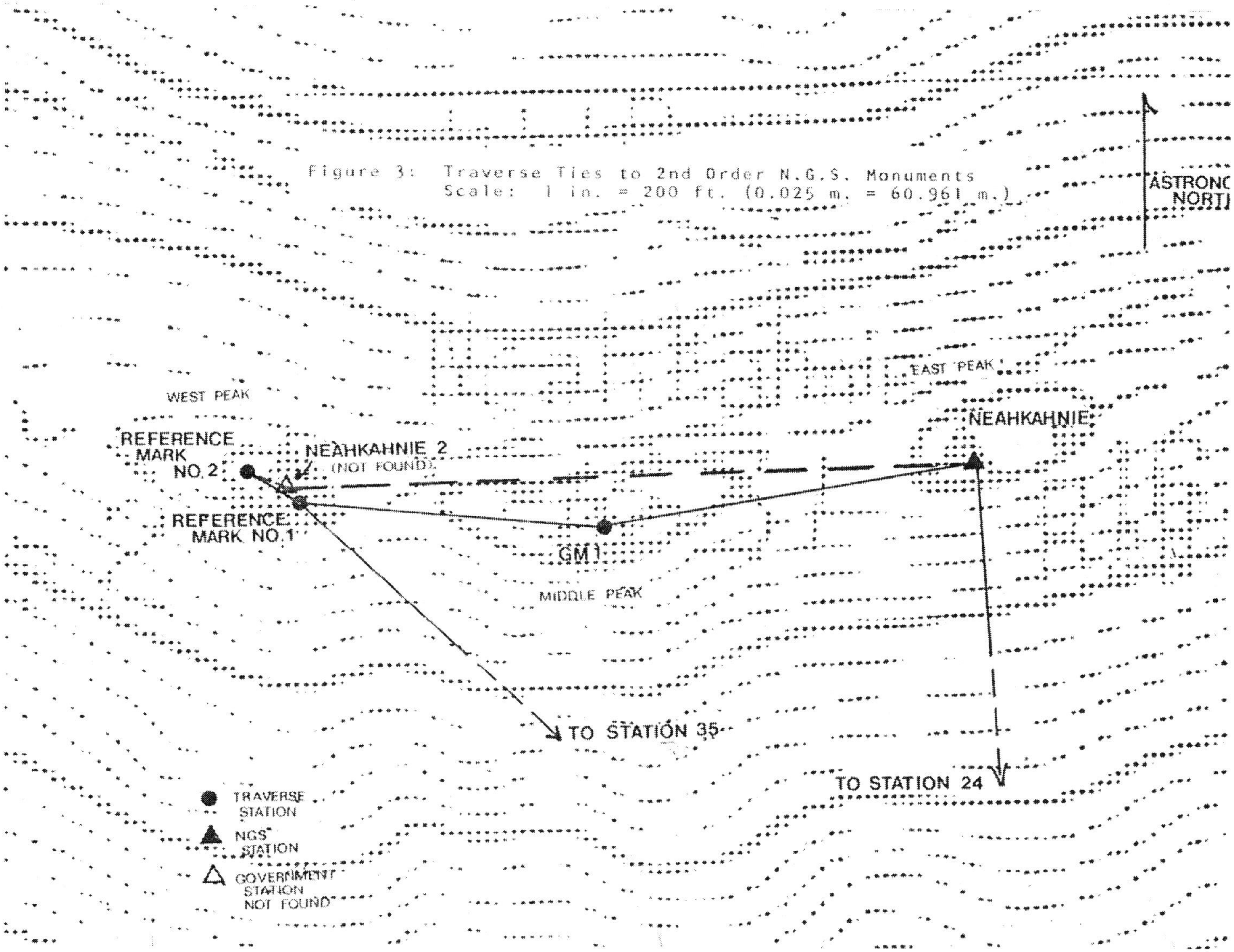
ASTRONO
NORTH
WEST PEAK
EAST PEAK
NEAHKAHNIE
REFERENCE MARK NO. 2
NEAHKAHNIE 2 (NOT FOUND)
REFERENCE MARK NO. 1
GM 1
MIDDLE PEAK
TO STATION 35
TO STATION 24
TRAVERSE STATION
NGS STATION
GOVERNMENT STATION NOT FOUND

Figure 3: Traverse Ties to 2nd Order N.G.S. Monuments
Scale: 1 in. = 200 ft. (0.025 m. = 60.961 m.)

12

Table 4: Computed and Published Data For N.G.S. Stations

Sta.	Computed Trav. Dist. Feet (Meters)	Published Grid Dist. Feet (Meters)	Published Geodetic Distance Feet (Meters)	Computed Traverse Azimuth ° ' "	Published Grid Azi. N--OSPC North Zone ° ' "	Published Geodetic Azimuth (S) ° ' "	Published Back Azimuth (S) ° ' "
Neah.							
Neah. 2	1,126.186 (343.266)	1,125.973 (343.201)	1,126.031 (343.218)	268 26 08.6	270 26 08.6	270 52 47.4	123 26 11.4

Table 5: Astronomic Azimuths, 6 Horizontal Circle Positions

Set	Position	Azimuth Polaris ° ' "	Horizontal Angle ° ' "	Astro Azimuth 24 to F ° ' "
1	1	359 14 20.6	33 44 27.0	325 29 53.6
1	2	359 11 18.6	33 41 33.5	325 29 45.1
1	3	359 08 51.0	33 39 00.5	325 29 50.5
1	4	359 06 39.2	33 37 01.1	325 29 38.2
2	1	359 06 35.3	33 34 54.5	325 29 40.8
2	2	359 02 40.3	33 33 08.0	325 29 32.3

171

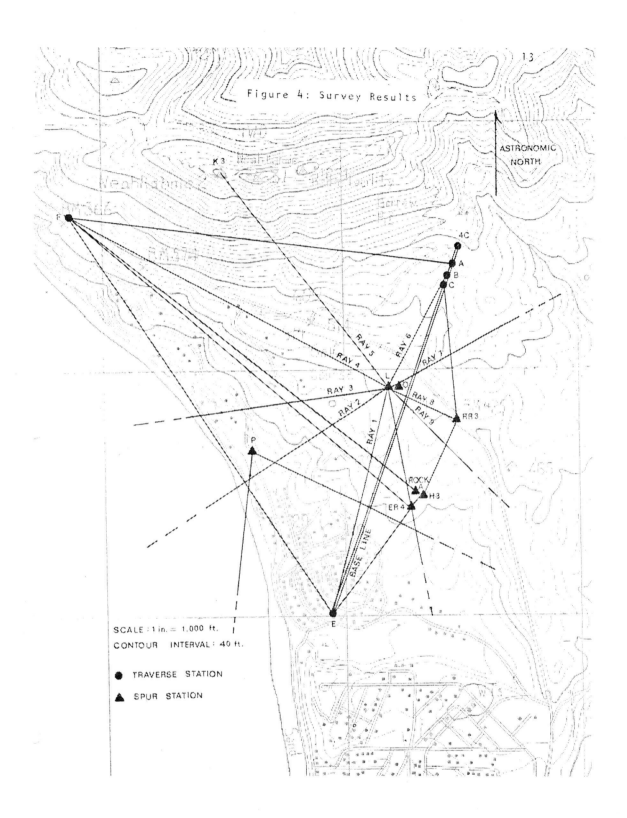

Figure 4: Survey Results
ASTRONOMIC NORTH
K3
F
4C
A
B
C
RAY 1
RAY 2
RAY 3
RAY 4
RAY 5
RAY 6
RAY 7
RAY 8
RAY 9
L
RR3
P
ROCK
H3
ER4
BASE LINE
E
SCALE: 1 in. = 1,000 ft.
CONTOUR INTERVAL: 40 ft.
TRAVERSE STATION
SPUR STATION

by any parties of record, nor was there any evidence suggesting any locations where treasures might have been buried or otherwise hidden.

2. The two cairns had apparently been placed deliberately, with a progressive size sorting of smaller rocks and stones at the bottom rising to the largest at the top. To reinforce the idea of deliberate placement, Mr. Jensen noted that each cairn location was several hundred feet from naturally occurring rock sites (in stream beds or draws). This suggests that the material was originally gathered and hauled to the cairn sites.

3. The rockshad been in place and undisturbed for well over one hundred years. Though this time period given is considered by Mr. Jensen as a minimum, the maximum is probably much more.

4. Under the North Cairn (A), was found a basalt stone, rectangular with square ends. The stone has a grooved line running longitudinally across the centers of two opposing rectangular faces, and a grooved line running across the center of one of the ends (so as to join the two other lines). The entire line measures 36 inches (0.91 m.) ±0.010 ft. (0.003 m.) when a cloth tape is stretched along the line. The stone as found had been chiseled or cut off (from a larger rock) at the other square end. The length of 36 inches (0.91 m.)--a yard--is important in the discussion about measurements below. Under the South Cairn (E) was found charcoal from burned wood. Radio carbon dating of this charcoal indicates an age exceeding 100 years from the discovery by Mr. Jensen in 1967.

Several inferences may be drawn from these observations.

It is certain that the cairns (A and E) were not created by acts or processes of nature. They were also not locations of treasures. There are four possible explanations for the cairns: burial sites, marks made by early explorers, marks made by native inhabitants and marks made by the white settlers of the 1800's.

In the Nineteenth Century, while it is true that some surveyors buried burned wood beneath rock mounds, there are three facts discouraging the idea that this group was responsible. First, the cairns are not anywhere near any U.S. Public Land Survey corners, Donation Land Claim corners, or even property corners of record. Second, the cairns are of such size (approximately 10 feet (3.05 m.) in diameter) as to make it unlikely that Nineteenth Century surveyors would have left such large monuments. Third, no written records exist of these monuments as being survey marks or corners. The explanation of the cairns as burial sites may be eliminated because no human remains were found. Further, no Indian artifacts were found. The remaining group responsible is the early explorers.

Three countries explored the west coast of present day Canada and the United States: Russia, Spain and England. Neither of the first two countries had explorers of record in the Neahkannie area. Among the English, Francis Drake stands out as a leading candidate for responsibility, although the scarcity of original written records lends more to speculation than solid proofs. It is known that Drake searched among the coastal inlets of present day California, Oregon and perhaps Washington in a vain attempt to find a shorter route back to England. It is

also known that, after reaching a northernmost point in the
Pacific, he backtracked and harbored his vessel *at a bad bay* ~~for 3 months~~
for repair. at a *unknown anchorage*
at some natural inlet in California or Oregon. The exact location is unknown (and is the subject of an intense debate), because Drake's written records of his circumnavigation were confiscated in England and remain lost to this day. A reading of
the written records extant indicates that Drake intended to claim
lands in the West for England, though it is not known what specific kind of claim he made or whether a survey was performed.
One tract mentions a single act--a plaque nailed to a tree--but
no other records survive as to exactly how Drake claimed land.
This plaque, so states the record, claimed land without any survey or formal demarcation. This type of claim falls into a cat-
egory known as an "act of possession," which, though largely
symbolic and ceremonial, was an important technique used by the
Sixteenth Century explorers to reserve lands for the crown. Among
the acts chronicled by these explorers were acts of building
rock mounds or cairns. But besides being acts of possession, the
Neahkahnie cairns, along with other evidence, suggest that some
sort of survey was performed.

The line joining the South Cairn (E) with the North Cairn
(A) lies at a bearing angle from Astronomic North of N 20° 32' 17" E,
very close to the current magnetic declination of the area
(N 20° 30' E). The U.S.C. & G.S. has declination data for Western Oregon from 1800 to the present, as shown in Table 6.

Table 6: Declination Data for Western Oregon, 1800-1979

Year (January 1)	Declination °	′
1800	15	56
1810	16	34
1820	17	13
1830	17	52
1840	18	29
1850	19	03
1860	19	32
1870	19	57
1880	20	15
1890	20	26
1900	20	30
1910	21	30
1935	22	30
1943	24	06
1975	20	45
1979	20	30

The trend of the declination is increasing westerly except since 1943, at which time the data indicates and easterly migration. The trend prior to 1800, then, is uncertain. Further study, perhaps employing a model to predict backwards, would be necessary before concluding that the line E to A was an intended North-South survey line. However, the assumption agrees with other research data.

A second feature of the line E to A is that is passes very close to three other survey points, C (offset distance 2.02 ft. (0.62 m.)), B (offset distance 8.34 ft. (2.54 m.))and 4C (offset distance 1.57 ft. (0.48 m.)).

Examining the distances for some possible significance begins with Wendle's Rock (see Figure 5). This rock, found on the beach in 1947 in the vicinity of the South Cairn (E), contains, among other marks, a grooved triangle, and a number, "1632" grooved along the shortest of the three legs. The triangle and

Figure 5: Wendle's Rock

1632
D.E.

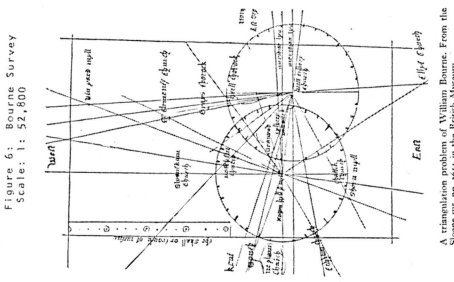

Figure 6: Bourne Survey
Scale: 1: 52,800

West
East

A triangulation problem of William Bourne. From the Sloane ms. no. 3651 in the British Museum.
(Courtesy of the Director.)

18

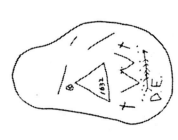

1632 have resisted credible explanations but have not been examined in the light of the survey data now available. It has been proposed that the number 1632 may refer to a year or to a measurement, or to something else. If the number refers to the year 1632, no Europeans could have been responsible since this year falls in the period between Drake and later known explorers in the area. Attempts to explain this number in terms of its relation to buried treasure have all been failures. If the number refers to a measurement, the questions remain as between what points and in what units. All distances on the plat (see figure 4) are drawn as the horizontal distances. It may be assumed that the early explorers measured along the ground surface and obtained data similar to slope measurements. This assumption is supported by the fact that, in Drake's time, stadia was unknown and the trigonometric reduction, though known, was not widely used. Utilizing this assumption, the slope distance E to A may be computed from the data and compared with the number 1632. From the survey data, the difference in elevation between E and A is:

(1) 682.686 ft. - 78.967 ft. = 603.719 ft.

(208.085 m. - 24.069 m. = 184.016 m.)

The horizontal distance E to A is 4,835.587 ft. (1,473.905 m.).

(2) $\text{Slope Distance EA} = \left((4835.587 \text{ ft.})^2 + (603.719 \text{ ft.})^2 \right)^{\frac{1}{2}}$

$= 4{,}873.128 \text{ ft.}$

Metric : $= \left((1473.905 \text{ m.})^2 + (184.016 \text{ m.}) \right)^{\frac{1}{2}}$

This slope distance, expressed in yards, is 1,624.376 yds. This number is about 8 yards (24 ft. or 7.32 m.) less than the number

1632 on the stone. To delve further into the speculative, if it were assumed that an early explorer stood on the cairn at E and sighted a man on the cairn at A, his surface measurement of 1,632 yards would appear to be fairly accurate (1 part in 200). That the number 1632 refers to yards may be also suggested in two other ways. First, the basalt stone found under the North Cairn may have been used to roll out the distance between E and A or, more likely, the stone might have been a yard standard to which lengths of survey ropes or wires were compared. Second, the yard was established as a unit of length and fixed as a standard in iron in the Twelfth Century, and has survived through time as equal to the same length as the yard of today.

Another important set of marks on the Wendle Rock is the triangle, whose sides measure 6 in. (0.152 m.), 6 in. (0.152 m.), and 5 in. (0.127 m.), with the number 1632 located along the 5 in. leg. Hence the proportions of the legs among themselves are 1 to 1 or 1.2 to 1. Following the assumption that the 5 in. side represents the line E to A, then the vertice opposite is most likely point Augur (F). In triangle EAF, a very close proportional relationship with Wendle's Rock triangle exists: FA to EA 1.1 to 1; FE to EA is 1.3 to 1 so that the average of FA and FE to AE is 1.2 to 1--the same as either of the 6 in. sides to the 5 in. side on the rock. Point F is an important point, due to its position of high visibility (south to Nehalem Bay and Tillamook) and due to the presence of grooved lines in the rock face next to it.

The above discussion suggests the hypothesis that the line E to A is a baseline, oriented in the North-South magnetic direction. The hypothesis is supported by the fact that this line contains the only cairns in the entire area, indicating a possible intent to monument the line (thereby imparting to the line a greater significance than to the other lines). The hypothesized base line, when compared to a triangulation problem of William Bourne (1) in the year 1578 (see Figure 6), indicates a strong resemblance to this type of survey work. In Bourne's sketch, the line from Kogon Hill to the West Elbery Church is a baseline (the only one in the survey), from the endpoints of which emanate lines of sight to intersected stations. Though the printing on Bourne's sketch is poor, it is seen that the baseline is oriented in a North-South direction (across the page). The scale of Bourne's sketch is 1:52,800 or about 1 in. = 4,400 ft. (0.025 m. = 1,341.136 m.). The ends of the baseline measure 1.1 in. (0.028 m.) on the map, or about 4,840 ft. (1,475.250 m.), which is only 33 ft. (10.058 m.) less than the 4,873 ft. (1,485.308 m.) of the proposed Neahkahnie baseline. The Bourne baseline is shorter than most of the lines to the intersected stations. The same characteristic is exhibited in the Neahkahnie baseline, with E to A being shorter than the lines to F.

If the baseline hypothesis is accepted, it may be argued that the survey's purpose, besides being an act of possession, was to indicate topography and/or area. Area computations were among the common surveying practices in the Sixteenth Century (1):

> ...two or three measurements are taken around the
> side of the hill or valley; then a straight line
> is run from the foot of the hill to its top or from
> the top of the valley to its bottom....The area of
> each triangle is computed, and the total area of the
> irregular figure is found by adding the separate areas.

180

The above procedure roughly fits the Neahkahnie survey east of
the baseline, with the topography broken into three sub-area
triangles: (1) LCRR-3, (2) LRR-3ER-4 and (3) LEER-4 (see Figure
4). These three sub-areas divide the subtended surface into
fairly equal topographical divisions. The northernmost triangle
contains 5.75 vertical contours (an elevation change of 230 ft.
(70.105 m.)) and is about 19.5 acres in area. The southernmost
triangle contains 4.50 vertical contours (an elevation change
of 180 ft. (54.865 m.)) and is about 25.3 acres in area. The
middle triangle contains 5 contour intervals (an elevation change
of 200 ft. (60.961 m.)) and is about 18.1 acres in area.

Analysis of the survey area west of the baseline reveals
that the Center Rock station (L) is an important point. Station
L might possibly have been a point for a radial survey. Station
L is physically near the center of the survey area. The grooved
lines on the rock, arranged like spokes on a wheel, emanate from
the center and if each is prolonged graphically they show a fairly thorough coverage of the survey area. Further, most of these
prolonged lines, or rays, intersect key survey stations. Rays 1
and 6 tie Station L to the baseline. Ray 5 intersects the top
of the western peak of the mountain. Ray 4 ties to station F,
Ray 8 ties to RR-3 and is presumably involved in the above discussed area computation. Ray 10 intersects ER-4. Rays 2 and 3,
which point out to the ocean, may indicate ties to anchored ships
near shore. This possibility is to be discussed below. The purposes of rays 7 and 9 are not readily apparent, though they may
reveal more artifacts if further field work is conducted.

The graphically obtained azimuths between Station L and the survey stations in Figure 4 show close agreement with inverses computed from the traverse data, as Table 7 depicts.

Table 7: Azimuths (from North) at L (to nearest minute)

Line	Azimuths From Graphical Projections*		Azimuths From Traverse Inverses	
	°	'	°	'
L--E	194	24	196	39
L--F	298	38	296	42
L--K3	322	26	325	44
L--ER4	170	18	173	30
L--4C	25	48	27	28
L--RR3	109	26	104	03

*These azimuths were obtained in the following manner: with the theodolite set up over the Center Rock L, the circle was oriented to the correct basis of bearings by backsighting the previous station. A string line was pulled taught along each grooved line, thereby extending each line to be sighted. Each azimuth so obtained was graphically prolonged.

Similarly, grooved lines on other rocks were graphically projected and compared with traverse inverses, with these results tabulated in Table 8.

Table 8: Azimuths (from North) of Key Stations

Line	Azimuths From Graphical Projections*		Azimuths From Traverse Inverses	
	°	'	°	'
H--RR3	25	58	26	25
P--E	151	03	152	25
Rock A--F	308	36	311	37
ER4--F	311	03	313	57
D--E	201	11	201	19
D--RR3	171	16	169	19

* These azimuths were obtained as described in the note to Table 7.

Analysis of the data in Tables 7 and 8 show good conformity of graphical to mathematical, which is supportive of the hypothesis of an ancient survey.

The long lines of sight necessary in the ancient survey could be achieved only in the presence of minimal vegetation, a condition which actually occurred at least once in modern history. Photographs of the mountain in the early 1900's reveal bared slopes and high visibility. The native inhabitants, in fact, burned the area frequently to aid their hunting.

Further work needs to be done in the Neahkahnie area. The area north and west of the mountain could be investigated. Ray 5 from Station L could be prolonged over the top of Neahkahnie to see if any additional artifacts exist. Rays 7 and 9, which point in the northeast and southeast directions, respectively, could yield more information if further investigation is conducted.

Concluding Remarks

Concluding remarks concern the question of who authored the ancient survey. It was stated above that Francis Drake is a leading candidate, though there is no certainly that he performed the survey. In fact, the case for Drake is largely circumstantial; the comparisons with the Bourne Survey and the formation of cairns are convenient in that they dovetail with the evidence, but as such they provide no solid proofs. One piece of written evidence exists, however, which makes a stronger case for Drake. In the 1890's a Neahkahnie treasure hunter dis-

covered a rock containing the word "DEOS" carved into it.
This word is a pseudonym for the Spanish word for God (Dios),
and is important because a crewman of Drake's, apparently una-
ware of the correct spelling, affixed the word "DEOS" to a map
made recently after the circumnavigation (see Figures 7 and 8).
This evidence certainly implies that the Spanish (who correctly
spelled the word in their transcripts) did not make the carving
but argues that Drake's charges were responsible. Figure 8
also provides a clue concerning Rays 2 and 3, which may have been
directed to (or from) anchored ships. As Figure 8 shows, ties
from ship to shore were made for orientation (or, as research
has indicated, to calculate longitude).

DE
DEOS
8 inches Thick
Sketch of rock at Nehalem, Oregon
B. F. H. Shephard Oct 22° 1895
37 years ago
B.C
F W Shephard
Nelson. BC.
Oct 22- 1895

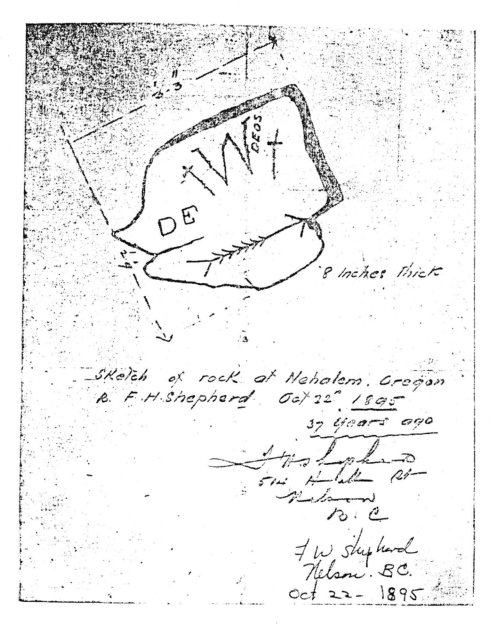

Figure 7: Sketch of Rock, Found in 1895, Containing the Word "DEOS".

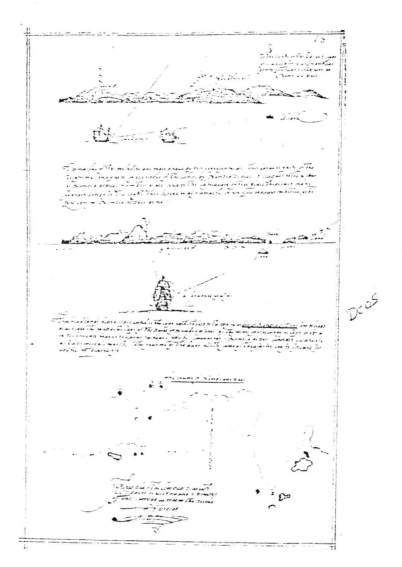

VIEW OF NOMBRE DE DIOS

This watercolor sketch, made during Drake's last voyage to the Spanish Main (1595-1596), shows the care with which the sixteenth-century seaman noted details of sea and shore. Today's sailor could easily orient himself by means of these graphic notes.

Courtesy of Bibliothèque Nationale, Paris

Figure 8: Sketch Made by Drake or One of His Crewmen.

28

Appendix 1.--References

1. Richeson, A. W., English Land Measuring to 1800: Instruments and Practice, MIT Press, 1966, p.51.
1. Ibid., p.38.

Appendix 2.--Bibliography

Andrews, Kenneth R., Drake's Voyages: A Reassessment of Their Place In Elizabethan Maritime Expansion. Chas. Scribners Sons, New York, 1967.

Barry, Austin, Errors in Practical Measurement in Science, Engineering and Technology, John Wiley & Sons, Inc., New York, 1978.

Benson, E.F., Sir Francis Drake. John Lanes, New York, 1927.

Blumenstein, Lynn, "Neahkahnie-Oregon's Historical Treasure Site," A.T. Evans 'Treasure Hunters' Yearbook, 1974-75 Edition (No publishing information- available from M. Wayne Jensen).

Boyce, William E., and Richard C. DiPrima, Elementary Differential Equations and Boundary Value Problems, 3rd Edition, John Wiley & Sons, Inc., New York, 1977.

Breed, Charles B., and George L. Hosmer, The Principles & Practice of Surveying, Vol I., Elementary Surveying, 11th Edition, Revised by Dr. W. Faig, P. Eng., John Wiley & Sons, Inc., 1977.

Brinker, Russell C., Elementary Surveying, 5th Ed., International Textbook Co., Scrantan, PA., 1969.

Brinker, Russell C., and Paul R. Wolf, Elementary Surveying, 6th Ed., IEP-A Dun-Donnelley Publisher, New York, 1977.

Brown, Curtis M., and Winfield H. Eldridge, Evidence and Procedures for Boundary Location, John Wiley & Sons, Inc., New York, 1962.

Clark, David, Plane and Geodetic Surveying for Engineers, Vol. I, Plane Surveying, Constable & Co., LTD, London, 1961.

Clark, David, Plane and Geodetic Surveying for Engineers, Vol., II, Higher Surveying, Constable & Co., LTD, London, 1963.

Corbett, Julian S., Drake and the Tudor Navy, 2 Vols. Burt Franklin, New York, Reprint of 1899 Publication.

Davis, John, Voyages and Works of John Davis, The Navigator Hakylut Society, Vol. 59, Burt Franklin, New York, 1880 (Reprinted, no date).

Davis, Lee W., Elements of Calculus for Technical Students, Canfield Press, San Francisco, CA, 1971.

Davis, Raymond E., and Francis S. Foote, Surveying Theory and Practice, 4th Edition, McGraw-Hill Book Company, Inc., New York, 1953.

El Hult, Ruby, Lost Mines and Treasures of the Pacific Northwest. Binfords and Mort, Portland, OR., 1957.

El Hult, Ruby, Treasure Hunting Northwest, Binfords & Mort, Portland, OR, 1971.

Ernst, Joseph W., With Compass and Chain: Federal Land Surveyors in the Old Northwest, 1785-1816. Arno Press, New York, 1979.

Ewing, Clair E., and Michael M. Mitchell, Introduction to Geodesy, American Elsevier Pub. Co., Inc., New York, 3rd Print., 1976.

Garland, G.D., The Earth's Shape and Gravity, Pergamon Press, Oxford, 1977.

Gunther, R.T., "The Astrolabe: Its Uses and Derivatives," Scottish Geographical Magazine, Vol. 43, No. 1, May, 1927, pp. 135-47.

Guye, Samuel, and Henry Michel, Time and Space: Measuring Instruments From the 15th to 19th Centuries. Praeger Pubs., New York, 1970.

Hakylut Society, The Three Voyages of Martin Frobisher, In Search of Passage to Cathaia and India By the Northwest AD 1576-78.

Hampden, John (Editor), Francis Drake, Privateer, University of Alabama Press, Alabama, 1972.

Hannah, Warren L., Lost Harbor: The Controversy Over Drake's California Anchorage, Univ. of California Press, Los Angeles, CA, 1979.

Hart, William L., College Algebra & Trigonometry, D.C. Health & Co., Boston, 1959.

Head, Lewis M., "Neahkahnie Mountain: The Most Beautiful Spot on the Pacific Coast," S.G. Reed Pub., Portland, OR, 1910.

Keller, Arthur S., Oliver J. Libsitzyn, and Frederick J. Mann, Creation of Rights of Soverignty Through Symbolic Acts 1400-1800, AMS Press, Inc., New York, 1967.

Kissam, Philip, Surveying for Civil Engineers, McGraw-Hill Book Co., Inc., New York, 1956.

Kline, Morris, Calculus: An Intuitive and Physical Appraoch, 2nd Edition, John Wiley & Sons, Inc., New York, 1977.

Lissitzyn, Oliver J., International Law Today and Tomorrow, Published for the Parker School of Foreign and Comparative Law, Columbia University, Oceana Publications, Ic., Dobbs Ferry, N.Y., 1965.

Mackie, J.B., The Elements of Astronomy for Surveyors, Sixth Edition, Charles Griffin & Co., LTD, London, 1964.

McEntyre, Land Survey Systems, John Wiley & Sons, New York, 1978.

McKee, Alexander, The Queen's Corsair: Drake's Journey of Circumnavigation 1577-1580. Souvenir Press, London, 1978.

Mikhail, Edward M., Observations and Least Squares, IEP Dun-Donnelley Harper & Row Publ., New York, 1976.

Mikhail, Edward M., and Gordon Gracie, Analysis and Adjustment of Survey Measurements, Van Nostrand Reinhold Co., New York, 1981.

Moffitt, Francis H., Photogrammetry, 2nd Edition, International Textbook Co., Scranton, Pennsylvania, 1967.

Moffitt, Francis H., and Harry Bouchard, Surveying, Sixth Edition, Intext Educational Publishers, New York, 1975.

Mueller, Ivan I., Spherical & Practical Astronomy as Applied to Geodesy, Frederick Ungar Publ. Co., New York, 1977.

Neter, John, and William Waserman, Applied Linear Statistical Models Regression, Analysis of Variance, & Experimental Designs, 7th Printing, Richard D. Irwin, Inc., Homewood, Illinois, 1974.

Nuttall, Zelia, Ed., Trans., New Light on Drake: A Collection of Documents Relating to His Voyage of Circumnavigation, 1577-80. Cambridge Univ. Press, London, 1914.

Ott, Lyman, An Introduction to Statistical Methods and Data Analysis, Duxbury Press, North Scitvate, MA, 1977.

Price, Derek J., "Medieval Land Surveying and Topographical Maps," The Geographical Journal, Vol CXXI, Part I, March, 1955, pp. 1-10.

Rainsford, Hume F., Survey Adjustments and Least Squares, Constable & Co., LTD., London, 1957.

Reasonover, John Roy, Land Measures: French, Spanish and English Land Measures of the U.S. and Canada. Houston, 1946, Privately Printed.

Richeson, A.W., English Land Measuring To 1800: Instruments and Practice, MIT Press, Cambridge, MA, 1966.

Salas, S.L., and Einar Hille, Calculus: One & Several Variables with Analytic Geometry, 3rd Edition, John Wiley & Sons, Inc., New York, 1978.

Settle, Dionyse, Laste Voyage Into the West and Northwest Regions By Martin Frobisher London 1577, (#88, "The English Experience: Its Record in Early Printed Books, Published in Facsimile). Da Capo Press, New York, 1969.

Shrestha, Ramesh L., "Least Squres Adjustment Computer Programs for Horizontal and Vertical Positions, Master's of Science Thesis, Oregon State University, Corvallis, Oregon, 1979.

Snedecor, George W., and William G. Cochran, Statistical Methods, 6th Edition, The Iowa State University Press, Ames, Iowa, 1978.

Taylor, E.G.R., "The Plane-Table in the Sixteenth Century," Scottish Geographical Magazine, No. 4, July, 1929, pp. 205-11.

Taylor, E.G.R., "Instructions to a Colonial Surveyor in 1582," Mariner's Mirror, Vol. 31, No. 1, January 1951, pp. 48-62.

Thomsen, Don W., Men and Meridians: History of Surveying and Mapping in Canada, Vol. I (Prior to 1867). Queen's Printer, Ottawa, 1966.

Thomson, George M., Sir Francis Drake. William Morrison, New York, 1972.

Wagner, Henry R., Sir Francis Drake's Voyage Around the World: Its Aims and Achievements. John Howell, San Francisco, 1926.

Ward, Robert, "Drake and the Oregon Coast," Published in England. The author sent copies to M. Wayne Jensen.

Waters, D.W., The Art of Navigation in England in Elizabethan and Early Stuart Times, Yale University Press, New Haven, CT, 1958.

Williamson, J.A., Sir Francis Drake. Archon Books, Hamden, Conn., 1966.

Appendix II   Wood Samples of ships in Nehalem Bay

The following documents describe the wood samples taken from the two reported shipwrecks which were seen at various times in the Nehalem Bay.

UNIVERSITY OF WASHINGTON
SEATTLE, WASHINGTON 98105

July 27, 1970

College of Forest Resources

E. W. Giesecke
318 North Rogers Street
Olympia, Washington   98501

Dear Mr. Giesecke:

After more than a week's work I more fully realize the lack of adequate keys for identifying samples such as yours. The detective work is not quick and easy. The limited amount of transverse surface (end grain) area in such small samples give inadequate information for some of the major identification features of tropical woods, namely pare patterns and parenchyma distribution. I have had to fall back on microscopic characteristics in the radial and tangential views, so it has been slow going.

The conclusions I reach are that samples No. 1 and 2 are both teak <u>Tectona grandis</u> but of quite different growth rates. No. 1 is more like a sample we have from Malaya, while No. 2 is closer to the growth of samples from the Philippines and India. This is no proof of origin as we know growth rates vary from tree to tree or within trees in one locality.

Sample No. 3 is Greenheart <u>Ocotea Sp.</u> probably from West Indies, Guiana or South America. This was very difficult to determine.

Sample No. 4 keys out to Lignum vitae, <u>Guaiacum officinale</u> or <u>G. Sanctum</u>, which is from the West Indies or Central America.

Sample #1 is from Ben Lane's table top — rut from sandspit wreckage.

As for origin of the wood you can say Sample No. 1 could have come from the Philippines or Malaya region. Sample No. 3 is West Indies or Central America.

I hope this information is helpful in your research. ~~If you are able to have sample which identified I would appreciate knowing what it is.~~

Yours sincerely,

Lawrence Leney
Associate Professor, Wood Science
and Technology

LL/n

P.S. I identified #3 when this letter was being typed so the last line should have been omitted. Do not want to take time for retyping if this is to get in the mail.

192

318 N. Rogers St.
Olympia, Wash.
98501

August 3, 1970

Alex Walker, Curator
Tillamook Pioneer Museum
Tillamook, Oregon

Dear Mr. Walker:

Enclosed is a very interesting letter from Dr. Lawrence
Leney, of the University of Washington. In it he
gives us some support for the "beeswax" ship being of
a Philippine origin. This is one step closer to the
wreck being identified as a Manila galleon, possibly the
San Francisco Xavier.

Sample #1 was sliced from the bottom of a table top, this
table being located in the Columbia River Maritime Museum,
Astoria. It is a small table; they keep it in their
office. The late Ben Lane, former Mayor of Manzanita, told
me several times that he had had this table made for him
some 40 years ago, from "a piece of teak from the wreckage
of the galleon at Manzanita." I have since searched high
and low for other pieces, but non can be found, so we have
to be content with the table top at Astoria.

I feel Dr. Leney's statement, "As for origin of the wood
you can say Sample #1 could have come from the Philippines
or Malaya region," is very important. As you know, the
Manila galleons were constructed in Manila out of locally
grown woods. The beeswax itself has already been radiocarbon dated as of 1685 and identified as being from the
Orient. Thus, this teak wood sample from southeast Asia
further supports the beeswax ship tradition. The next
step is to obtain a large enough piece from Rolf Klep to
have the wood radio-carbon dated, to establish the cutoff
date before which the ship could not have been built.
As you know, I have a copy of the cargo listing of the
Xavier showing that it actually did carry large amounts of
wax (the list provided by Dr. Warren Cook.)

(Sample #2, for your information, was a "control" piece of
teak. I obtained this from an India built ship which now
rests at the bottom of Sydney Inlet, Vancouver Island. This
ship was built in Bombay in the 1830's. The samples #3 and
#4 were given me by Wayne Jensen of your city. He had
obtained these from an old lady in Rockaway, who stated that
they came from the Manzanita wreckage; unfortunately, their
origin being given as West Indies or Central America does
not on the surface help with the Manila location, unless
certain hardwoods (Lignum vitae is the hardest and heaviest
known wood, 89 lbs per cubic foot) were exported from Mexico
to Manila for the construction work in the Philippines.)

I have full confidence in the Sample #1 being just what Ben
Lane told me that it was, that it came from timbers on the
Nehalem sandspit, not far from where most of the beeswax
was found. You may wish to help obtain a larger piece from
the table top at Astoria for radio carbon dating. If you
wish to make this news known to the press, you may do so.

Sincerely,
E. W. Giesecke

There were 2 shipwrecks at the mouth of the Nehalem Bay of which Wayne Jensen
received the wood samples from one of the wrecks. Giesecke ignored samples 3 & 4

because he was looking for wood from the Philippines where Spanish galleons were built. Sample # 3 & 4 may be from Tello's Bark, built near Nicaragua, Central America.

illuminators, might have been a theme to treat of, but the beeswax of Nehalem had pounded in the surf until battered and blackened out of all recognition, and had no essential claim for inspiration until its history developed to cause imagination and fancy to wonder at its origin.

When Lewis and Clark wintered at the mouth of the Columbia—a century ago—they learned the first we knew officially of this flotsam of the seas, for they told of seeing it in the hands of natives. In 1814, one Henry, connected with the fur trade, who travelled and wrote of what he saw, published to the British world that beeswax had been dug out of the sands and was found drifting on the ocean shore, to his great wonder. It is thus evident that the memory of living man goes not back to the time when this beeswax was not known to the natives at the mouth of the great river.

My personal cognizance of it goes back to 1870, when my family made a summer trip from the Willamette to Tillamook, fifty or sixty miles south of the Columbia, and brought back small pieces of the beeswax, as also various traditions concerning the ancient wreck that might have left it there. The bones of two wrecks were then to be seen at the mouth of the Nehalem River, that enters the ocean a few miles north of Tillamook Bay.

Clark, Samuel A., Oregon Native Son and Historical Magazine, Legend of Nehalem, Vol. II, No. 1, pg 169, Native Son Publishing, Portland, Oregon May

Appendix III Oregon Geography and Archaeological Institute of America Reports

These documents verify Indian archaeological sites and Nehalem Bay geological changes over the last three hundred years.

I A S
Institute for Archaeological Studies

October 15, 1989

Leland Gilsen, Ph.D.
Historic Preservation Office
State Parks and Recreation
525 Trade Street
Salem OR 97318

Dear Dr. Gilsen:

Enclosed is a research plan for archaeological work, which we would like to apply to a limited area of the Nehalem Bay State Park. The area that we have designated for investigation is illustrated on the enclosed map, and is located within the Park boundaries, as defined by the USGS Nehalem Quadrangle, 7.5 minute, 1985 Provisional Series.

The preferred periods of field work would be June 14-30 and August 1-15, 1990. These dates would allow for the avoidance of on-site work during the periods of maximum Park usage, as suggested by Park personnel. During the interim period, Institute archaeologists would attempt to monitor both this area and 35-TI-4b.

The preliminary report for the 1989 work at 35-TI-4b, and the reports for the other sites observed, are in process. The expected date of completion is October 15, 1989, with the final report to be submitted to the State-designated recipients by November 30, 1989. It is the findings of the multi-disciplinary investigation of the sand spit area that have indicated a need for the work proposed for 1990. The findings by Portland State University geologist Leonard Palmer, Ph.D. and University anthropologist Daniel Scheans, Ph.D., resulted in the identification of a pre-existing river channel, as well as other pertinent features. These findings, discussed in the project description, are also illustrated in the enclosed Appendix.

Please let us know if any other information is needed, prior to the approval of this request for permit for 1990. Proof of insurance will be provided, prior to the onset of field work, in the amount provided during our 1989 investigation on State lands.

Sincerely,

Alison T. Stenger
Research Director

ATS/tt

cc:
State Historic Preservation Office
Division of State Lands
National Park Service
University of Oregon
Portland State University
File

4235 S.W. Westdale Dr.   Portland, OR 97221   (503) 292-5862

I A S
Institute for Archaeological Studies

PROJECT BACKGROUND

In 1989, the Institute for Archaeological Studies initiated an investigation of a portion of the Nehalem Bay sand spit (see Appendix I). Based upon a survey of the existing literature, and upon previously documented work in the area, deposits of prehistoric and historic materials were anticipated. Field work, involving survey and limited data collection, verified the existence of these deposits. The findings of this 1989 project, with recommendations and conclusions, are expected to be submitted to the appropriate agencies by the end of November.

The occurrence of intrusive investigations of the sand spit over a period of years had resulted in broad zones of erosion. These deflated surfaces, while yielding numerous artifacts, also acted to encourage some archaeologists and members of the public to continue probing the fringes of the shoreline. Thus, in an effort to examine the area without continuing to impact the fragile environment, the Institute for Archaeological Studies chose to utilize remote sensing equipment. The GeoRadar II was selected for its subsurface profiling capabilities, and because of its documented success in locating specific types of non-metallic materials. Stratified subsurface areas were often recorded in detail by this device (see Appendix II). However, although the angles and spacing of the signals were adjusted to accommodate the areas of inspection, the salinity in some regions resulted in signal interference. In an effort to calibrate the machine, and to correctly interpret the resulting printouts, selected areas distant from the present tidal zone were examined. The GeoRadar II reliably demonstrated its ability to document numerous subsurface intrusions, including the utility pipes that currently service Nehalem Bay State Park.

While the goal of the 1989 project was to compile and add any information that might be beneficial to National Register nomination, the immediate need was to ascertain the source(s) of the materials that occurred within the site area. The 19th century artifacts would subsequently be sourced to the Donation Land Claim and Homestead era residences of Cronen and White, as well as to the lumber business that also occupied the area. The prehistoric assemblage, which will be discussed at length in the November report, reflected a "use" area. An occupation area was not indicated in this area, although houses and a midden were documented to the north of our research area. The Asian porcelains, which were responsible for many of the initial concerns about the area, maintained several important attributes that indicated some form of 17th century contact.

4235 S.W. Westdale Dr.   Portland, OR 97221   (503) 292-5862

196

The exposure of indigenous people to populations from distant regions may have been indirect. Cargo, in the form of crates of porcelains, may have drifted into the shallows and then been recovered by the Indians. Alternately, these porcelains may have reached the sand spit through trade with other tribes. Another explanation for the occurrence of the wares may have been through the wreck of a ship within an area accessible to the Indians. Were this to have occurred, the contents of the ship would have provided a resource for additional materials, making any attempts at recovery worth pursuing.

Many legends surround the proto-contact period. Yet, a common theme exists within each of these accounts. Contact, or at the very least, exposure to foreign materials, occurs through an association with the ocean. All of the accounts include descriptions of the vessels, usually discussed as whale-like forms. Often, these "whales" have trees on top, while many also carry men. Vessels with masts, a-typical of coastal Indian crafts, would have been representative of both European and Asian ships.

Ethnohistorical accounts, documented within the earliest periods of western contact, further indicate exposure to foreign populations. Some of these accounts specifically describe foreign peoples coming in contact with local populations. Also, ethnographers observed and recorded refined and worked metals, in the possession of Indians who did not have the technology to manufacture these items.

The research questions have begun to focus upon the potentials of early contact. The people, methods of contact, and locations of occurrence have become primary in the investigations of this region of the coast. Because Asian porcelains have been the primary indicator of contact, it has become necessary to explore the routes by which this material may have arrived. And based upon the many accounts of maritime contact, in combination with the high frequency with which the porcelains have been observed on the sand spit, it seems appropriate to investigate potential shipwreck locations within the immediate area of Nehalem Bay State Park.

Based upon the results of the work in the area by the Institute for Archaeological Studies, an access route from the Pacific Ocean to the Bay may have been located. If this route is legitimate, then the ship discussed in early newspaper accounts may be entrenched in this old channel. The location and verification of this ship would allow for nomination to the National Register, and protect this historically significant vessel from exploitation.

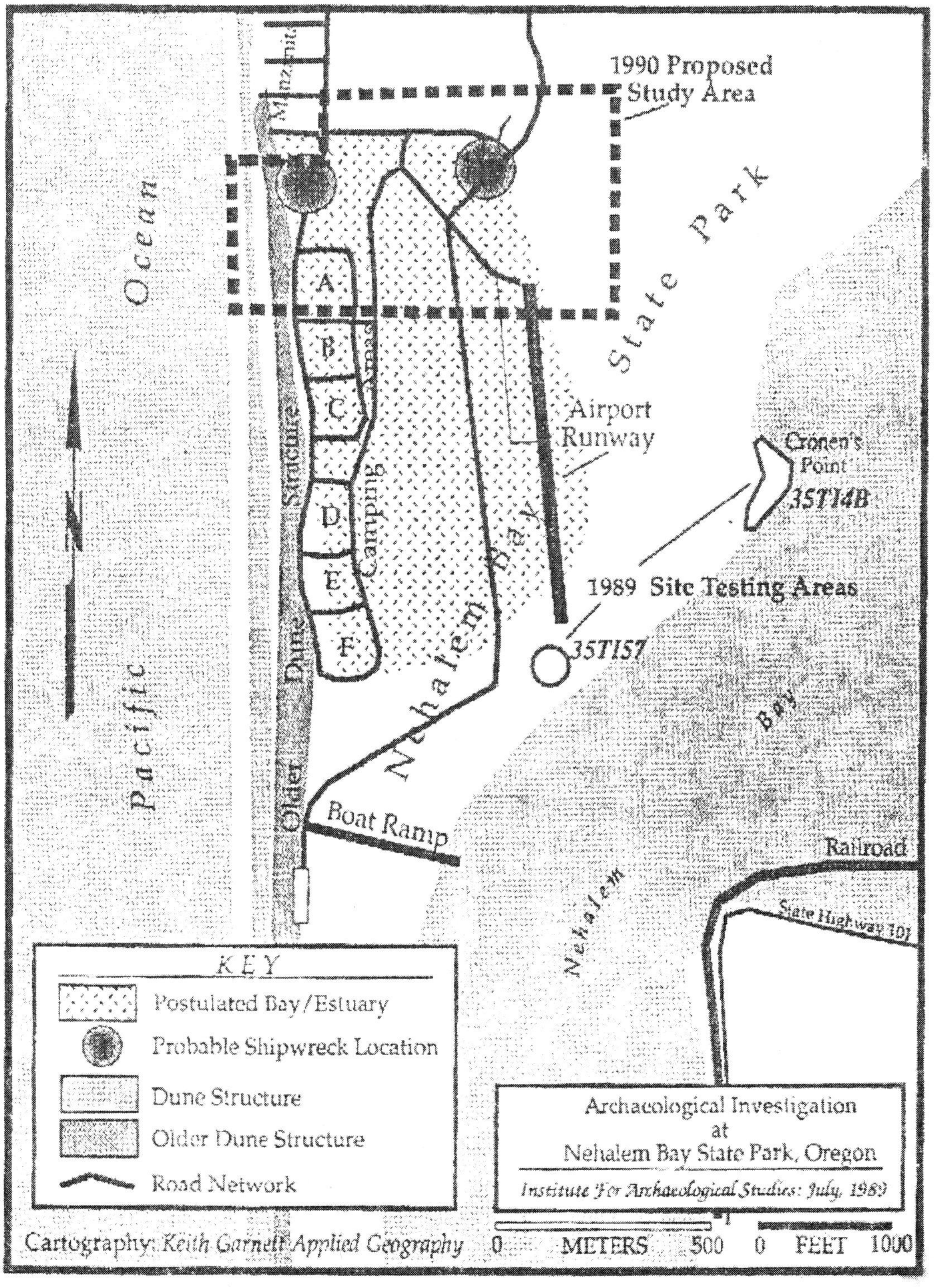
1990 Proposed Study Area
Manzanita
Pacific Ocean
State Park
Airport Runway
Cronen's Point
35TI48
1989 Site Testing Areas
35TI57
Older Dune Structure
Camping Areas
A
B
C
D
E
F
Nehalem Bay
Bay
Nehalem
Boat Ramp
Railroad
State Highway 101
KEY
Postulated Bay/Estuary
Probable Shipwreck Location
Dune Structure
Older Dune Structure
Road Network
Archaeological Investigation at Nehalem Bay State Park, Oregon
Institute For Archaeological Studies: July, 1989
Cartography: Keith Garnett Applied Geography
0 METERS 500
0 FEET 1000

APPENDIX III: AREAS OF INVESTIGATION FOR 1990. THE PROBABLE SHIPWRECK LOCALES ARE THE PRIMARY FOCUS.

Paleoseismicity and the archaeological record: Areas of investigation on the northern Oregon coast

by John Woodward, archaeologist, Mount Hood Community College, 26000 SE Stark, Gresham, Oregon 97030; James White, consultant and shell expert, P.O. Box 795, Portland, Oregon 97207; and Ronald Cummings, archaeological technician, 11933 SE Foster Road, Portland, Oregon 97266.

INTRODUCTION

"Then everything got dark; no one could see anything. The men could not go fishing, women were unable to go root digging, nothing could be done. Very soon the water began to rise. Many small things were drowned, small people.... That little muskrat came back. He carried that sun.... Everywhere there was daylight again, and all the flood went down" (Jacobs and Jacobs, 1959, p. 83-84).

This quotation is from a Nehalem-Tillamook myth recorded in 1934 by anthropologist Elizabeth Jacobs. The storyteller was Clara Pearson, probably the last fluent speaker of the Nehalem language on the northern Oregon coast. According to Mrs. Pearson, this story with its catastrophic flooding belonged to the earliest time period of the Tillamook oral literature. Stories of the myth age were assigned to happenings long before the 19th century.

Although great flood myths are frequently encountered worldwide, can this Nehalem version have originated in an actual event that happened on the northern Oregon coast between 300 and 400 years ago? Recently, geological, dendrochronological, and archaeological evidence has been produced to support the theory that coastal areas of Oregon and Washington have experienced catastrophic earthquake-generated subsidence or tsunami flooding (known popularly as "tidal waves") or both at least twice in the last 1,000 years.

This theory has now been widely reported in both scientific and popular literature. Yeats (1989) writes, "The submergence of archaeological sites indicates that earthquakes affected Native American communities prior to the establishment of a culture that kept written records."

The earthquake-subsidence record evidence for the Oregon and Washington coasts first received widespread public interest following publication of a paper by B.F. Atwater in *Science* in 1987 (Atwater, 1987). Atwater presents the results of a geologic study of the Washington coast, showing that during the last 7,000 years intertidal mud has rapidly buried coastal marshes at least six times. Atwater writes, "Nothing other than rapid tectonic subsidence readily explains the burial of the peat layers." At Willapa Bay, a sand sheet extending 3 km inland and covering a marsh surface is attributed to an earthquake-generated tsunami.

Tsunamis, or seismic sea waves, can take several forms. Seismic sea waves are very low and long, with sea heights of less than 1 m. Moving as shallow-water waves, their velocity and coastal crest height vary greatly due to bottom contours, headland refraction, and other local variables. These multiply or reduce wave height and may result in either a huge cresting wave front or simply an unusually rapid rise in water level. Another variable of a tsunami's local effect on estuaries is the magnitude of the seiching, or shore-to-shore ("bathtub") wave action, that occurs in wave-disruptive bodies of water that are partially enclosed. Bascom (1980) writes, "A Pacific tsunami will usually succeed in exciting all the bays and harbors around its rim. Often these will oscillate for days." Tsunami-generated seiches can occur harmonically, with water-level changes in a bay happening every few minutes and exceeding in height the normal tidal fluctuations. Such events in shallow estuaries could result in significant bank erosion and mud deposition.

The source of the rapid subsidence and earthquake-generated tsunamis is likely to be a megathrust earthquake on the Cascadia Subduction Zone that extends less than 100 km off the coast of Washington and Oregon. Although there is no historic precedent, Heaton and Hartzell (1987) indicate that earthquakes of great magnitude might occur on the Cascadia Subduction Zone, generating ground shaking lasting longer than two minutes and causing tsunamis of significant size. Subduction zone megathrust earthquakes in an analogous situation in Japan have generated local tsunami heights of greater than 6 m. A great subduction megathrust earthquake in Chile in 1960 generated local run-up heights exceeding 20 m.

At Netarts Bay (Figure 1) on the Oregon coast, Peterson and others (1988) have also shown the presence of rapidly buried marshes that they attribute to episodes of abrupt coastal subsidence. Twelve core sites in marsh lands of this bay showed several episodes of marsh burial in the last 3,300 years. Radiocarbon analysis indicates that the most recent events occurred less than 400 years before the present (B.P.). A date of A.D. 1580±60 was obtained from the top of a marsh surface that is overlain by a sediment-capping layer associated with "catastrophic sheet floods over the subsided marsh system" (Peterson and others, 1988). In another, more recent paper, Darienzo and Peterson (1990) present additional data derived from sediment and diatom analyses that further support the presence of tectonic subsidence and tsunami deposition at Netarts Bay.

COLUMBIA RIVER
ASTORIA
SEASIDE
NEHALEM BAY
TILLAMOOK BAY
NETARTS BAY
0
10
MILES
N
WASHINGTON
PORTLAND
OREGON
0
150
MILES
NORTHERN OREGON COAST

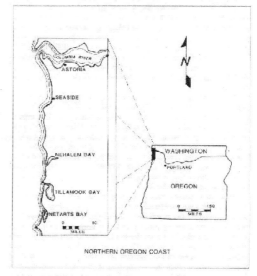

Figure 1. Map of the northern Oregon coast showing locations discussed in the text.

Grant and McLaren (1987) describe a similar buried marsh at the Salmon River estuary, approximately 40 km south of Netarts Bay, with evidence of a landward-directed surge of sandy water that deposited a thin layer of capping sand for at least 2 km along the Salmon River estuary. At Nehalem Bay, Grant found a marsh buried beneath sand and silt that she attributes to an episode of rapid subsidence.

nonshell midden are more numerous and include both stemmed and leaf-shaped forms (Figure 3). The largest number of arrow points are stemmed forms recovered from the mixed upper deposits, where they were redeposited during the 20th century by leveling and filling of the site.

The midden deposits at the Wilson River site appear to show very significant environmental changes in Tillamook Bay over at least the last 1,000 years. These changes resulted in shifts in the availability of shellfish obtained within the catchment area of the site's inhabitants. Such shifts were apparently not viewed by the prehistoric inhabitants as sufficiently disruptive to bring about abandonment or relocation of the site. Also, they do not necessarily indicate abrupt subsidence at this location. (The inundated materials might be interpreted as the result of prehistoric trash disposal into the Wilson River rather than as changes in sea level.)

Yet, while there is no direct support for earthquake-generated catastrophic change at this locality, the abrupt disappearance in shellfish utilization can be interpreted as indicating that the rapid habitat change resulted from the periodic building and breaching of the sand spit protecting Tillamook Bay. That breaching and disappearing of the sand spit could have been caused by wave erosion from tsunamis and/or bay seiching.

NEHALEM BAY

With a surface area of 4,100 acres, Nehalem Bay is Oregon's fifth largest estuary (Figure 4). This estuary is unusual in that it does not contain the major beds of native shellfish found farther south. The only abundant clam is the softshell, *Mya arenaria* (Linne), found in tidal flats common along the northern and eastern edge of the bay. Although originally thought to have been introduced, its wide range suggests that it may be native. Unlike the other clams found in the estuaries, it has the ability to withstand significant changes in salinity (White, 1976). Because it can survive in low salinity, it is found as far up the Nehalem River as the town of Nehalem. This clam might survive geological changes that would eliminate an estuary or an environment of a very limited estuary. However, its absence in the Nehalem middens suggests that it was recently introduced or was scarce in prehistoric times.

Near the mouth of the Nehalem estuary, we find a relative abundance of native littleneck clams (*Protothaca staminea*). Although this clam prefers a high salinity and is also found in sheltered coves along the open coast, its limited presence in Nehalem Bay would be consistent with a relatively new or re-established estuary. These clams occur in Nehalem middens with a scattered and limited distribution. Gapers, butterclams, and cockles also occur in Nehalem middens in small numbers, where they are intermingled with barnacles, ocean mussels, limpets, and sea snails. This suggests that they are not a nearby resource but were transported to Nehalem Bay through trade or infrequent visits to adjoining waters. In fact, Nehalem Bay, unlike Oregon's other major estuaries, lacks identified shell middens despite the presence of numerous late prehistoric house sites and a significant native population during the early historic period, probably because of the fragile nature of the protecting sand spit. This sand spit many have broken down at intervals sufficiently frequent to prevent the development of those conditions favorable to clam beds.

The oldest documented archaeological site of the group of sites at Nehalem Bay (Site 35TI4) is fully inundated and consists of a layer of fire-cracked rock overlain by a 35-cm-thick stratum of silt (Figure 5). The upper 10 cm of the silt include waterlogged organic materials containing leaves of willow, *Salix* sp., and red alder, *Alnus rubra*. Also present is moss (*Sphagnum* sp.), a cone of red cedar (*Thuja plicata*), and numerous seeds of Sitka spruce (*Picea sitchensis*). Wood fragments and small logs also occur at the top of the silt and include Douglas fir (*Pseudotsuga menziesii*). These plants are found around Nehalem Bay at forested wetland margins located at present no closer than 0.9 km from this site. Fragments of a waterlogged twinned mat woven from Douglas fir root were found at the top of the silt. A portion of the mat has been radiocarbon dated to 380±60 years B.P., with a calibrated range of A.D. 1410-1635 (Woodward, 1986). This date is consistent with the radiocarbon date of 370±60 years B.P., with a calibration range of A.D. 1431-1660, obtained from the top of a buried marsh at Netarts (Peterson and others, 1988). The silt layer is interpreted as having formed in a sheltered tidal marsh that developed behind a prehistoric sand spit. Sand dunes bordering this marsh stabilized and were invaded by a dense growth of Sitka spruce, willows, red alder, and shrubs, creating a spruce swamp/tidal channel habitat. Leaves and other vegetation fell, were washed directly into a body of quiet shallow water, and there covered with silt. This phase ended abruptly between 300 and 400 years ago

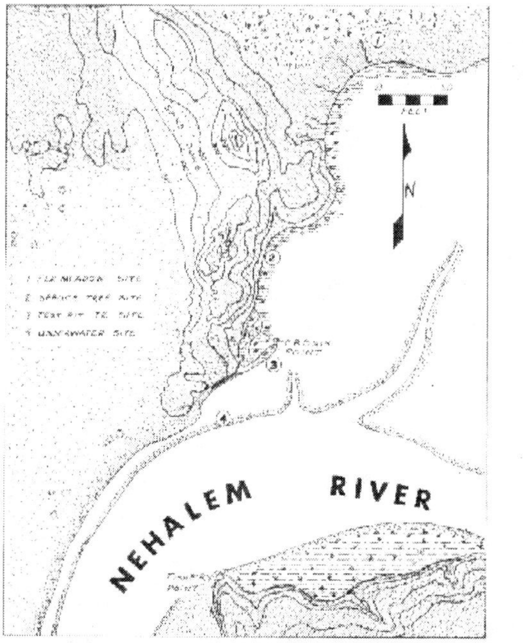
N
NEHALEM RIVER

Figure 4. Nehalem Bay redrawn from 1875 map (U.S. Coast Survey Chart, 1875), showing sites discussed in text.

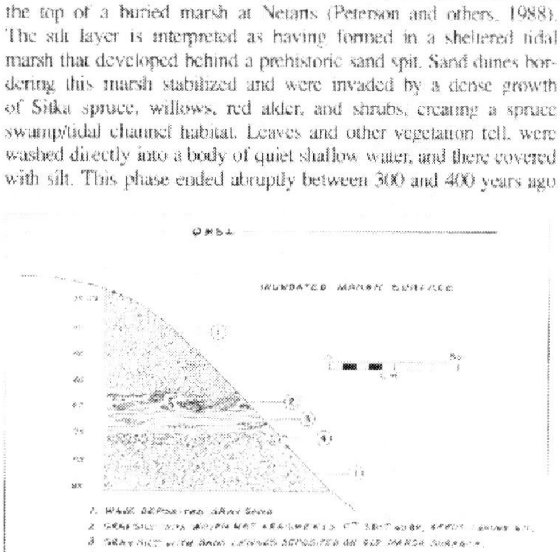

Figure 5. Underwater site, Nehalem Bay. MSL = Mean Sea Level.

with the disappearance of the sand spit and burial of the spruce swamp with wave transported sand. This was a potentially catastrophic event for any prehistoric community at this location. More recently, channel shifts have cut into the deposits and exposed the edge of the site.

A portion of Nehalem Bay Site 35T14 is on Cronin Point, which is shown as a tidal marsh in an 1875 geodetic survey of the bay (U.S. Coast Survey Chart, 1875) (Figure 4). At present, a portion of the southern edge of this marsh is experiencing seasonal tidal bank erosion, but other areas are being invaded by wave deposited alluvium including both sand and cultural material eroded from the bank. These processes occur primarily during the fall and winter. During the spring and summer, silt tends to cover the site, which is largely stabilized by the growth of grasses.

Archaeological testing of this site in 1980 consisted of the excavation of four 1-m by 2-m test pits that were excavated to the summer low-tide water table. Stratigraphic profiles of two of these test pits are shown in Figures 6 and 7. They show evidence of repeated burial of marsh surfaces by wave-deposited sediments. The most recent episode of this process began during the late 19th century and is continuing today. Materials currently moving across the site include a partially sorted deposit consisting primarily of sand, lithic rubble, and mixed cultural materials of all ages. The first author has observed materials, including fist-sized rocks and recent debris, to have been transported at least a meter to the north-northeast by a single intense storm. In 1980, experiments conducted near the site showed that modern ceramic fragments between 1 cm and 5 cm in diameter were transported by incoming tidal action between 2 and 3 m a year in this direction, even without intense storm-tidal action. This rate suggests that much of the fire-cracked rock and artifacts observed at this site originated 200-300 years B.P. and were originally in situ about 550 m southwest of Cronin Point. The rate of littoral transport would, of course, be much more rapid if the Nehalem sand spit did not exist and the location were an open beach. Experiments cited in Bascom (1980) show that some of 600 radioactive pebbles tracked during an experiment on the east coast of England were moved as much as a mile from their original location.

The pattern of frequent episodic marsh burial at Cronin Point during late prehistoric and historic times makes the identification of possible tsunamis difficult because their effects are not easily differentiated from local effects of intense wave action generated by Pacific storms.

At the Spruce Tree site of 35T14, in situ cultural material occurs beneath a sand dune (Figure 8). At the time this site was occupied, a Sitka spruce swamp existed at this locality.

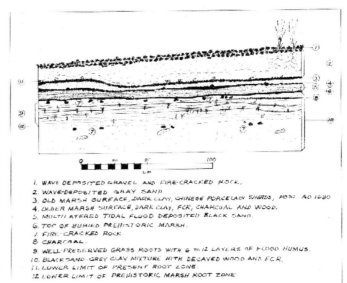

1. WAVE DEPOSITED GRAVEL AND FIRE-CRACKED ROCK.
2. WAVE-DEPOSITED GRAY SAND.
3. OLD MARSH SURFACE, DARK CLAY, CHINESE PORCELAIN SHERDS, POST AD 1680
4. OLDER MARSH SURFACE, DARK CLAY, FCR, CHARCOAL AND WOOD.
5. MULTI-LAYERED TIDAL FLOOD DEPOSITED BLACK SAND.
6. TOP OF BURIED PREHISTORIC MARSH.
7. FIRE-CRACKED ROCK.
8. CHARCOAL.
9. WELL-PRESERVED GRASS ROOTS WITH 6 TO 12 LAYERS OF FLOOD HUMUS.
10. BLACK SAND-GREY CLAY MIXTURE WITH DECAYED WOOD AND FCR.
11. LOWER LIMIT OF PRESENT ROOT ZONE.
12. LOWER LIMIT OF PREHISTORIC MARSH ROOT ZONE.

Figure 6. Cronin Point stratigraphy, West Wall Test Pit T2P1, Site 35T14, Nehalem Bay.

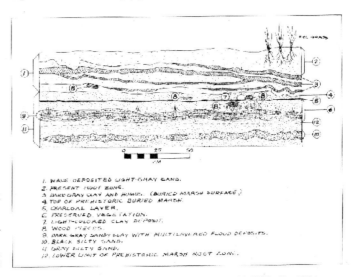

1. WAVE DEPOSITED LIGHT-GRAY SAND.
2. PRESENT ROOT ZONE.
3. DARK GRAY CLAY AND HUMUS. (BURIED MARSH SURFACE.)
4. TOP OF PREHISTORIC BURIED MARSH.
5. CHARCOAL LAYER.
6. PRESERVED VEGETATION.
7. LIGHT-COLORED CLAY DEPOSIT.
8. WOOD PIECES.
9. DARK GRAY SANDY CLAY WITH MULTILAYERED FLOOD DEPOSITS.
10. BLACK SILTY SAND.
11. GRAY SILTY SAND.
12. LOWER LIMIT OF PREHISTORIC MARSH ROOT ZONE.

Figure 7. Nehalem Bay stratigraphy, West Wall Test Pit T2P2, Site 35T14.

which is now marked by partially inundated roots of these trees. Fire-cracked rock and artifacts occur here on the present marsh surface. A radiocarbon date of 260±40 years B.P. with a calibration of A.D. 1490-1670 has been obtained from charcoal associated with cultural materials (Woodward, 1986).

In 1989, the first author conducted test excavations at the Elk Meadow site of 35T14

(Figure 9). This site is at the same elevation as the Spruce Tree site on the edge of a sand terrace that extends above sea level at least 2 km north. This site also has inundated spruce tree roots and is shown as forested on the Nehalem Bay survey of 1875. Since 1875, this forest has been replaced by a tidal marsh that has moved north at least 35 m since the site was occupied. The archaeolog-

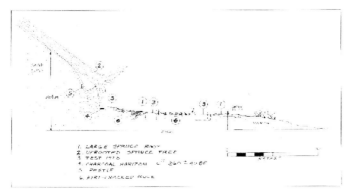

Figure 8. Spruce Tree site, Nehalem Bay.

OPEN MEADOW
SPRUCE TREE
METERS
SAND AND
EEL GRASS
MUD - TIDE FLATS

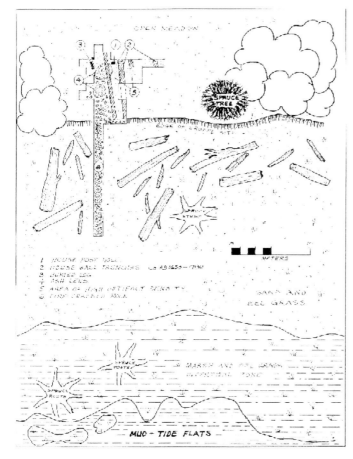

Figure 9. Elk Meadow site, Nehalem Bay.

ical excavations show that a plank(?) house at least 8.5 m long had been constructed fully above ground on the sand sheet. Evidence of food preparation includes a large amount of fire-cracked rock and small fragments of mammal and fish bones. The only bone large enough for identification was identified as from a Roosevelt elk (*Cervus roosevelti*). It is significant that shellfish are entirely absent.

The lithic artifacts recovered from the site include two pestles, eight small arrow points, a stone knife, and 25 hide scrapers (Figures 10, 11, and 12). Beeswax, Chinese ceramics, and iron, lead, and bronze artifacts that were found on the house floor are attributed to a shipwreck (or more) on the Nehalem sand spit (Figures 13 and 14). Absent are glass beads, rolled copper ornaments, or other artifacts associated with the early historic period. This house site, with its primary emphasis on hunting, fishing, cooking, and hide preparation, is dated to ca. A.D. 1650-1780.

The tidal archaeological sites around the Nehalem estuary show that rapid habitat and land-form changes have been ongoing since at least ca. 400 years B.P. Many of these are probably cyclic and associated with the position of the Nehalem River channel and the form of the Nehalem sand spit. At one earlier dated site, however, fully inundated cultural materials were found in association with a wetland pond/Sitka spruce swamp rapidly buried by a massive sand sheet. This burial may be interpreted as evidence of seismic-generated subsidence, a tsunami, or both. Such events would probably have brought about wave erosion of any protecting sand spit and would have exposed Nehalem Bay directly to ocean waves. One result of this could have been the formation of the beach-sand terrace on which the Spruce Tree and Elk Meadow sites are situated.

Geodetic survey maps and photographs made between 1868 (U.S. Coast Survey Chart, 1868) and 1940 show the Nehalem sand spit as a low, narrow, wind-deflated surface almost entirely devoid of vegetation. During the 19th century, the wrecks of possibly two ships were periodically visible on the spit following episodes of wind erosion. The last recorded time that a wreck was visible was 1926. Between 1890 and 1916, one wreck with exposed ribs, a keel, and teak wood decking was partially stripped of its wood, which was then locally used to make furniture and souvenir walking canes. In 1989, the Quaternary Isotope Laboratory of the University of Washington obtained a radiocarbon date of A.D. 1638±21 (M. Stuiver, personal communication, 1989) from one of these Asian teak-wood (*Tectona grandis*) canes that had been in museum storage. With the age calibration of Stuiver, two age ranges were obtained: A.D. 1517-1593 and A.D. 1620-1639. The Quaternary Isotope Laboratory has also recorded a date of A.D. 1640±20 (M. Stuiver, personal communication, 1990) from a ship's pulley that was made

of an Asian wood (*Calophyllum* sp.) (Figure 15). Calibration of this date is A.D. 1519-1589 or A.D. 1622-1639. The pulley was found in 1896 on or near the teak-wood wreck.

The presence of shipwreck debris on the Nehalem spit indicates

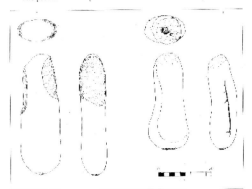

Figure 10. Stone artifacts, Elk Meadow site.

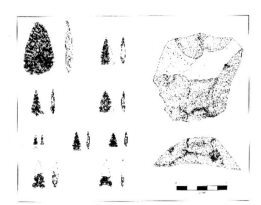

Figure 11. Flaked stone artifacts, Elk Meadow site.

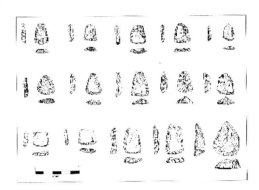

Figure 12. Hide scrapers, Elk Meadow site.

that the present spit has been in place in some form since at least the early 17th century. The teak-wood wreck lay on its side and is at present buried beneath about 3 m of wind-blown sand. This suggests that at the time of the wrecks, the spit assumed a far lower, more barlike configuration than it now has.

SEASIDE

At Seaside, Clatsop County, a three-site cluster situated on an old beach terrace was excavated by amateur archaeologists in the 1970's (Phebus and Drucker, 1979). Although a complete report is not available, some data concerning these shell middens have been published.

Radiocarbon dates show that the earliest occupation was established on a cobble terrace by at least 600 B.C. This culture, in addition to fishing and the hunting of land and sea mammals, collected bay clams (described as *Schizothaerus nuttallii*, *Saxidomus giganteus*, and *Protothaca staminea*), cockles (*Cardium* sp.), and sea mussels (*Mytilus californianus*). The likely source of the bay shellfish was the now-filled Necanicum estuary.

The site's stable occupation continued with no observed changes in midden composition until site abandonment about 185 B.C. Brief reoccupation is indicated about A.D. 200. A second period of intensive use of the locality occurred between A.D. 245 and 915. The shell middens from this second period lack the estuary shellfish but instead are composed primarily of sea mussels. Sea snails, barnacles, and

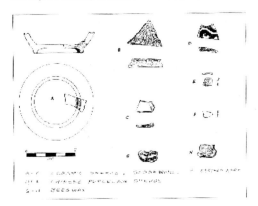

Figure 13. Ceramic and beeswax artifacts, Elk Meadow site.

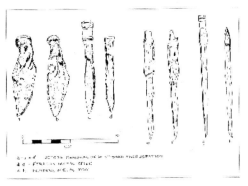

Figure 14. Iron artifacts, Elk Meadow site.

64

Figure 15. Ship's pulley from prehistoric shipwreck on Nehalem sand spit. Photo courtesy of Wayne Jensen, Jr.

razor clams were also observed, indicating that, at this time, the Necanicum estuary no longer was extant, and an open-beach environment existed similar to that found at Seaside today.

Although artifacts from both the bay-clam and the mussel-collecting cultures exhibit similar bone and stone tool types, there are enough significant differences in house form, artistic expression, and woodworking technology to indicate that the littoral mussel collectors may not have been the direct descendents of the earlier bay clam collectors. There is archaeological evidence that a population replacement occurred between A.D. 200 and 300 and was directly linked to a relatively rapid change in the Necanicum estuary and loss of its major shellfish resources. Phebus and Drucker (1979) conclude that "...the Seaside area, north of Tillamook Head, has undergone some dramatic topographical alterations that must have certainly required some serious economic adjustment on the part of the native population."

CONCLUSIONS

Archaeological sites located near four present or prehistoric estuaries on the northern Oregon coast show evidence of landform/habitat changes associated with sand-spit stability during the last 2,000 years. Shellfish utilization by prehistoric inhabitants is an important indicator of estuary change that may be the result of rapid subsidence, tsunamis, or intense-storm waves. At Netarts, Tillamook, and Nehalem Bays, we find inundated archaeological materials that suggest sea-level changes resulting from subsidence. However, prehistoric human occupation at Netarts and Tillamook

Bays appears to have continued without being affected by catastrophic events. One of the archaeological sites on Nehalem Bay shows an episode of rapid microenvironmental changes and sand burial attributed to a tsunami, subsidence, or both. The result of this episode, which likely occurred between 300 and 400 years B.P., may have been catastrophic for any inhabitants of the site.

ACKNOWLEDGMENTS

We wish to express our special appreciation to Sharon Woodward for her assistance with excavation supervision, artifact drawing, and typing of this report. Barbara McCorkle also helped with artifact analysis and drawing, and Wayne Jensen of the Tillamook Pioneer Museum provided important support for archaeological research in Tillamook Bay. C. Dale Snow kindly took time to review the report, and Steve Cragg located funds for radiocarbon dating. Susan Foster and Jack Foster of Mount Hood Community College assisted in identification of faunal remains.

REFERENCES

Atwater, B.F., 1987, Evidence for great Holocene earthquakes along the outer coast of Washington State: Science, v. 236, p. 942-944.

Bascom, W., 1980, Waves and beaches: New York, Doubleday, Anchor Press, 366 p.

Carver, G.A., and Burke, R.M., 1987, Late Holocene paleoseismicity of the southern end of the Cascadia subduction zone [abs.]: EOS, v. 68, no. 44, p. 1240.

Darienzo, M.E., and Peterson, C.D., 1990, Episodic tectonic subsidence of late Holocene salt marshes, northern Oregon central Cascadia margin [abs.]: Tectonics, v. 9, no. 1, p. 1-22.

Grant, W.C., and McLaren, D.D., 1987, Evidence for Holocene subduction earthquakes along the northern Oregon coast [abs.]: EOS, v. 68, no. 44, p. 1239.

Heaton, T.H., and Hartzell, S.H., 1987, Earthquake hazards on the Cascadia Subduction Zone: Science, v. 236, p. 162-168.

Hill, R., 1989, NW coast tree rings hold clues to quakes: The Oregonian, December 14, 1989, p. 61, 63.

Jacobs, E.D., and Jacobs, M., 1959, Nehalem Bay tales: Eugene, Oreg., University of Oregon Monographs, Studies in Anthropology, 216 p.

Newman, T., 1959, Tillamook prehistory and its relation to the Northwest coast culture area: Eugene, Oreg., University of Oregon doctoral dissertation, 118 p.

Oregon Department of Fish and Wildlife, 1982, Oregon's captivating clams: Corvallis, Oreg., Oregon State University Extension Service, Sea Grant Publication 28, 10 p.

Peterson, C.D., Darienzo, M.E., and Parker, M., 1988, Coastal neotectonic field trip guide for Netarts Bay, Oregon: Oregon Geology, v. 50, no. 9/10, p. 99-106.

Phebus, G.E., and Drucker, R., 1979, Archaeological investigations at Seaside, Oregon: Seaside, Oreg., Seaside Museum and Historical Society, n. pag.

Sauter, J., and Johnson, B., 1974, Tillamook Indians of the Oregon coast: Portland, Oreg., Binford and Mort, 196 p.

Steele, H., 1986, Nonferrous objects from 35TI1 metallurgical and metallographic comparisons: Unpublished manuscript, available from Harvey Steele, P.O. Box 13293, Portland, OR 97213.

U.S. Coast Survey Chart, 1868, Oregon Historical Society Manuscript 775: Portland, Oreg., Oregon Historical Society Library.

———. 1875, Oregon Historical Society Manuscript 782: Portland, Oreg., Oregon Historical Society Library.

Vaughan, W., 1852, An early history of Tillamook, 1851-1852: Tillamook, Oreg., Tillamook County Pioneer Museum manuscript.

White, J., 1976, Seashells of the Pacific Northwest: Portland, Oreg., Binford and Mort, 127 p.

Woodward, J.A., 1986, Prehistoric shipwrecks on the Oregon coast? Archaeological evidence, in Ames, K., ed., Oregon Archaeologists Association, Third Annual Symposium, Portland, Oreg., 1985, Proceedings: Albany, Oreg., Social Science Department, Linn Benton Community College, p. 219-264.

Yamaguchi, D.K., Woodhouse, C.A., and Reid, M.S., 1989, Tree-ring evidence for synchronous rapid submergence of the southwestern Washington coast 300 years B.P. [abs.]: EOS, v. 70, no. 43, p. 1332.

Yeats, R., 1989, Current assessment of earthquake hazard in Oregon: Oregon Geology, v. 51, no. 5, p. 90-91. □

204

The case of the counterclockwise river

by John Eliot Allen, Emeritus Professor of Geology, Portland State University, Portland, Oregon 97207-0751

INTRODUCTION

A tiny creek appears just east of Cochran, a former Southern Pacific Railroad station located at the summit elevation of 1,808 ft in a little-known pass through the northern Coast Range of Oregon. For 6 mi, the creek flows east to the town of Timber, where the valley widens and the creek, gathering water from several tributaries, meanders north for almost 10 mi across narrow flood plains and then turns northeast for 4 mi to Vernonia.

Within slightly incised meanders through a narrower valley, the creek continues from Vernonia north-northeast for 5 mi, then north-northwest for 5 mi, and northwest 4 mi to the town of Mist. There it takes a 6-mi arc to the west and southwest to arrive at Birkenfeld, where it begins a generally southwest-trending and deeply incised meandering course for 25 mi to the mouth of the Salmonberry River, a stream that completes the oval, since only 14 mi upstream to the east, the headwaters of one of its tributaries begin just south of Cochran, within a mile of where our river began!

This is the peculiar 65-mi-long counterclockwise loop made by the Nehalem River around the heart of the northern Coast Range before it turns west-southwest for the last 15 mi through deeply incised meanders to Nehalem Bay and the Pacific Ocean. The width of the Coast Range between Forest Grove and Tillamook Bay is less than 40 mi; the Nehalem River valley is more than 90 mi long.

DISCUSSION

The purpose of this essay is to develop multiple hypotheses, one of which might account for this apparently anomalous course of the Nehalem River, a minor geomorphic puzzle that has intrigued me for more than 40 years, ever since the publication of the first geologic map of the area (Warren and others, 1945). Old fashioned armchair geomorphic analysis, "reading the contours" of topographic maps, which I have sometimes indulged in since my retirement (Allen, 1975, 1989a,b) can occasionally furnish valuable insights into the geologic history of an area.

I have heard that the course of the Nehalem River caught the attention of interpreters scanning satellite images, looking for "astroblemes," structures produced by the impact of large meteorites or comets. Although this hypothesis (no. 1) can be quickly discarded, another hypothesis (no. 2) is suggested by similar drainage patterns that can form within giant calderas produced by great volcanic explosions.

Structural uplift or doming, as in the Black Hills of South Dakota, is a third more likely explanation (no. 3); its implications will be explored later. Still another hypothesis (no. 4) suggests that the Miocene Nehalem River, originally flowing east into the Columbia, was diverted north and then west by flows of Yakima Basalt filling the ancestral Columbia River valley.

Geographic factors that can be investigated during a study of these hypotheses are statistics on relative rainfall, length and gra-

drainage divide
Seaside
Nehalem
Birkenfeld
Mist
Sunset
Highway
Jewell Junction
Vernonia
River
Nehalem
North
Fork
River
Salmonberry
Nehalem
Nehalem
Creek
Timber
Cochran
divide
drainage
Nehalem
0 5 10
MILES

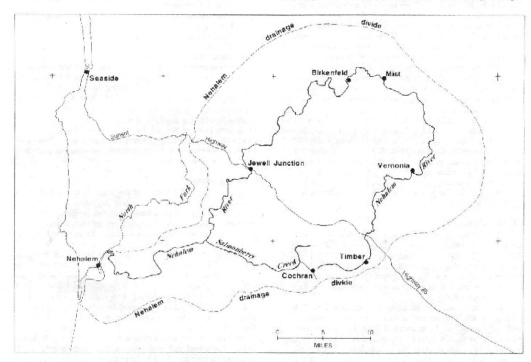

Figure 1. Index map showing counterclockwise course and drainage area of the Nehalem River in northwest Oregon.

dients of stream channels, and changes of drainage divides. Geomorphic features to be studied include presence or absence of meanders (especially when incised), different valley-wall slopes and benches or terraces, upland surfaces of low relief (which used to be called "peneplains"), and barbed tributaries.

Along the Oregon coast, geologic and geomorphic features were studied by Lund (1971, 1972a,b, 1973a,b, 1974a,b, 1975), but within the northern Oregon Coast Range, possibly due to heavy vegetation, the geologic maps of Warren and others (1945), Wells and Peck (1961), and Niem and Niem (1985) are the only ones that have been published, and no geomorphic studies have been made.

Areal geology and bedrock structure ("ground truth") must always be considered whenever geologic maps are available, since bedrock characteristics can affect drainage patterns and result in drainage changes due to differential erosion. Dipping strata can cause lateral migration of valleys. Vertical beds or a fault zone may result in a straight valley course. Tight folding may result in an Appalachian type trellis pattern, and domal uplift may produce both radial and concentric patterns.

GEOGRAPHY

Careful map measurements on seven 15-minute quadrangles (Birkenfeld, Cathlamet, Enright, Nehalem, Saddle Mountain, Timber, and Vernonia) gave the length of the Nehalem River valley as 88 mi, with a valley gradient of 20 ft per mi (determined by dividing the change in elevation between the start and end of the river, which is 1,808 ft, by the length of the river, which is 88 mi, giving a gradient of approximately 20.5 ft per mi). Repeated, more precise measurements following each meander gave a "channel length" of 121 mi. The average river gradient (1,808 ft divided by 121 mi = 14.9 ft per mi) itself is thus approximately 15 ft per mi.

One tributary of the Salmonberry River rises near Cochran and joins the river, which flows 14 mi westerly to its mouth on the Nehalem at an elevation of 231 ft. The Salmonberry River thus completes the southwest 55° of the 305° Nehalem loop, with a channel gradient of 113 ft per mi (1,808 ft – 231 ft = 1,577 ft divided by 14 mi = 113 ft per mi), 7.53 times that of the Nehalem. The area within this loop is nearly 300 mi², while the area within the Nehalem River drainage (excluding the North Fork) is a little more than twice that.

Average annual rainfall in the northern Coast Range is higher than anywhere else in Oregon, being 110 in. at Nehalem near the mouth of the river and 130 in. at Glenora on the Wilson River, 10 mi southwest of Cochran. West of the main drainage divide of the Coast Range, adiabatic/orographic rainfall is greater than to the east, and stream gradients are steeper since they travel a much shorter distance to the sea. Erosion on the west side of the northern Coast Range could well have been more rapid than anywhere else in the state.

GEOMORPHOLOGY

Barbed tributaries in the Coast Range can indicate stream capture of the headwaters of streams flowing east into the Willamette River. Barbed tributaries on both the South and North Forks of the Salmonberry River suggest that at least 8 mi of the Nehalem has been captured and that the North Fork before its capture at a point 1½ mi west of Cochran once formed the headwaters of the Nehalem River.

The result of such stream captures is that the Coast Range drainage divide here lies farther to the east than anywhere else north of Eugene. At its easternmost limit, the divide now lies within 12 mi of the Columbia River; south of the Nehalem drainage basin, the Coast Range divide lies 15 mi farther to the west. At its northern limit, the Nehalem drainage divide lies only 2 mi south of the Columbia River.

Usually a stream will constantly adjust its course so as to run on the most easily eroded bed rock. The location of a stream then is nearly always a result of such differential erosion of the various kinds (stratigraphy) and the folding and fracturing (structure) of the bed rock. Thus the stream may follow a bed of soft shale lying between more resistant sandstone layers, or it may follow a zone of broken rock caused by a fault or sets of closely spaced joints.

Within the Nehalem drainage basin, upland areas of gently rolling surfaces can be observed on several of the quadrangles. These could be interpreted as remnants of a once continuous, late mature or early old-age erosion surface. Elevations on this surface usually lie between 800 and 1,200 ft, with few ridges and prominences rising above them to above 2,000 ft.

The Nehalem drainage divide is marked by several basaltic prominences reaching nearly 3,000 ft or more. Among these are Saddle Mountain, Humbug Mountain, Onion Peak, Pinochle Peak, Rogers Peak, Larch Mountain, and Round Top.

STRATIGRAPHY AND STRUCTURE

The cast of our detective story must include the geologic formations making up the northern Coast Range, whose names and ages are as follows (Baldwin, 1981):

Miocene (5.3 to 23.7 million years):
 Yakima Basalt Subgroup of the Columbia River Basalt Group
 Astoria Formation
Miocene and Oligocene:
 Scappoose Formation
Oligocene (23.7 to 36.6 million years):
 Pittsburg Bluff Formation
Eocene (36.6 to 57.8 million years):
 Keasey Formation
 Goble Volcanics
 Cowlitz Formation
 Yamhill Formation
 Tillamook Volcanics
 Siletz Volcanics

The most important player in this "Case of the Nehalem Loop" is certainly the Keasey Formation, an easily eroded mudstone and shale, with the underlying resistant lavas of the Goble and Tillamook Volcanics and the overlying Pittsburg Bluff sandstones as supporting players and possibly the Yakima Basalt also entering into the plot.

Faulting appears not to have significantly interrupted the contacts of the formations or affected the course of the Nehalem. The relatively straight 25-mi-long, generally east-west course of the Salmonberry and upper Nehalem might suggest this, but such a fracture has not yet been mapped.

CONCLUSIONS

A much simplified history of the main structural feature involving the above formations, as first suggested by Warren and others (1945) and later presented on the state geologic map (Wells and Peck, 1961), indicates that beginning perhaps in late Miocene time, the formations named above began to be arched up into a north-northeast-plunging geanticline.

Millions of years of slow erosion then beveled off this giant fold, reducing it to a surface of low relief, with streams meandering near sea level. Eocene volcanic rocks were exposed in the core of the fold, and outcrops of the later sedimentary formations formed arcuate belts around the plunging north end of the fold. Pliocene and later uplift eventually rejuvenated the streams and incised their meanders into the rising lowlands, etching out valleys in the weaker Keasey Formation.

One resulting deduction (hypothesis no. 3, modified) is that during this second period of uplift and resulting orographically increased rainfall, the Nehalem River captured all the streams that occupied the arcuate belt of Keasey shale during the rapid clockwise

206

headward erosion of most of the upper part of its valley.

For the 45 mi from Timber to Jewell Junction, the Nehalem River follows this Keasey belt, with the exception of a 10-mi stretch north of Vernonia, where its meanders have cut less than a mile into the Pittsburg Bluff Formation. The lower 40 mi of the valley, from Jewell Junction to Nehalem Bay, is mostly carved in resistant Tillamook Volcanics. The river originally meandered across a surface of low relief, now uplifted to 800–1,000 ft, upon which the major drainage pattern was established as the range began to rise.

The lower course of the river became fixed within the underlying volcanic rocks, but the upper course migrated down-dip on the "slip-off" contact at the base of the Keasey shale, moving the Coast Range drainage divide 10 to 15 mi to the north and east.

Still another possible deduction (hypothesis no. 4) proposes that a middle Miocene Nehalem River, which originally flowed east across a topography of low relief, was diverted north and west by flows of Yakima Basalt that filled a former broad valley of the Columbia River, then located 10-20 mi west and south of its present course. Today, numerous erosional remnants of basalt lie less than 10 mi from the Nehalem River along most of its course.

Whichever hypothesis is finally chosen (and the main purpose of this discussion is to spur further investigation), the Nehalem River remains the longest river within the Oregon Coast Range and the only one with 305° of counterclockwise course.

REFERENCES

Allen, J.E., 1975, The Wallowa "ice cap" of northeastern Oregon, an exercise in the interpretation of glacial landforms: Oregon Department of Geology and Mineral Industries, Ore Bin, v. 37, no. 12, p. 189-202.
——— 1989a, Ice age glaciers and lakes south of the Columbia River Gorge: Oregon Geology, v. 51, no. 1, p. 12-14.
——— 1989b, Northwest topographic maps: Geological Society of the Oregon Country Newsletter, v. 55, no. 11, p. 153-156.
Baldwin, E.M., 1981, Geology of Oregon, 3rd ed.: Dubuque, Iowa, Kendall/Hunt, 170 p.
Lund, E.H., 1971, Coastal landforms between Florence and Yachats, Oregon: Oregon Department of Geology and Mineral Industries, Ore Bin, v. 33, no. 2, p. 21-44.
——— 1972a, Coastal landforms between Tillamook Bay and the Columbia River, Oregon: Oregon Department of Geology and Mineral Industries, Ore Bin, v. 34, no. 11, p. 173-194.
——— 1972b, Coastal landforms between Yachats and Newport, Oregon: Oregon Department of Geology and Mineral Industries, Ore Bin, v. 34, no. 5, p. 73-91.
——— 1973a, Landforms along the coast of southern Coos County, Oregon: Oregon Department of Geology and Mineral Industries, Ore Bin, v. 35, no. 12, p. 189-210.
——— 1973b, Oregon coastal dunes between Coos Bay and Sea Lion Point: Oregon Department of Geology and Mineral Industries, Ore Bin, v. 35, no. 5, p. 73-92.
——— 1974a, Coastal landforms between Roads End and Tillamook Bay, Oregon: Oregon Department of Geology and Mineral Industries, Ore Bin, v. 36, no. 11, p. 173-195.
——— 1974b, Rock units and coastal landforms between Newport and Lincoln City, Oregon: Oregon Department of Geology and Mineral Industries, Ore Bin, v. 36, no. 5, p. 69-90.
——— 1975, Landforms along the coast of Curry County, Oregon: Oregon Department of Geology and Mineral Industries, Ore Bin, v. 37, no. 4, p. 57-76.
Niem, A.R., and Niem, W.A., 1985, Oil and gas investigation of the Astoria Basin, Clatsop and northernmost Tillamook Counties, northwest Oregon: Oregon Department of Geology and Mineral Industries Oil and Gas Investigation 14, 8 p., 1 map, 1 correlation chart.
Warren, W.C., Norbisrath, H., and Grivetti, R.M., 1945, Geology of northwestern Oregon west of the Willamette River and north of latitude 45° 15′: U.S. Geological Survey Oil and Gas Investigation Map OM-42.
Wells, F.G., and Peck, D.L., 1961, Geologic map of Oregon west of the 121st meridian: U.S. Geological Survey Miscellaneous Geological Investigations Map I-325. □

Hungarian appeals to mineral collectors

We have received a request from a mineral collector in Budapest, Hungary, and we are passing it on, hoping to reach some collectors interested in contacting this person. His letter is printed below, with a few editorial changes needed to clarify the writer's English.
(Editors)

Budapest, October 30, 1989

I am sorry I cannot write to you in my poor English.

I am a Hungarian mineral collector. That is unusual in Hungary, so it's very difficult for me. In Hungary, we have only few people whose profession is mineral collecting.

In early 1989, the Society for Popularization of Scientific Knowledge approached me, because I have a considerable collection, and they want to make a comprehensive exhibit of my collection. I was happy, but I haven't one perfect, good mineral from your country.

If it were possible for you to send me any mineral from the U.S.A., I would be very happy and grateful, and it would be a great help for my exhibit.

I offer to send Hungarian minerals in exchange. Accurate scientific names with precise locality information (e.g., pegmatite deposits, mineralogy of Nb, Ta, Ti, REE minerals, pegmatite phosphates, feldspars, and minerals of the zeolite group).

In Hungary, we hear very rarely about American minerals. So you can send us what you want. We trust you. Any assistance you can give me in locating literature will also be most appreciated.

Sorry for my poor English again, but I am looking forward to hearing from you soon. Should you wish to send us minerals or literature for our collection, please send them to this address:

> Gabor Tompai
> Geology
> Körösi Csoma ut. 5.
> 9. em. 27.
> H-1102 Budapest
> Hungary.

> Thanks for your kindness!
> Yours very sincerely,
> Gabor Tompai □

Financial assistance for geologic studies in Washington available

Awards to help defray expenses will be available in the 1991 fiscal year for original geologic mapping and other geologic studies that are useful to the Washington Division of Geology and Earth Resources in compiling the new geologic map of Washington.

Available funds will be approximately $15,000 for fiscal year 1991, and awards will be made on the basis of proposals submitted. First priority will be given to proposals for work in areas lying within the northwest and southeast quadrants of the new state geologic map that are currently unmapped, poorly mapped, or poorly understood geologically. Proposals are due by June 4, 1990.

For additional information and suggestions, interested persons may consult with Division staff, specifically J. Eric Schuster, Assistant State Geologist, State Geologic Map Program, Division of Geology and Earth Resources, Department of Natural Resources, Mail Stop PY-12, Olympia, WA 98504, phone (206) 459-6372 or SCAN 585-6372; or Keith L. Stoffel, Geologist, Spokane Field Office, Division of Geology and Earth Resources, Department of Natural Resources, Spokane County Agricultural Center, N. 222 Havana, Spokane, WA 99202, phone (509) 456-3255 or SCAN 545-3255. □

207

Appendix IV John Drake Depositions

John Drake, the young cousin of Francis Drake after having sailing with William Fenton in 1582 and after his capture in South America gave two depositions to the Spanish Inquisition, in 1584 and 1587.   Drake was a imprisoned for the rest of his life by the Spanish and under constant threat of death. These depositions state they sailed to 44° and 48° on each occasion.

On the same day that they released the vessel of the monks, they saw another ship of 120 tons which was going to Panama. They captured her at seven or eight in the evening, although some defence was made with arquebuses and her pilot was wounded. They guarded the ship all night till the morning, when they went below decks (debaxo de cubierta), where they found a great quantity of silver and a little gold, all of which they transferred to the English vessel. They also took a quantity of flour and salted hams. Captain Francis divided among the people of that (? or ' his ' ship) ship some of the plate (baxilla) which she carried. Two or three days after unloading her Captain Francis allowed her to proceed, and continued his voyage towards Mexico (la vuelta de Mexico). The first place he reached was some islands near Nicaragua, the name of which he does not know. Shortly before reaching there they took a ship of fifteen tons laden with maize, which was going to Panama. As soon as they got to these islands they took in water and wood, and remained five or six days. There were Indians there who were hostile, so that they did not land, but continued to follow the coast to Guatulco, taking on the passage a ship that was going to Lima on which was a gentleman named Don Francisco de Zarate, whom they took from his ship and detained for three days. He was captured at seven in the morning without making any defence. His ship was of sixty tons. As far as the deponent remembers, they took five or six bales of cloth and silk from a Flemish merchant on the vessel, but they took nothing from Don Francisco. They took out of the vessel a great quantity of dry biscuit. Captain Francis was very gracious to Don Francisco, and gave him his own poop cabin to sleep in. He took from him a negress whose name was Maria, and they also took the pilot from the vessel.

They saw no other ship until Aguatulco, where they found a vessel of a hundred tons, laden with woollen cloth (ruanes) and linen (lenceria). They took nothing but four or five bales of cloth and various ship's nails. They remained two days in this port, during which they landed and took two or three Spaniards, whom they let go at once, as well as the Portuguese whom they had taken in the island of Mayo.

They continued their voyage with only their own countrymen, the negress named Maria, a negro taken at Payta, another taken at Aguatulco as well as one brought from England. He does not know on what day they left Aguatulco beyond that it was April. They put to sea, making for the N.W. and N.N.E. (?), and sailed during the whole of April and May and half June from Aguatulco.

which lies in fifteen degrees, until they reached eighteen degrees. On the way they met with great storms : the whole sky was obscured and covered with clouds ; they saw five or six islands, to one of which Captain Francis gave the name of St. Bartholomew and to another St. James. These islands were situated in forty-six and forty-eight degrees. Captain Francis gave to the land which lies in forty-eight degrees the name of New England. They remained there a month and a half, taking in wood and water and repairing the ship. From there they went to the islands of Los Ladrones. On account of the cold they went no higher than forty-eight degrees. From New England they steered to the S.W. to the island of Los Ladrones, which is in nine degrees. In these islands there are Indians, very warlike, of whom they killed twenty, as a hundred of their canoes came out. They go about naked. From the islands of Los Ladrones they went, in nine days, to an island the name of which he does not know : it lies in seven degrees, and they steered to it towards the south and the south-west. They remained a day at this island, taking in wood and water. From there they went to the Moluccas, steering to the south-west, and taking twenty days on the voyage. They remained there eight days, buying from the Indians and Moors cloves and ginger ; there is little gold or silver there. There was a Portuguese ship there, but they did not take her or attack her. These islands are well furnished with arms. They took in meat and supplies. They then had sixty men on board. The supplies consisted of cassave, plantains and fowls, which were given in exchange for cloth. From there they went to an island which lies in four degrees north ; as it was uninhabited, they took nothing but wood, water and some crabs. They remained there a month and a half, on account of contrary winds, and left there the two negroes and the negress Maria, with some rice, seeds and fire, in order that they should populate the place. From there they reached an island in eight degrees called Java, populated with Indians. They remained there fifteen days. These Indians gave them rice, cows, fowls and cassave. There were two Portuguese there who hid themselves. In exchange for the supplies they gave the Indians linen (olandas) and cloth. A Portuguese came on board the ship with Indians to see if he could take it. The Indians went about clothed.

From there, without touching land, they went to the Cape of Good Hope. They took two months and a half from the island until they doubled the Cape. They reached it in thirty-five or thirty-six degrees, and came to the mainland in the country of Guinea, but did not anchor, as they did not find a good port and the wind was

The 1584 Deposition says they were at 46 and 48° where Francis Drake named the new land New Albion (New England) in this translated version of the book which also contains the Spanish version.

The Family and Heirs of Sir Francis Drake by Lady Eliott-Drake, Volume II, London 1911

Captain Francis called to them to strike their sails in the name of the Queen of England, and fired a shot which carried away her mizen. A volley of arrows was then fired at the San Juan de Anton, which surrendered. They captured the vessel, with a great quantity of silver, and took her with them for three days, when a calm fell and the silver was transferred to Captain Francis's ship. The San Juan de Anton was then left : on board were the people belonging to her and the other people who had been taken during the voyage from Payta.

Continuing their course, they came to the Island of Cano, where they anchored in order to careen the vessel to clean her (?).¹ While they were there a ship passed, coming from Nicaragua laden with maize and sarsaparilla : they captured her with the launch, although some resistance was made. They left the people of the vessel in the launch in order that they might go away, but they took the vessel and the pilot belonging to the crew, which numbered three or four.

After passing eight or more days at this island, and while in the Gulf of Papagayo, before reaching that place, they fell in with a ship from Mexico in which was Don Francisco de Zarate ; they took out of her some cloth and biscuit, and because the ship was of small value Captain Francis wished to hang the pilot. Because there was a nobleman like Don Francisco on board, Captain Francis received him at his table during the time which he detained him, and then allowed him and his people to go with their vessel, and put on board the pilot of the other vessel which he had previously taken. They took out of Don Francisco's vessel a seaman whose name was Juan Pasqual (sic). They then sailed to the port of Guatuco (sic) where they found a ship. By means of the small vessel he had with him he put some of the people on the land, where he captured a judge, a priest and others and took them off to his ship. They supplied themselves with water and wood, and took some cloth from the vessel as well as a negro : they then set the people at liberty, together with the Portuguese pilot Silvestre whom they had captured before getting to the Straits.

From there they sailed in a N.W. and N.N.W. direction and covered a thousand leagues as far as 44 degrees, always on the bowline, then the wind changed, so they made for the Californias and found land in 48 degrees. They disembarked and made huts, remaining there a month and a half to repair the ship. Their food consisted of cockles (? mexillones) and wolves'² flesh. While they

¹ 'Dar lada' for 'dar la vanda.' ² Seals' flesh.

were there the Indians often came, and when they saw the English they wept and drew blood with their nails from their faces as if they were doing reverence and worshipping them. Captain Francis explained to them by signs that they should not do this, as the English were not gods. The Indians remained peaceful without doing them any harm, although they gave them no food. They are a race of the colour of these Indians (? here in Lima), well disposed : they carry bows and arrows and go naked. The country is temperate, cold rather than hot : a very rich country to the eye.

They repaired their large ship here, and left the one from Nicaragua which they had captured ; they then went away, leaving the Indians apparently sorrowful. Thus they sailed with only one ship in the direction of the Moluccas, but on account of the currents which opposed them they altered their course towards China before reaching one and a half degrees of latitude. They proceeded to the Island of Los Ladrones, which is in nine degrees. There many Indians came to them with fish, and gave it to them in exchange for beads (cuentas) and other trifles. The Indians embarked in canoes which were very well made, with short oars with which they rowed very well ; they were naked and carried darts and stones. They took from each other the beads and things which were given to them in payment : the strongest remained in possession while the quarrelling went on the whole time.

They sailed to a large island called Bosney, where they took in water and wood, and then made for the Moluccas. On the voyage they met a ship and asked for provisions, saying that they were English, that they had the greatest need of the provisions, and that they must take them if the others would not sell them. The people in the ship refused to give them any, on the ground that the English were Lutherans. They followed the ship for that day and night and part of the next day without obtaining any provisions, after that they got to some shallow water where Captain Francis did not dare to enter. On this they left the other ship and went away : they never knew what sort of people were on her, whether Portuguese or from some other country.

They then sailed to another island and took from it two or three Indians to direct them to the Moluccas, keeping these men with them until they reached there. In one island a Portuguese halfbreed promised to take them to a place where provisions might be procured. A Moorish gentleman (? Moro Cavallero), who wished to travel in the ship, came to it in his costume, with a chain, apparently of gold, round his neck and some keys on a small chain of silver.

The 1587 Deposition states they made for California and found land at 48°. There were no places named Oregon, Washington or British Columbia because everything north of New Spain or Mexico was considered an island called California. Additionally, Drake implies they left the Bark of Rodrigo Tello by stating they left with but one ship.

The Family and Heirs of Sir Francis Drake by Lady Eliott-Drake, Volume II, London 1911

Appendix V Charcoal under Monument Measurement Rock

This Appendix contains an exchange of documents between Wayne Jensen and the University of Georgia, Geochronology Laboratory, Athens, Georgia pertaining to charcoal pieces from a fire which had been built under the north cairn of which the Measurement Rock Monument was place atop the cairn. The carbon dating of the charcoal from the north cairn arrived at a date of 855 + or - 55 years old before present.

Sample Report form for Radiocarbon Age Determination

Please submit with Samples

Sample # 1

 Sample Name (location or other)
 NORTH MOUND - NEAH-KAH-NIE MT.

 Material (i.e. wood, charcoal, bone, shells)
 CHARCOAL
 Location, including lat. & long.
 45° 44.50' LATITUDE
 123° 75' LONGITUDE

Occurrence and stratigraphic and/or archaeological history.
 A PIT DUG AND WOOD BURNED AND COVERED OVER WITH DIRT, A MOUND BUILT
 OF STONE OVER THIS TO MARK ANCIENT SURVEY. BELIEVE TO BE DONE IN 1579

Name of Collection and Date of Collection
 SAMPLE OF CHARCOAL COLLECTED MARCH 29,1975
Name and Address of person submitting sample
 M.WAYNE JENSEN JR.
 2250 NEILSEN ROAD, TILLAMOOK, OREGON 97141

Comments

Bibliographic references, if any

Authorization to release this data for publication in date list.

                    Signature _M Wayne Jensen Jr_
                    Date _April 6, 1975_

THE UNIVERSITY OF GEORGIA
GEOCHRONOLOGY LABORATORY
ATHENS, GEORGIA 30601

4 GGS BUILDING
404-542-5579

June 2, 1975

Mr. M. Wayne Jensen, Jr.
2250 Neilsen Road
Tillamook, Oregon 97141

Dear Mr. Jensen:

The date of your sample is: UGa-1003 855 ± 55

A.D.1095

I appreciated the reprints you sent, but am also interested
in your comments after receiving the radiocarbon date.

Thank you!

Sincerely,

Betty Lee Brandau

Betty Lee Brandau
Associate Director

BLB/jcn
enc.

211

Bibliography

I've chosen to sort the bibliography in alphabetical order by author. I know most scholarly books (in my humble way I've tried to make this a scholarly work) are divided into categories such as cartography, geology, surveying, navigation, Spanish and English journals, etc., but I have found during my research that it was much more convenient to have the information presented in this way.

Abendroth, Jack, *The Naming of Gervais Creek Wheeler*, Oregon, 1998

Aikens, C. Melvin, *Archaeology of Oregon*, U.S, Dept. of the Interior, Portland, Oregon 1993

Aker, Raymond and Von der Porten, Edward, *Discovering Francis Drake's California Harbor*, Published by Drake Navigators Guild, Palo Alto CA 2000

Aker, Raymond, *Sir Francis Drake at Drakes Bay, A summation of Evidence Relating to the Identification of Sir Francis Drake's Encampment at Drakes Bay, California*, Based on the Research of the Drake Navigators Guild., Copyright 1978 by Drake Navigators Guild pp 32-34 photo by Robert Allen

Allen, D., *Indians of the Northwest Coast*, Hancock House Publishers, Seattle, WA 1977

Anderson, Irma, Chair of Editorial Committee, *100 Years of the Nehalem Country Reminiscences of Early Days in One of Oregon's Pioneer Coastal Areas*, Compiled and Edited by the Nehalem Bay United Methodist Church, 1970

Andrews, Ralph W., *Indian Primitive, Bonanza Books*, NY 1960

Ashwell, Reg., *Coast Salish, Their Art Culture and Legends*, Hancock House Press, Seattle, WA 1978

Bancroft, H.H., *History of California*

Barnett, Homer G., *Culture Element Distributions: VII Oregon Coast, Anthropological Records*, Volume 1, No.3, pp. 155-205, 2 figures in text, 1 map, University of California Press, Berkeley, California 1937

Bartroli, Tomas, *Brief Presence, Spain's Activity on America's Northwest Coast 1771-1796*, Published by author 1991

Bawlf, Samuel, *Sir Francis Drake's Secret Voyage to the Northwest Coast of America, AD 1579*, Sir Francis Drake Publications, Salt Spring Island, BC 2001

Bawlf, Samuel, *The Secret Voyage of Sir Francis Drake 1577 - 1580*, Published by Douglas & McIntyre, Vancouver/Toronto 2003

Beals, Herbert K. and Steele, Harvey, *Chinese Porcelains From Site 35-TI-1, Netarts Sand Spit Tillamook County, Oregon*, University of Oregon Anthropological Papers No. 23 1981

Beals, Herbert K., *For Honor & Country, The Diary of Bruno de Hezeta*, Translation and annotation by Western Imprints, Press of the Oregon Historical Society 1985

Beck, Giles, *Lost Treasures of Oregon*, Salem OR, copyright 1956

Bennett, Robert A.; *A Small World of Our Own*, Pioneer Press Books, Walla Walla, Washington 1985

Blundevil, M(aster). (Thomas Blundevill), *A New and Necessary Treatise of Navigation*, London 1613

Blundevill, Thomas, *A Very Briefe and most plaine Description of Mr Blagrave his Astrolabe*, London 1636

Boas, Franz, *Chinook Texts*, Washington, Government Printing Office 1894

Boas, Franz, *Notes on the Tillamook*, University of California Publications in Am. Arch, and Ethn. Vol. 20, Kraus Reprint 1965 1923

Boas, Franz, *Traditions of the Tillamook Indians*, The Journal of American folk-lore, XI, 23-38, 133-150, United States, 1920, 1929

Bordwell, Constance, *Delay and Wreck of the Peacock: An Episode in the Wilkes Expedition*, Oregon Historical Quarterly pp 117-198, Summer 1991

Bouchard, David, *The Journal of Etienne Mercier*, Orca Book Publishers, Victoria, BC 1998

Bourne, William, *A Book Called the "Treasure for Traveilers, devided into five Books or parts, contaynyng very necessary matters, for all sorts of Travailers, eyther by Sea or by Lande"*, Imprinted at London for Thomas Woodcocke, 1578, published in 1979 by Theatrum Orbis Terrarum, Ltd., Amsterdam

Bowditch, LL.D., N., *American Practical Navigator*, 1966 Corrected Print, US Government Printing Office, WA 1966

Brooks, Charles Wolcott, *Early Migrations Japanese Wrecks Stranded and Picked up Adrift in the North Pacific Ocean*, Ethnologically Considered, San Francisco 1876

Buan, Carolyn M. and Lewis, Richard, *The First Oregonians*, published by Oregon Council for the Humanities 1991

Byram, R. Scott, *The Work of a Nation-Richard D. Cutts and the Coast Survey Map of Fort Clatsop*, Oregon Historical Quarterly pp 254-271, Vol. 106, No. 2 Summer 2005

Canniff, KiKi, *Sauvie Island A Step Back in Time*, KI2 Enterprises, Portland, OR 1981
Willard, Carrie M. Among the Tlingits Letters of 1881-1883, Published by Mountain Meadow Press 1995

Chapman, Ph. D., Charles E., *A History of California - The Spanish Period*, Macmillan Company 1921 1939

Churchill, Claire Warner, *Slave Wives of Nehalem*, Metropolitan Press, Portland, Oregon 1933

Clark, Samuel A., Oregon Native Son and Historical Magazine, *Legend of Nehalem*, Vol. II, No. 1, pg 36-40, Native Son Publishing, Portland, Oregon May 1900

Clark, Samuel A., Oregon Native Son and Historical Magazine, *Wrecked Beeswax and Buried Treasure*, Vol. I, pg 245-249, Native Son Publishing, Portland, Oregon September 1899

Conversations with Wayne Jensen 2002

Cook, James, *Captain Cook's Approach to Oregon*, Introduced by T.C. Elliott, Oregon Historical Society 1974

Cook, Warren L., *Flood Tide of Empire, Spain and the Pacific Northwest, 1543-1819*, New Haven and London: Yale University Press 1973

Cooper, William S., *Coastal Sand Dunes of Oregon and Washington*, The Geological Society of America, Memoir 72, June 18, 1958

Coote, Captain John O., *The Norton Book of the Sea*, Edited by Norton & Company, New York 1989

Cortes, Martin, *The Arte of Navigation*, translated by Eden, London 1561

Costaggini, Phillip A. and Schultz A.S.C.E, Robert J., *Survey of Artifacts at Neahkahnie Mountain Oregon*, Oregon State thesis, 1976-81

Cotton, S.J., *Stories of Nehalem*, M.A. Donohue & Co., Chicago 1915

Cox, Ross, *The Columbia River*, London 1831, University of Okalahoma Press 1957

Cressman, L.S., Williams, Howel and Krieger, Alex D., *Early Man in Oregon, Archaeological Studies in the Northern Great Basin*, University of Oregon Eugene 1940

Crockett, Hugh, *The Wreck of the ship Georgiana*, 1892, Pioneer Press Books, Walla Walla, Washington 1985

Cutter, Donald C., *The California Coast A Bilingual Edition of Documents from the Sutro Collection*, University of Oklahoma Press Norman 1969

Cutter, Donald C., *Malaspina in California*, Published by John Howell Books 1960

Cutter, Donald C., *Journal of Tomas de Suría of His voyage with Malaspina to the Northwest Coast of America in 1791*, Ye Galleon Press, Washington 1980

Daugherty, Dr. Richard D., *The Yakima People*, Published by Indian Tribal Series, Phoenix 1973

Davenport, Henry, *Indian Horrors or Massacres by the Red Men*, Northrop, D.D., 1899

David, Andrew, *Vancouver's Survey Methods and Surveys, Maps to Metaphors the Pacific World of George Vancouver*, Edited by Robin Fisher and Hugh Johnson,

Davidson, George, *Francis Drake on the Northwest Coast of America in the Year 1579*, The Geographical Society of the Pacific, Vol. V. Series II, 1908

Dee, John, *The Elements of Geometxia of the most Ancient Philosopher Euclide of Megara*, London 1570

Dee, John, *The Perfect Arte of Navigation*, London 1577

Densmore, Frances, *How Indians Use Wild Plants for Food, Medicine & Crafts*, Dover Publishing, NY 1974

Dickens, Samuel N., *Pioneer Trails of the Oregon*, Oregon Historical Society, Portland, OR, 1971

Digges, Leonard, *A Booke Named Tectonicon* 1556

Digges, Thomas, *A Geometrical Treatise Named Pantometria*, London 1571

Drake, Lady Elizabeth Elliott, *The Family and Heirs of Sir Francis Drake*, Appendix I, pg. 3567 and Appendix II, pg. 392. These depositions of John Drake are also printed in the original Spanish as well as English given to the Inquisition.

Ellis, Captain Henry, *Considerations on the Great Advantages which would arise from the Discovery of the North West Passage*, Sutro Library, San Francisco, California MDCCL

Erlandson, J.M., Losey, R.J. and Petersen, N., *Early Maritime Contact on the Northern Oregon Coast*, 2001

Fink, Colin G. & Polushkin, E.P., *Drake's Plate of Brass Authenticated, The Report on the Plate of Brass*, California Historical Society, San Francisco MCMXXXVIII

Fletcher, Master Francis Preacher, *The World Encompassed By Sir Francis Drake*, Printed for Nicholas Bourne, London 1628

Frisius, Gemma, *Libellus De Regionum Et Locurum Desriptione, Addendom to: Cosmographicus Liber,* by Apian, Antwerp 1533

Frisius, Gemma and his Treatise on Triangulation pg 469-485, 1935

Frisius, Gemma, *De principiis astronomiae & cosmographiae (1553)*, Scholars' Facsimiles & Reprints, Delmar, New York 1992

Frost, Joseph, *Joseph H. Frost's diary of 1841*,MSS, Oregon Historical Society Collection

Garnett, Cartographer Keith, *Archaeological Investigation at Nehalem Bay State Park, Oregon*, Institute for Archaeological Studies, Portland, OR, July 1989, Applied Geography

Gerhard, Peter, *Pirates on the West Coast of New Spain 1575-1742*, Arthur H. Clark Company, Glendale, Calif. 1960

Giesecke, E.W., Letter to Alex Walker, Curator Tillamook Pioneer Museum, August 3, 1970, MS Jensen Collection

Gitzen, Garry, *Real Treasure Discovered on Neahkahnie Mountain, The Secret Voyage of Sir Francis Drake to the North Oregon Coast*, Ekahni. Pub., Wheeler, Oregon 2003

Greenhood, David, *Mapping*, University of Chicago Press 1944 1951

Gunther, E., *Ethnobotany of Western Washington; the Knowledge and Use of Indigenous Plants by Native Americans*, University of Washington Press, Seattle, WA. 1973

Gunther, Dr. R. T., *The Astrolabe: its Uses and Derivative*, Scottish Geo Magazine, vol. 43, no. 1, May 1927

Haasbroek, N.D., Former Lecturer at the Technological University of Delft, *Gemma Frisius, Tycho Brahe and Snellius and Their Triangulations*, Printed in the Netherlands by W.D. Meinema N.V., Delft 1968

Hakluyt, Richard, *Principal Navigations, Voyages and Discoveries*, Penguin 1972

Hakluyt, Richard, *The Principal Voyages, Traffiques and Discoveries of the English Nation*, Published by Alfred A. Knopf, New York 1927

Hakluyt, Richard, *"The discoveries made by M. Arthur Pet and M. Charles Jackman, of the Northeast parts, beyond the Island of Vaigatz, with two Barkes: the one called the George, the other the William, in the year 1580*, by Huge Smith, www.ebooks,adelaide,edu.au/h/hakluyt/voyages/v40/chapter32.html#note246

Hariot, Thomas, *The New Found Land of Virginia; A brief and true report*, The History Book Club, Inc., New York 1951

Harvey, Neva Mae, *Wappato, Ancient Food from the Marsh*, Northwest Magazine, May 30, 1971

Heizer, Robert F., *Elizabethan California*, Ballena Press, Ramona California 1974

Heizer, Robert F., *Francis Drake and the California Indians, 1579*, University of California Press 1947

Holmes, Kenneth L., *The Historiography of the Activities of Francis Drake Along the Pacific Coast of North America in 1579*, Albion, Proceedings of the Conference of British Studies, pg 30-36 Volume I Number 1, Published by The Washington State University Press 1969

Holmes, Kenneth L., *Sir Francis Drake in the North Pacific*, The Geographical Bulletin pp 5-41,Vol 17 June 1979

Howay, Frederic W., *Voyages of the "Columbia" to the Northwest Coast 1787-1790 and 1790-1793*, Oregon Historical Society Press 1941 1990

Hyde, Dayton O., *Yamsi*, Dial Press NY 1971

Irving, Washington, *The Conquest of Spain and Spanish Voyages of Discovery*, Published by R. F. Fenno & Company, NY,NY 1900

Jackson, John, *Children of the Fur Trade Forgotten Metis of the Pacific Northwest*, Mountain Press Publishing, Missoula, Montana 1995

Jacobs, Elizabeth D., *The Nehalem Tillamook An Ethnography*, edited by William R. Seaburg, Oregon State University Press, Corvallis, Oregon 2003

Jewitt, John R., *White Slaves of Maquinna*, Heritage House Publishing, B.C., 1815 2000

Jilek, Wolfgang G, MD, *Indian Healing Shamanic Ceremonialism in the Pacific Northwest,* Hancock House Publishing Ltd., Washington, Fifth printing 1997

Jones, Roy E., *Wappato Indians Their History and Prehistory*

Keddie, Grant, *Aboriginal use of Tobacco in British Columbia and its Origin Areas to the South*, MS Curator of Archaeological Royal B.C. Museum, May 1, 2005

Kelleher, Brian T., *Drake's Bay, Unraveling California's Great Maritime Mystery*, Published by Kelleher & Associates, Cupertino, CA, 1997

Keller, Arthur S. and Lissitzyn, Oliver J. and Mann, Frederick J., *Creation of Rights of Sovereignty through Symbolic Acts 1400 - 1800*, Columbia University Press, NY 1938

Kelsey, Harry, *Sir Francis Drake: The Queen's Pirate*

Kenyon, Malcolm Hall, *Naval Construction and Repair at San Blas, Mexico, 1767-1797,* Masters Thesis University of New Mexico 1965

Kortejarvi, Dr. Arnold, *Handbook of Treasure Symbols*, Galleon Publications, Florida 1969

Kroeber, A. L., *Handbook of the Indians of California*, Dover Publications, NY, 1925 1976,

L'ecluse, Charles, *CAROLI CLVSSII ATREB ALIQVOT NOTE' IN CARCIA*, (Some notes of a native of Gaul, upon the history of spices by Garcia), Antwerp, From the printery of Christopher Plantin 1582.

Lane, Mrs. Ben, *General History Beeswax Observations Manzanita Beach Jan 1938*, Wayne Jensen Collection

Lee, Daniel & Frost, Joseph, *Ten Years in Oregon (1837-1847)*, Galleon Press 1968

Leigh, Valentyne, *The Most Profitable and commendable science, of Surveying of Lands, Tenementes, and Hereditamentes: Drawen and Collected*, Imprinted at London for Andrew Maunsell 1577, published 1971 by Theatrum Orbis Terrarum Ltd., Amsterdam

Leney Ph. D. Lawrence, University of Washington, Seattle, WA, Associate Professor, Wood Science and Technology, July 27, 1970, personal correspondence, Wayne Jensen

Collection

Lessa, William A., *Drake's Island of Thieves Ethnological Sleuthing*, University Press of Hawaii 1975

Library of Congress; www.loc.gov/rr/rarebook/catalog/drake-4-famourvoy.html

Lives and Voyages of the Famous Navigators Drake and Cavendish, Blackie & Son, London

Lockley, Fred, *History of the Columbia River from The Dalles to the Sea*, Clark Publishing 1928

Loxodrome, www.en.wikipedia.org/wiki/rhumb_line

Luthin, editor Herbert W., *Surviving Through the Days*, University of California Berkeley 2002

Lynam, Edward, *British Maps and Map-Makers*, Collins Publisher London MCMXLVII

MacKinnon, Pojar, J. and A., *Plants of the Pacific Northwest Coast; Washington, Oregon, British Columbia and Alaska*, Lone Pine Publishing, Redmond, WA. 1994.

Mahn, Wm., *Early Spanish Treasure Signs & Symbols*, Little Treasure Publishing Texas 1963

Mathes, W. Michael, *Vizcaino and Spanish Expansion in the Pacific Ocean, 1580-1630*, California Historical Society, San Francisco 1968

McArthur, Lewis A., *Oregon Geographic Names*, revised by Lewis L. McArthur, Oregon Historical Society 1982

McLuhan, T. C., *Touch the Earth, A Self-Portrait of Indian Existence*, Promontory Press, NY 1971

Meany, Edmond S., *History of the State of Washington*, Publisher Macmillan 1909

Morison, Samuel E., *The European Discovery of America The Northern Voyages A.D. 500 – 1600*, Oxford University Press NY 1971

Morison, Samuel Eliot, *The European Discovery of America The Southern Voyages 1492-1616*, Oxford University Press NY 1974

Mozino, Jose Mariano, Noticias *De Nutka, An Account of Nootka Sound in 1792*, University of Washington Press Seattle 1970

Neasham, V. Aubrey & Pritchard, William E., *Drake's California Landing, The Evidence for Bolinas Lagoon*, Published by Western Heritage, Inc., Sacramento, California 1974

Nehalem Valley Historical Society, *Tales of the Neahkahnie Treasure*, Prepared by the Treasure Committee 1991

Nehalem Valley Historical Society, *A Patchwork History of Nehalem Bay*, Compiled circa 1995

Nehalem Wetlands Review A Comprehensive Assessment of the Nehalem Bay and River Oregon Summary Report, U.S, Army Engineer District, Portland 1977

Newman, Thomas A., *Tillamook prehistory and its relation to the Northwest coast culture area*, Ph.D. Thesis Oregon State University, 1959

Nichols, Philip, *Sir Francis Drake Revived*, London 1626

Nokes, Richard J., *Columbia's River, The Voyages of Robert Gray 1787-1793*, Washington State Historical Society 1991

North America Historiography 1982

Nuttall, Editor Zelia, *New Light on Drake*, Translated and Printed for the Hakluyt Society, London MDCCCCXIV

O'Crouley, Sir Don Pedro Alonso, *A Description of The Kingdom of New Spain 1774* , Translated and edited by Sean Galvin, published John Howell Books 1972

Olson, Julius E. and Bourne, PhD, Edward Gaylord, *Original Narratives of Early American History, The Northermen Columbus and Cabott*, Charles Scribner's Sons New York 1906

Olson, Wallace M., *Through Spanish Eyes Spanish Voyages to Alaska, 1774-1792*, Heritage Research 2002

Oregon Geology, Volume 52, pg 57, May 1990

Parker, David N. & Turner, Robert D., *Captain James Cook and the Pacific Voyages*, British Columbia Provincial Museum 1978

Penzer, N.M., *The World Encompassed and Analogous Contemporary Documents Concerning Sir Francis Drake's Circumnavigation of the World*, Cooper Square Publishers New York 1969

Peterson, Curt, PhD., Conversations, Nehalem Shipwreck, www. captainrick.com, 2007

Plate of Brass, http://en.wikipedia.org/wiki/Drake%27s

Pogo, A., *Gemma Frisius, his method of determining differences of longitude by transporting timepieces (1530), and his treatise on triangulation (1533),* Abstract, Harvard Library 189,

Power, Robert H., *Early Discoveries of San Francisco Bay*, 2nd Printing Nut Tree, California 1968

Ray, Verne F., *Lower Chinook Ethnographic Notes*, University of Washington 1938

Richeson, A. W., *English Land Measuring to 1800: Instruments and Practices*, Published by The society for the History of Technology and M.I.T. Press 1966

Riesenberg, Felix, *Cape Horn*, Readers Union, London 1950

Roberts, Mark A., *Riddle of the Viking Cryptograms*, Science Digest, January 1969

Rogers, Thomas H., *Nehalem – A Story of the Pacific A.D. 1700*, H.L. Heath Publisher, McMinnville Oregon 1898

Rogers, Thos. H., *Beeswax and Gold, A Tale of the Pacific A.D. 1700*, J.K. Gill Co., Publishers, Portland Oregon 1929

Roles of Certain Indian Tribes in Washington and Oregon, Ye Galleon Press, Fairfield, Washington 1969

Ross, Alexander, *Adventures of the First Settlers on the Columbia River*, Published by Smith, Elder and Co., Cornhill, London 1849

Rowett, Frank A., *The Treasure of Neahkahnie Mountain*, 1976

Ruby, Robert and Brown, John, *A Guide to the Indian Tribes of the Pacific Northwest.*

Sagittaria latifolia, Wild Wapato, Arrowhead Family, www.plants.usda.gov

Schafer, Joseph, *Documents Relative to Warre and Vavasour's Military Reconnaissance in Oregon 1845-6*, Oregon Historical Society, pg 29-30, Vol. X, No. 1, March 1909

Seaman, N.G., *Indian Relics of the Pacific Northwest*, Published by Binfords 1946

Senungetuk, Vivian, *Wise Words of Paul Tiulana An Inupiat Alaskan's Life*, Grolier Publishing, NY 1998

Smith, Honorable Silas B., Oregon Native Son and Historical Magazine, *Tales of Early Wrecks on the Oregon Coast*, Vol. I, pg 443-446, Titular Chief of the Clatsops, Native Son Publishing, Portland, Oregon January 1900

Spencer, Robert F. & Jennings, Jesse D., *The Native Americans,* et al., Harper & Row Publishers, NY 1965

Strong, Emory, *Stone Age on the Columbia River*, Binford & Mort Publisher, Portland OR 1959

Summaries of Statements before the State Historical Resources Commission Francis Drake in California Hearings, October 1978, Wayne Jensen Collection

Swan, James G., *The Northwest Coast or Three Years' Residence in Washington Territory,* Harper & Brothers Publisher, New York 1857

Taylor, E.G.R. and Richey, M.W., *The Geometrical Seaman A book of early nautical instruments*, Hollis & Carter, Ltd. Publisher, London 1962

Taylor, E.G.R., *The Haven-Finding Art, A History of Navigation from Odysseus to Captain Cook*, Hollis & Carter, London 1956

Taylor, E.G.R., *The Earliest Account of Triangulation*, Scottish Geographical Magazine 43 pg 341-345, 1927

Taylor, Jr., Herbert C., *Aboriginal Populations of the Lower Northwest Coast*, Pacific Northwest Quarterly Vol. 54, No. 4, pg 158-165, 1963

Taxus brevifolia, Western Yew-Pacific Yew,www. en.wikipedia.org/wiki/western_yew

The Craftsman in America, Published by The National Geographic Society 1975

The Flight of the Nez Perce ...through the Bitterroot Valley 1877, The US Dept. of Agriculture (USDA), R1-95-79

The Golden Hinde, 1986 Golden Hinde Ltd.

The Mighty Chieftains, by Time-Life Books, Alexandria, VA 1993

The Plate of Brass Reexamined 1977, A Report Issued by The Bancroft Library, University of California, Berkeley 1977

The Story of Natsalane A traditional Tlingit Myth, No author, publisher, or date listed

Thomas, Hugh, *The Slave Trade, The Story of the Atlantic Slave Trade 1440-1870*, Simon and Schuster 1997

Vancouver, John, *A Voyage of Discovery to the North Pacific Ocean*, 3 V & Atlas, Reprinted Amsterdam and New York 1967

Vaughn, Thomas, *The Western Shore Oregon Country Essays*, Oregon Historical Society 1976

Vaughn, Warren N., *Till Broad Daylight A History of Early Settlement in Oregon's Tillamook County*, Bear Creek Press 2004

Viles, Don M., *North America's Hidden Legacy at Neah-Kah-Nie Mountain 1579*, by Hidden Heritage Series 1982

Viles, Donald M. and Jensen, M. Wayne, *Drake Cermeno Vizcaino*, 1971

Viles, Donald M. and Viles, Charlene, *North America Land with a Counterfeit History*, Garibaldi, Oregon 1973

Viles, Donald M., and Viles, Charlene, *Quatuorcentennial Aurora Borealis, Francis Drake Northwest 1579 - 1979*, Garibaldi, Oregon 1978

Viles, Donald Speech Titled: *Sir Francis Drake Colony Found Neah-Kah-Nie Mountain*, - Neah-Kah-Nie Community Club Jan. 1971

Villiers, Alan, *James Cook*, Published by Charles Scribner's Sons, New York 1967

www.gocreate.com/history/ra16.htm

Wagner, Henry R., *Early Franciscan Activities on the West Coast*, Reprinted from the Quarterly, September-December, 1941 Los Angeles

Wagner, Henry R., *Cartography of the Northwest Coast of America to the year 1800*, Volume 1, N. Israel, Amsterdam 1968 reprinted from the edition Berkeley 1937

Wagner, Henry R., *Drake on the Pacific Coast*, Published for the Zamorano Club, Los Angeles, California 1970

Wagner, Henry R., *Spanish Voyages to the Northwest Coast of America in the Sixteenth Century*, San Francisco, California Historical Society 1929

Wagner, Henry R., *Creation of Rights of Sovereignty Through Symbolic Acts*, The Pacific Historical Review 1938

Wallis, Helen, *The Voyage of Sir Francis Drake Mapped in Silver and Gold*, By

Keeper of Maps, The British Library, Published by The Friends of the Bancroft Library, University of California, Berkeley 1979

Ward, Bob, *Lost Harbour Found, The Truth about Sir Francis Drake's Movements along the American Coast,*

Waters, D.W.,*The Art of Navigation in England in Elizabethan and Early Stuart Times,* Yale University Press New Haven 1958

Wickersham, James, Oregon Native Son and Historical Magazine, *Pre-Historic North Pacific Wrecks,* Vol. II, No. 10, pg 5405-42, Native Son Publishing, Portland, Oregon March 1900

Williams, Glyn, *Voyages of Delusion, The Quest for the Northwest Passage,* Yale University Press, New Haven 2003

Younker, J., Tveskov, M.A. and Lewis, D., *Changing Landscapes: Telling Our Stories,* pg 45-54, Coquille Indian Tribe, North Bend, Oregon

INDEX

B

C

D

F

I

J

K

L

M

N

O

P

Q

R

S

T

U

V

W

Y

Z